THE MILLIONAIRE
FROM
NAZARETH

"THE MILLIONAIRES OF THE BIBLE" Series

THE MILLIONAIRE FROM NAZARETH

His Prosperity Secrets for You!

CATHERINE PONDER

DeVorss Publications

ISBN: 0-87516-370-X
Library of Congress Catalog Card Number: 79-51218

DeVorss & Company, Publisher
P.O. Box 550
Marina del Rey, CA 90294

Printed in The United States of America

CONTENTS

What to do when you are being pressured by negative appearances. How the author's need was supplied. *Step Two*: To handle the possibility of new good, prepare inwardly. *Step Three*: Go to Cana by speaking words of abundance. How she became a successful union negotiator. *Step Four*: By treating the available supply as the desired supply, water becomes wine. *Step Five*: How to pour forth specific prosperity into the stony waterpots. How a wife transformed her rocky marriage into a happy one. *Step Six*: How not to reject your good. How a farmer used unusual available supply to prosper. His last minute rescue from East Africa. *Step Seven*: To persist in filling "to the brim" can produce healing and abundance. *Step Eight*: How to draw out your abundant good from the hard experiences of life. How she drew health out of illness. *Step Nine*: Why the good that comes last is satisfying and enduring. How a businessman turned his life around. *Step Ten*: How to fill your life to the brim with abundant good.

The Prosperous Matthew. Jesus was an educated mystic. Jesus was a master and a great initiate. The mystical training of the Bible's earlier millionaires. Nothing new about the Bible's prosperity symbology. Why Galilee was a proper setting for the Beatitudes. The abundance and beauty of prosperous Galilee. The significance of the "Beautiful Attitudes." He experienced a new venture in prosperous living, and you can, too.

How to handle a financial need. The *first* prosperous Beatitude: A summary of the power of prosperous thinking. How a Texas businessman prospered. The *second* prosperous Beatitude: The basic prosperity law is that man should look to God as the source of his supply. How they were forced from mourning into prosperity. The *third* prosperous Beatitude: The prospering power of forgiveness and release. How meekness prospered a formerly bitter divorcee. How they experienced the vast benefits of forgiveness and release. How you can inherit the earth. The *fourth* prosperous Beatitude: The will of God for man is wealth.

How she was healed and prospered. A maid in Colorado became a museum executive in California. The *fifth* prosperous Beatitude: The prospering power of love. He converted a raging customer into a good one. How a lawyer collected two large accounts. How mercy saved a marriage and brought prosperity. The *sixth* prosperous Beatitude: The prospering power of pictures. How they prospered through pictures. The *seventh* prosperous Beatitude: The prospering power of peace and blessing. Her success secret was "peace." How the act of blessing brought peace and prosperity. The *eighth* prosperous Beatitude: Chemicalization is a healing, prospering process that brings joyous results. Chemicalization started his healing. Chemicalization brought her a far better job. How he attracted an $800,000 business transaction. In conclusion, the most "Beautiful Attitude" of all: use often the prospering power of joy.

The secret of her health, youth and success. The early Christians' success secrets can be yours. An incurable condition was healed. The secret for overcoming hard conditions. A businesswoman dissolved hard conditions. Why the Lord's Prayer has prospering power. The inner and outer benefits. *Prosperity: Part I*—the prospering power of God's nature, both universally and within man. The *first* prosperity secret from the Lord's Prayer: the basic law of prosperity. From a job layoff to a bigger company within one week. The *second* prosperity secret from the Lord's Prayer: how to become attuned to the prosperous nature of God. Two businessmen prospered from this method. The *third* prosperity secret from the Lord's Prayer: the prospering power of God's kingdom. How this prayer brought a better job. Are you willing to receive the surprises and changes this prayer may bring? The *fourth* prosperity secret from the Lord's Prayer: the prospering power of God's will. How this prayer brought healing and prosperity. *Prosperity: Part II*—How man's specific daily needs can be met. The *fifth* prosperity secret from the Lord's Prayer: the power of specific prosperity decrees. Jesus' secret for manifesting rich supply. How a housewife manifested an abundance of food during a job layoff. The *sixth* prosperity secret from the Lord's Prayer: the result-getting power of forgiveness. The healing power of forgiveness helped her return to work. The *seventh* prosperity secret from the Lord's Prayer: there is prospering power in claiming divine protection. A "woman driver" was divinely delivered. The prospering power of initiation periods. The *eighth* prosperity secret from the Lord's Prayer:

They got into an unrestricted state of mind, and prospered when they shared with others. The *fourth* step in the "money miracle": deliberately get into a prosperous "Capernaum" state of mind. How he paid off an $800,000 indebtedness and began making $200,000 a year. The *fifth* step in the "money miracle": use the prospering power of faith. How a divorcee went through a stringent financial period, then remarried well. *Part II:* Prosperous actions for tapping unrestricted supply. The sixth step in the "money miracle": go to the sea of rich ideas. The *seventh* step in the "money miracle": cast a specific hook. From a screeching halt to abundance. Improvement came along all lines when she got definite. When a bankrupt contractor cast a hook, he was prospered. A two-part formula for results. Cast specific hooks to prosper. They cast a hook through list-making. They cast a hook through affirmations. She cast a hook through picturing. The *eighth* step in the "money miracle": how to prosper from the first fish. He was talked out of becoming a millionaire. He kept mental company with an idea and prospered. The *ninth* step in the "money miracle": ways to open the fish's mouth. The author's single prosperous shekel. The *tenth* and last step in the "money miracle": use what comes as promised. How they stopped their prosperity. In closing: the rich benefits to be found in the fish's mouth.

The Prosperity Parable, Part One: How to get out of the far country of limited thinking. The magical powers of divine order. The success power of peace. No one gave unto him. The prospering power of release. The importance of literally getting back to the Father's house. She went from "rags to riches" by getting back to the Father's house. Why a famine occurs. How to overcome famine. How $8,000 became $25,000. *The Prosperity Parable, Part Two:* The lavish abundance that awaits you in the Father's house. Carry yourself as one who owns the earth. How a divorcee and her children built a satisfying new life. She proved that you can have everything! How he became a multimillionaire by returning to the Father's house. *The Prosperity Parable, Part Three:* The prospering power of joy and forgiveness. The destructive power of "incurable condemnation." She went on to a wealthy life style while her critics remained in lack. Joy prospers and love envieth not. Release of envy brought vast improvement. In conclusion: the prospering, freeing power of forgiveness. Your personal prosperity promise.

How supply can be made to increase. The widow with the prosperity
consciousness. Do something drastic and prosper. The modern widow
who did something drastic and prospered. Why the widow was one of
the great personages of her time. How to obtain special blessings. A
modern businessman's prosperity secret. How Jesus tried to prosper the
poor. The early Christians' secret for their vast success. How others
have prospered through using this ancient success principle. How a
blessed penny multiplied to become millions. How your money can do
far more for you than you thought possible. How a young girl found
work and prospered mightily. The prospering power of expectation. Do
not hurry past your supply. The invaluable prosperity lesson he learned
early. When they used what they already had, they became millionaires.
How a gold nugget manifested. How a $100 gift brought a $1,000
return. To overcome the consciousness of lack: send out in faith, then
expect replenishment. Giving thanks in advance draws happy results to
you. Jesus' last prosperity lesson at the end of his earth life. A special
note from the author.

The prosperity miracle of the second draught. Steps that can lead you
to the right side of life. *Step One:* ask the help of the prosperous Christ.
How to tap a success power for overcoming life's hard experiences. The
success power that was poured out upon a businessman's life. *Step Two:*
go to Galilee with high vision and orderly thoughts, words, and actions.
Step Three: instead of trying hard from a human standpoint, look up from
your tasks, and reaffirm your faith. Why they did not immediately prosper. How to make your catch of unlimited abundance. *Step Four:* cast
your mind in a sea of rich ideas by getting definite. The prospering
power of right attitudes. She went from a rented house to her own
elegant home. *Step Five:* make the effort to move toward your goals in
faith. Why Peter had to make the first move toward results. She moved
forward into success one day at a time. *Step Six:* to make the effort to
share what you already have develops your prosperity consciousness,

strengthens your character, and opens the way to super-abundance. The secret of the bountiful breakfast feast. How she finally got a job. What Jesus' last mystic prosperity formula can do for you. *Step Seven:* divine substance (bread), the foundation of all wealth, is a rich gift that can bring a feast of abundance. The prospering power of the mystical bread made one family rich. *Step Eight:* ideas of increase (fish) are a rich gift that can bring a feast of abundance. What a professor learned from the prospering power of the mystical fish. *Step Nine:* the prospering power of release. Jesus' last prosperity message. How the prospering power of release worked for the author. *The Last Step:* after release, comes new success and satisfying abundance. Their success story was just beginning, and so is yours!

Introduction . . . .

THERE IS GOLD IN
THE GOSPEL FOR YOU!

A Special Message from the Author

The word "gospel" means "good news," and the good news is that there is gold in the gospel for you! We have often thought of Jesus as the great healer, which he was. We have regarded him as an expert in prayer, which he was. *But Jesus also understood, used and taught the mental and spiritual laws of prosperity in a way that no one before or since ever has!*

Not only did he know the great, eternal truths about universal abundance, but he dared to reveal how the average person of his time—or any time—could develop an *inner* consciousness of supply that would tap that universal abundance. Because the political situation of Jesus' era controlled the economic welfare of his followers, teaching prosperity was an especially bold and fearless thing for him to do. Yet *Jesus seemed to know that a part of his mission in becoming Saviour of the world was to save mankind from its erroneous beliefs*

1

about financial limitation being a spiritual necessity. That he dared to teach the spiritual principles of true abundance was a part of his greatness.

Not only did Jesus' prosperity teachings catch on during his lifetime, but history reveals that the early Christians and the early church followed through on his prosperity teachings to such an extent that *early Christianity was a prosperous Christianity.* It was only in later centuries, for political reasons, that the pagan idea arose that it was virtuous to be poor. This pagan idea was deliberately used to again enslave the masses during the Middle Ages. Unfortunately this false idea has been passed down from generation to generation so that it has continued with us until this day in some religious circles.

If you have been enslaved to pagan poverty beliefs, the time has come to declare your freedom from them, and from all the financial havoc they have probably caused in your life. Indeed, *the prosperous truth is that, as a child of God, it is a sin to be poor, and it is your spiritual birthright to prosper and succeed!*

JESUS' WEALTH

Quite contrary to what most of us have been led to believe, *Jesus certainly was not poor. Instead, Jesus was the wealthiest man who ever trod this earth because he was one with all interior and exterior wealth.* A wonder-working mind that could turn ordinary water into the finest of wine, multiply bread and fish at will to feed thousands, raise the dead to life, and heal all manner of disease could hardly be counted poor—especially if these invaluable services were being performed at today's prices! Indeed, a man who had the ability to manifest money from the fish's mouth with which to pay

taxes, and who could cause large and valuable drafts of fish
to appear for the fishermen, where previously there had
been none, would be considered a multimillionaire on today's economic scene.

Although he manifested literal financial supply, both for
himself and his followers, *Jesus also symbolized the Divinity in
every man that is never poor.* "I came that they may have life,
and may have it abundantly." (John 10:10) He reminded
his followers of their own divinity through stressing the Old
Testament teaching, "Ye are gods and all of you sons of the
Most High." (Psalms 82:6; John 10:34)

*It was the purpose of the Christ nature in Jesus to succeed, and to
rest in divine bounty.* It is the divine purpose of the Christ
nature in all mankind to also be an instrument of that success and bountiful abundance. In this great age of enlightenment, nothing less can possibly satisfy the evolving soul of
an illumined individual. An *inner* consciousness of wealth includes all of the vast benefits of outer, material wealth—
"the earth . . . and the fullness thereof" (Psalms 24:1)—but
it encompasses much more. To learn and apply the prosperity principles Jesus taught is to become at one with all interior and exterior wealth, and to reap the peaceful, soul-
satisfying benefits that such a consciousness brings.

THE GOLDEN RESULTS OBTAINED BY OTHERS

Here are some of the golden results obtained on all levels
of life by those who have studied and applied the prosperity
teachings of that millionaire from Nazareth:

A businessman from Pennsylvania got out of debt and
prospered. A California businessman went from doing
business out of the back of a pickup truck in a poverty-
stricken area to a millionaire clientele in a prosperous area

known as "the playground of the rich." Peace and harmony were restored in the previously chaotic business office of a worker in California. A man in New York, who had been in a wheelchair for nine months, got up out of it and walked again. An out-of-work college professor in Texas was shown how to develop his real estate holdings into a mobile home park, and to live handsomely in the process. He was even able to build and pay cash for his own beautiful home.

A housewife in New York was shown how to avoid an operation and obtain healing. Another housewife was able to transform her rocky marriage into a happy one. A businesswoman in Nevada became a successful union negotiator, and her income grew to ten times what it had been! At a time when he had no native currency left for a required travel tax, a member of the Hollywood film industry was shown how to leave East Africa anyway. A widow with a severe heart condition, and no family or funds, was able to regain her health and become a successful dress designer.

Still another housewife was shown how to overcome her painful arthritis, and to lead a happy, normal life again. A discouraged businessman in Maryland was shown how to turn his life around after going through the heartbreak of divorce. A retired businessman in the State of Washington was shown how to come out of retirement and establish his own new business at the age of sixty-two. A businessman in Utah was able to turn a former sorrow into a blessing. And so it goes. As related throughout the pages of this book, *the list of the varied results one can obtain through applying the prosperity teachings of Jesus seems endless.*

THE PROMISE OF INEVITABLE PROSPERITY

People are "down" on what they are not "up" on. It is unfortunate that traditional religion has long been inclined to "put down" prosperity from the pulpit. Religious leaders have often told their followers in one breath that it was a sin to be rich, and quite spiritual to be poor. Yet, in the next breath, they did not hesitate to financially burden their followers by calling for increased offerings to be taken for expensive building programs, expanded missionary outreaches, and other undertakings of financial significance. Ministers in traditional religious circles have often declared that Jesus was poor and that in some strange way his true followers should always be poor, too. Yet the churches and cathedrals of the past have often stood as monuments of prosperity and untaxed wealth. No wonder so many people have been turned off by such a contradictory point of view!

No such contradictory point of view existed in the Bible. The idea of material prosperity as a reward to the faithful was a common teaching of the Old Testament. It was pointed out often that should Israel forget God as the Giver of all life's blessings, the Hebrews would perish. But if Israel were faithful, there would be no poor. *A righteous and God-revering people meant a healthy and prosperous people. Loyalty to Jehovah would bring inevitable prosperity.*

In the New Testament, Jesus gave many successful formulas. Perhaps his most famous is found in these words: "The kingdom of God is within you." (Luke 17:21) He then told his followers to seek first this inner kingdom and the right use of it, and "all these things shall be added . . . It is your Father's good pleasure to give you the kingdom." (Matthew 6:33; Luke 12:31-32) Here he was again reiterating the Old Testament belief that loyalty to Jehovah would bring inevitable prosperity.

Through his many prosperity miracles and parables,[1] Jesus pointed out simple ways to employ the right use of the

---

1. Two-thirds of his parables were "prosperity parables."

inner kingdom of God *within* man, both in attitudes and actions; thereby bringing prosperity and success. The early chapters of this book clarify some of Jesus' most famous sayings about wealth versus poverty, which have so often been grossly misunderstood. Because of this lack of understanding, these fine teachings have erroneously added to the poverty and misery of the world in the name of religion, whereas Jesus meant for them to add to mankind's progress and success.

THE MILLIONAIRES OF THE BIBLE

Certainly the great people of the Bible had no psychological hang-ups on the subject of money, prosperity or success being a part of their spiritual heritage. Instead, *the Bible is the greatest prosperity textbook that has ever been written!* Next to the subject of salvation, more is written in the Bible about money, giving, stewardship and financial matters than on any other subject. The word "gold" appears more than four hundred times in the Bible. There are between three thousand and four thousand promises in the Bible, many of them literal prosperity promises. You have probably regarded Abraham, Isaac, Jacob, Joseph, Moses and Joshua as among the great spiritual leaders of their time, which they were. They also became literal millionaires as described in my books, *The Millionaires of Genesis,*[2] *The Millionaire Moses,*[3] and *The Millionaire Joshua.*[4] The success of these best-selling

---

2. Catherine Ponder, *The Millionaires of Genesis* (Marina del Rey, Calif.: DeVorss & Co., 1976).

3. Catherine Ponder, *The Millionaire Moses* (Marina del Rey, Calif.: DeVorss & Co., 1977).

4. Catherine Ponder, *The Millionaire Joshua* (Marina del Rey, Calif.: DeVorss & Co., 1978).

books has already indicated to me how eager people are to learn the true, *inner* secrets of prosperity from some of the greatest millionaires of all times!

Many of our present-day millionaires could hardly conceive of the affluent life style of the millionaires of the Bible, with their vast flocks, huge land holdings, large families, and unlimited staffs of servants. It was a gracious, leisurely way of life that might be difficult for even a person of wealth to maintain at today's prices. The frantic, hard-work competitive consciousness of modern man can hardly imagine it. Yet the abundant prosperity consciousness—which the millionaires of the Bible symbolize—is still available to us today!

A housewife from Pennsylvania wrote:

> "Your new series of books about 'the millionaires of the Bible' is delightful. However, I am having a hard time trying to accept the spiritual principles of prosperity advocated in them, because I was reared according to the New Testament, which is the foundation of Christianity. I am a 'New Testament Christian.'
>
> "It appears to me that the Gospel writers constantly condemned the rich. I find it inconsistent and confusing that it seems all right for the Old Testament figures to have been rich Jews, while the New Testament principles seem to forbid wealth for all true Christians."

When I read the above letter, it brought back my own early religious training which had left me with similar, mixed ideas. Although we regard Jesus as the founder of Christianity, he was also a Jew, having been reared by devout parents according to Old Testament law. That so much of Jesus' teaching was based upon the Old Testament is reflected in both the New Testament, and in the teachings of early Christianity.

It is true that Jesus spoke out strongly against many of the rich people of his time who had only a material consciousness of supply. They had often gained their wealth wrongly, through political corruption, and then used it selfishly. (See Chapter One.)

It is also true that Jesus spoke out just as strongly on the subject of prosperity, emphasizing that it was man's spiritual heritage. He gave numerous prosperity formulas which could be used by the common man to produce true abundance. It was a revolutionary idea to the people of that era—as it still is today—that *true prosperity has a spiritual basis*; that God is the Source of man's supply.

It is true that Jesus did not possess many of the outer trappings of wealth, as did some of the illustrious millionaires of the Old Testament. Instead, he developed an *inner* consciousness of wealth that made it possible for him to manifest supply as the need arose—without any of the burdens and responsibilities that sometimes accompany vast material wealth. In this present era of "instant everything," his rich mentality of "instant supply" can be especially appreciated since it reflects a consciousness of true prosperity at its best.

A "millionaire" is usually regarded as one who has a million dollars or more, but in its root, the word "millionaire" means "abundance and happiness." Increased health, wealth, happiness and spiritual understanding are all possible when you begin to use the prosperity secrets that were taught by Jesus.

THE AUTHOR'S PROSPERITY STORY

I have been waiting for more than twenty years to share the prosperity secrets of Jesus with you in these pages! During the past two decades, I have gradually moved lecture notes and research material on the subject with me from coast to coast, over a three-thousand-mile span, in preparation for the writing of this book.

I began researching the prosperity teachings of Jesus while living in one room when serving my first ministry in Alabama. Later, I carefully moved those files of research to Texas, where I lived in a series of apartments for more than a decade while founding two churches. My expanding research was finally moved into my first home, a little Mexican hacienda, in San Antonio. As my own prosperity consciousness slowly evolved, I later moved my growing research notes into a somewhat more comfortable home in the Palm Springs, California area, located near the global ministry I now serve. It is a pleasure to finally be writing about the prosperity teachings of Jesus while living and working in the midst of the lavish tropical beauty of this famous resort area. This mystical desert terrain is reported to be similar to that of the Holy Land that was enjoyed by the millionaires of the Bible so many centuries ago.

I can still feel the initial excitement I first experienced when I did the original research for this book while in my first ministry in Alabama in the late 1950's. It was only at the urging of the chairman of the church's board of trustees, who was a very prosperous-minded lady, that I found the courage as a new minister to present a series of lectures on the prosperity secrets of Jesus to that local congregation. Having never heard a minister lecture on the prosperity philosophy of Jesus, I felt very bold in describing him as a "prosperity teacher." I would not have dared describe him as a "millionaire" in those days.

The enthusiastic response I received even then encouraged me to continue studying the subject. As my research developed over the years, I became more convinced than ever that *Jesus was among the greatest prosperity teachers of all times—and that his prosperity story should finally be told!*

It has been startling to discover how hungry people are to learn the prosperous truth taught by the millionaire from Nazareth. Their reaction has often been, "Why didn't someone tell me long ago that Jesus was prosperous, and that I should be, too?" Again and again people have seemed relieved to learn that *true prosperity always has a spiritual basis, and that true spirituality has prospering power!* When I began the actual writing of this book, my prayer partner predicted: "The gratitude from the readers of *The Millionaire from Nazareth* will overwhelm you, Catherine. People will be so happy to find someone who has finally dared to write about the prosperity secrets of Jesus."

THE AUTHOR'S PROSPERITY INVITATION
TO YOU

As you get acquainted with the millionaire from Nazareth and apply his prosperity secrets in your own life, I trust that your progress will far exceed any of the success stories found in this book. *For most of us, the development of a prosperity consciousness is an evolving process.* It is not usually a "get-rich-quick" experience.

The word "wealth" means "to fare well." *Your potential wealth includes all the good your soul desires.* Your health, prosperity, happiness, peace of mind, spiritual awareness, and growth into expanded good are all a part of your wealth. As you open your mind to claim this abundance, your life can take on more and more of the blessings you desire, so that you "fare well" or become wealthy.

You *should.* It is simply not possible to live a normal, well-balanced life today unless you are prosperous. An expanded prosperity consciousness is a necessity in this age of increasing economic demands. Rising prices, inflationary recessions, uncertain political and economic world conditions are all indications that we must raise and expand our consciousness to a new level of universal supply. Jesus had access to and shared such a consciousness.

So again I say: It is perfectly right and proper that you should give your attention to the science of acquiring wealth, in both *inner* and *outer* ways, as taught by Jesus. It is certainly a noble and necessary occupation in these times, as it was in his. I hope you will write me about the prosperous impact that the man from Nazareth has had upon your life.

As you go quickly now to Chapter One and meet the millionaire from Nazareth, I invite you to join me and countless others in boldly declaring often: "THERE IS GOLD IN THE GOSPEL FOR ME, AND I CLAIM IT NOW!" May that statement prove to be a "mind-blowing" idea to you—one that "blows" all limited, restricted, poverty-infesting concepts out of your thinking and from your life, now and forever.

Catherine Ponder

P.O. Drawer 1278
Palm Desert, California 92261
U.S.A.

FROM CARPENTER TO LORD
OF PLENTY

— Chapter 1 —

Jesus, a millionaire? Shocking, isn't it? Yet it is true. That humble carpenter from Nazareth became Lord of Plenty. What may seem even more shocking is that *you can become Lord of Plenty, too!* The Christ-nature in Jesus symbolizes the Divinity that is within you which is never poor.

In the past, Jesus has had bad "p.r." on the subject of prosperity. He's had some "bad press" by those who should have known better. So, again, let us set the record straight:

Quite contrary to what most of us have been taught to believe, *Jesus was not poor. He was one of the most prosperous thinkers who ever lived! He was a master teacher of prosperity. Yes, he even became Lord of Plenty.*

A businessman wrote from Singapore:

"For years I have read books on success. Each helped, but none managed to get me going until I found some of your

12

books, which stressed that *true prosperity always has a spiritual basis*; and that the great spiritual leaders of the Bible were prosperous. Through that realization I have been shown the way to start all over again, and to succeed.

"*It is thrilling to realize that Christianity and prosperity are synonymous,* translating 'the good life' and 'the abundant life' into practical terms, challenging all who dare. I now realize this is what the teachings of Jesus were all about, and I am taking up that dare!''

JESUS' ENTIRE LIFE SHOWED HIS INTEREST IN PROSPERITY

Jesus had a prosperous background. He was born of royal blood, having descended from a long line of Hebrew prophets and kings. Even at birth, the wealthy Wise Men from the East presented him with the richest of gifts: gold, frankincense, and myrrh. Although Jesus has been described as being so poor that he had no place to lay his head, he had a home with his parents in Nazareth, and was gladly welcomed into the homes of both rich and poor all over Palestine. At the time of Jesus' birth, his father, Joseph, had been a landowner. This is evidenced by the need to appear for tax assessment.

The events of Jesus' entire life showed his interest in prosperity. Early in his ministry, Jesus received the anointing of the Holy Spirit. This symbolized his receiving the fullness of a rich and loving Father, or a consciousness of divine abundance. (John 1:33) Jesus obviously had nothing against money because he unhesitatingly called Matthew, a tax collector, to be one of his disciples. He indicated his appreciation for the orderly handling of money when he appointed Judas as treasurer for himself and the disciples.

Furthermore, he did not hesitate to use his deeper powers to promote earthly prosperity. He had no qualms about using the mental and spiritual laws of prosperity to produce an abundance of food to feed the five thousand in a desert place. (See Chapter 6) He willingly supported the twelve who traveled with him from day to day. Imagine the payroll that would represent today! When the Roman government inquired as to his tax status, Jesus willingly paid taxes with money from the fish's mouth—a further sign of his acceptance of prosperity as his divine right. (See Chapter 7)

He believed that prosperity was a blessing which was available to all mankind as indicated in his famous line from the Lord's Prayer, "Give us this day our daily bread. And forgive us our debts, as we also have forgiven our debtors."[1] (Matthew 6:11-12) This statement is still a powerful prosperity prayer. (See Chapter 5)

The teachings of Jesus are filled with prosperity formulas. When he declared in the Beatitudes, "Blessed are the poor in spirit, for theirs is the kingdom of heaven," (Matthew 5:3) he was not approving poverty as a spiritual virtue, as has so often been implied. By "poor in spirit" he meant free from egotism, pride and all the attitudes of mind that keep one from being humble and receptive to divine ideas and their consequent blessings. (See Chapter 4)

One of Jesus' most popular parables was the prosperity parable in which the Prodigal Son spent his substance in riotous living in a far country. Nevertheless, he was welcomed home by a loving father who clothed him with the best robe, placed an elegant ring on his finger, valuable shoes on his feet, and fed him the abundance of the fatted calf. Those acts contained important prosperity symbolism. (See Chapter 8)

---

1. Bible passages quoted herein are from the American Standard Version or the King James Version of the Holy Bible.

One of the first steps in the attainment of prosperity is to have the right attitude of mind and heart toward worldly wealth. Jesus had nothing against luxurious living. He dined on occasion with those of wealth. Such social events included dining with the well-to-do Pharisees, who were considered the religiously educated of his time. (Luke 11:37; 14:1) Mary of Bethany, a special friend of Jesus, was considered a woman of wealth and social position, not only in her own village, but also in Jerusalem. While dining with Mary and her family, Jesus allowed his feet—symbolizing his expanding understanding of the material world—to be anointed with precious oils. This gracious act was not only literally a rich gift from his hostess, but also a symbol of the prosperity consciousness that was being poured out upon him. (John 12) Jesus even invited himself to dine at the home of the controversial Zacchaeus, who had amassed a fortune as head tax collector in the important road center of Jericho. During Jesus' visit in his affluent home, Zacchaeus was converted. (Luke 19) This symbolized a conversion from a material consciousness of prosperity to a spiritual one.

Jesus was sometimes addressed as "Rabbi." This was a term of respect denoting knowledge, prestige and wealth. As pointed out in my books, *The Millionaire Moses* and *The Millionaire Joshua,* the priests of the Old Testament became millionaires. The instructions given Moses by Jehovah were that the priestly tribe of Levi would not receive *any* of the rich Promised Land, as had the other tribes of Israel. Instead, they received *all* of the tithes from *all* of the Promised Land. In turn, they gave a tithe of all the tithes they received (known as a "heave offering") for the support of the places of worship. Their private wealth was then passed on within this priestly tribe of Levi from generation to generation. In New Testament times, the rabbis were still considered to be among the wealthy class.

Jesus' seamless robe was regarded as so valuable that the Roman soldiers cast lots for it at the cross. After his crucifixion, the Scriptures say it was "a rich man," the affluent Joseph of Arimathaea, who begged Pilate for Jesus' body. He wrapped it in expensive linen cloth and buried it in his own elaborate tomb. (Matthew 27:57–60)

EVEN AFTER HIS RESURRECTION, JESUS' INTEREST IN PROSPERITY CONTINUED

Jesus continued to be aware of the prosperity needs of his followers, even after his resurrection. When the fishermen had fished all night without success, the resurrected Jesus appeared and instructed them to cast their nets on "the right side" of the boat. Their nets were then laden with fish. (John 21) (See Chapter 10)

After his resurrection, the disciples gathered in an upper room in Jerusalem and dwelled upon Jesus' name and presence for a number of weeks. It is little wonder that they were transformed from the common, ignorant disciples of an earlier age into the bold, illumined apostles of the early Christian era, because the word "Jerusalem" means "abode of prosperity." It symbolizes "divine substance," which is the body of God and the foundation of all wealth.

Through dwelling upon Jesus' name and prosperity consciousness, a handful of ordinary men were able to tune in on his consciousness of universal substance, and spread the extraordinary message of the prosperous Truth to the whole ancient world. That was a colossal achievement for those times! Imagine how many millions of dollars that feat would cost today in terms of radio, television, newspaper, direct mail marketing, and other media expense.

Later, it was prosperous women who boldly invited the controversial Christians to use their comfortable homes as meeting places:

1. The prominence of Mary, the mother of Mark, is indicated by the real estate holdings she held in her own name. It was her maid, Rhoda, who first greeted Peter and many others who came to pray together in Mary's home. (Acts 12:13)

2. The affluent businesswoman, Lydia of Thyatira, also bravely invited the early Christians to use her home as a meeting place. The illustrious Paul and Silas were among her houseguests. Described as a "seller of purple," Lydia was engaged in selling purple-dyed textiles used for coloring materials in the Macedonian city of Philippi. She and her prosperous household became the first recorded Christian converts in Europe. (Acts 16:14–15) She quietly helped Paul spread the message of the prosperous Truth throughout the ancient world.

Thus, the impact of Jesus' prosperity teaching is shown in the fact that *businessmen became some of his first disciples,* and *businesswomen were some of his early apostles.*

JESUS' MINISTRY BEGAN AT
PROSPEROUS CAPERNAUM

Jesus began his ministry in Capernaum, a prosperous port town, located on the shores of the Sea of Galilee. During Jesus' era, Capernaum was considered a large and rich city. Since it lay on the well-traveled highway between Damascus and Jerusalem, this port town of Capernaum tapped the rich commerce of the entire area. It was a Roman military outpost and tax-collecting station. The town of

Capernaum not only was a ship-building center, it was also a center of pickling, salting and packing fish for shipment to such far away markets as Spain. Capernaum enjoyed the thriving fish-packing industry because fish abounded in the waters of Lake Galilee. In fact, this lake yielded an extraordinary amount of fish.

The thriving city of Capernaum was surrounded by gentle rolling hills. Olive and citrus trees thrived on the abundance of water found in the area. Violent storms sometimes arose on the Sea of Galilee, but a wall of mountains shielded Capernaum, giving it an atmosphere of peaceful, sheltered comfort. It was entirely fitting that Jesus should begin his ministry in this place of beauty, peace and literal prosperity.

Everything needed for Jesus' physical comfort was there: He headquartered in the home of Peter and Andrew. When the throngs began to crowd in upon him, Jesus had a boat in which he would go out on the lake, or over to the other side for quiet meditation. He often taught from the boat as it anchored a short way offshore. This enabled him to address many more people at one time. He sometimes taught on a plain just outside the city. At other times he spoke in the elegant synagogue which some believe was constructed for him by the wealthy centurion, whose servant Jesus healed. (Matthew 8:5–13) This prominent centurion was a commander in the Roman Army, a most imposing job in those days.

That it was engaged in the fishing industry indicated that *Capernaum was also a place of metaphysical prosperity.* Fish symbolize the idea of increase, and it is significant that much of Jesus' teaching had to do with fish and fishermen. It was also fitting that early Christians later used the prosperous sign of the fish as their secret symbol. How that secret symbol of increase worked to prosper them! The prosperity theme of both Jesus and the early Christians might have been taken from the wise old saying: "Give a man a fish and you feed him for a day. Teach him how to fish and you feed him for a lifetime."

JESUS' FIRST PROSPERITY MIRACLES: PRIVATE AND PUBLIC

I find it of prosperous significance that Jesus did not call the typical spiritually-minded of his day to be his disciples. Instead, he deliberately called ordinary businessmen, including a tax collector and fishermen.

I also find it of prosperous significance that most of Jesus' parables were prosperity parables, and that some of his most prominent miracles were prosperity miracles. It is of further significance that he performed a prosperity miracle *before* he called his first three disciples. It was not Jesus' healing power, but his prospering power, that convinced Peter, James and John to follow him. It was only when he had first proved to them that he had prospering power that they became his "instant disciples." (Luke 5) Without any hesitation, they then left their boats, bulging with an abundance of fish, and went forth to follow Jesus.

This, his first *private* prosperity miracle, occurred when the disciples had fished all night without results. Jesus then appeared, and told them where to cast their nets. When they followed his instructions, they filled two boats with so many fish that both boats almost sank with such unaccustomed abundance!

Why were Peter, James and John so impressed by Jesus' ability to demonstrate prosperity? Because in the time of Jesus, the poor were despised by the general public. *Poverty was considered a curse and wealth was considered a spiritual blessing.* When Peter, James and John realized that Jesus taught the good news about plenty—that the kingdom of abundance was at hand—they quickly left the ranks of the despised poor to follow him.

It is also of prosperous significance that among Jesus' first *public* miracles was a prosperity miracle. It occurred at the wedding feast in Cana when Jesus turned ordinary water into the finest of wine. (John 2:1-11) This was quite a prosperity demonstration for the host. (See Chapter 2)

JESUS ENDORSED WEALTH ATTAINED
BY HONORABLE METHODS

It was not wealth that Jesus condemned, but the methods by which it was acquired, and the way in which it was so often used. There were more dishonorable people of wealth in Jesus' time than honorable ones. They often amassed their wealth—not by honest work in a business or profession—but more often by unjust means through bribery, extortion, or confiscation of someone's property.

There were all too few of the other type of men of affluence in the East: the kind who acquired their wealth in honorable ways during the prosperous years, then held that wealth in trust, sharing it with the common people during the lean years. In times of famine, the "honest rich" shared generously with the less fortunate. Such men of honor often lived simply, making no great display of their success.

Through his teaching, Jesus was trying to show his followers that they could again become prosperous by the honorable, age-old methods that had been used by their prosperous forebears of the Old Testament.

When the rich young ruler came to Jesus to inquire about eternal life, the Scriptures report that "Jesus looking upon him, loved him." (Mark 10:21) Jesus told this rich man to sell what he had and share the proceeds with the poor, if he wished to experience eternal life. The young man went away sorrowfully because he had many possessions which he was unable to emotionally release. Jesus then commented that it was easier for a camel to go through a needle's eye than for a rich man to enter the kingdom. But he explained that anyone who was able to release for Christ's sake would receive a hundredfold blessing.

This statement was not an indictment against wealth, possessions, or family. Please note that Jesus did not say that the rich man could not enter the kingdom, but that it would be hard for him to do so. Jesus knew the man was controlled by his possessions rather than being in control of them. Later Jesus commented sadly to his followers, "How hard it is for them that *trust* in riches to enter the kingdom." (Mark 10:23)

I can understand why Jesus made this observation. I regret to say that some of the stingiest people I have met were literal millionaires who were bound to their material wealth without the benefits of an *inner* consciousness of supply. Like this rich young ruler, they could not turn loose and enjoy what they had, much less share it with others. They just never entered the kingdom of true abundance where peace and plenty go hand in hand. Instead, life for them was a series of endless problems. They unwittingly proved that old saying: "If you do not give voluntarily to the constructive experiences of life, you will be forced to give involuntarily to the destructive experiences of life. But give you must, because it is the law of the universe."

Various schemes are often devised for getting rich quick. Yet most of them do not endure because they have no spiritual basis. Through his teaching, Jesus pointed out again and again that true prosperity must have a spiritual basis; that God is the Source of man's supply. This is why he said: "Lay not up for yourselves treasures upon earth, where moth and rust consume, and where thieves through and steal; but lay up for yourselves treasures in heaven.'' (Matthew 6:19-20) As you study the *inner* methods of prosperity which he employed, you, too, will be laying up treasures in the heavenly realms of your thinking. You will gain a true knowledge of how to prosper from within outwardly—through the action of the mind—and this is a method which no one can take from you.

HOW JESUS' PROSPERITY FORMULAS PROSPERED A BUSINESSMAN

Jesus said, ''You cannot serve God and mammon,'' (Matthew 6:24) because he knew that mammon is ''riches regarded as an object of worship or a false god.'' People serve mammon who leave God out of their financial affairs and try to go it alone. When you realize that God wants you to prosper, and that God, as the Creator of this rich universe, is the Source of your prosperity, then you are not worshipping mammon. You are not making a false god of prosperity. Instead, you are claiming your prosperous heritage from the divine Source of all your blessings.

A businessman wrote from Pennsylvania:

''Years ago, my financial affairs were in bad shape. I was suffering from unsteady work and the bills piled up. Even when money came in, it did not go very far. In desperation I cut out this statement and put it in my billfold: 'MY SUPPLY COMES TO ME FROM GOD, AND IT IS ALWAYS WITH ME WHEREVER I AM.'

''In all these years since, I have placed that statement in all the billfolds I have had. The good news is that *we have never been without funds since! There has always been enough money on hand to meet our needs.*''

HOW JESUS' PROSPERITY FORMULAS
PROSPERED THE AUTHOR

Soon after I was left a young widow with a small son to rear alone, I prayed over and over for guidance about how to prosper. For two years the only answer to my prayer came in the promise of Jesus, ''Be not therefore anxious, saying, 'What shall we eat?' or 'What shall we drink?' or 'Wherewithal shall we be clothed?' . . . for your heavenly Father knoweth that ye have need of all these things. But seek ye first his kingdom, and his righteousness; and all these things shall be added unto you.'' (Matthew 6:31-33)

When I finally began to fathom what it meant—that I was to seek first the inner kingdom of rich divine ideas—I took up the study of Practical Christianity, and began to employ the power of prosperous thinking. Gradually, ''all these things'' began to be added to my life. That prayer of so long ago has now been answered, and I discovered along the way that *Jesus' teachings are filled with prospering power!*

During that bleak period of my life, I also discovered that some of Jesus' most famous promises were prosperity promises. Among them, I have found these to be especially inspiring.:

''All things whatsoever the Father hath are mine.'' (John 16:15)

''I came that they may have life, and may have it abundantly.'' (John 10:10)

''If ye shall ask anything of the Father, he will give it you in my name. Hitherto have ye asked nothing in my name; ask, and ye shall receive, that your joy may be made full.'' (John 16:23,24)

''The hungry he hath filled with good things.'' (Luke 1:53)

"All things whatsoever ye pray and ask for, believe that ye receive them, and ye shall have them." (Mark 11:24)

"Nothing shall be impossible unto you." (Matthew 17:20)

"Ask and it shall be given you; seek and ye shall find; knock and it shall be opened unto you. for every one that asketh receiveth; and he that seeketh findeth; and to him that knocketh it shall be opened." (Matthew 7:7-8)

"If ye abide in me, and my words abide in you, ye shall ask what ye will, and it shall be done unto you." (John 15:7)

"If ye shall ask anything in my name I will do it." (John 14:14)

"These things have I spoken unto you, that my joy may be in you, and that your joy may be full." (John 15:11)

WHY JESUS PLACED SO MUCH EMPHASIS
UPON PROSPERITY

The four Gospels are filled with good news about prosperity. There are definite reasons for this:

First: As stated previously, the poor were despised in the time of Jesus. Poverty was considered a curse and wealth a spiritual blessing. Unorganized and without leadership, the masses were in a sad economic condition. They seemed helpless to protest the unjust system of taxation that had been placed upon them by the Roman government, or to revolt against it. The world seemed a hopeless place where they found relief from their miseries only by believing they would find comfort in the life hereafter.

Jesus came to show his followers that the kingdom of God is at hand here and now; that it is within. He emphasized that they did not have to wait until some future time to reap life's blessings. *Through his various prosperity miracles, parables, and promises, Jesus tried to teach the good news about plenty: that they could have it now!*

Second: There was another reason why Jesus put so much emphasis in his teachings upon the fact that true prosperity always has a spiritual basis; that man must look to God for guidance and enduring supply. The Romans did not strictly require them to observe the laws of the Jewish religion. Only the small towns, villages, and communes of Galilee retained their Jewish identity. This meant that many of the Jews had become lax in their tithe-paying to the Temple in Jerusalem, and to the observance of spiritual methods that would have continued to prosper and guide them, regardless of the political situation of the time.

Jesus came to remind his followers that they must begin to put God first financially, and again observe the tithing laws of their own religion if they were to prosper and succeed in life—regardless of whether the Romans demanded it or not.

Throughout Hebrew history, their sharing of tithes and offerings had brought peace and plenty. In the Old Testament, the payment of tithes was believed to have purged one of sin, illness, and even to deliver one from death. During that era, the tithe was considered to be the hedge of the Hebrews' riches, or the secret of their vast wealth. So long as the people of the Old Testament had put God first financially, they prospered exceedingly. No other group of people has even been able to surpass their wealth! But *when they became lax in their giving, they came upon hard times and want.* This was the condition in which they found themselves at the time Jesus appeared on the scene. It had been the wise prophet, Malachi, who had earlier reminded them that they could again tithe their way out of their problems into abundant success:

"From the days of your fathers ye have turned aside from mine ordinances, and have not kept them. Return unto me, and I will return unto you, saith Jehovah of hosts. But ye say, 'Wherein shall we return?' Will a man rob God? Yet ye rob me. But ye say, 'Wherein have we robbed thee?' In tithes and offerings. Ye are cursed with the curse; for ye rob me, even this whole nation.

"Bring ye the whole tithe into the storehouse, that there may be food in my house, and prove me now herewith, saith Jehovah of hosts, if I will not open you the windows of heaven, and pour you out a blessing, that there shall not be room enough to receive it." (Malachi 3:7-10)

Through his strong prosperity teaching, Jesus was trying to again bring to the attention of his followers that basic secret of success. (See Chapter 9)

THE PROSPEROUS MESSIAH'S EARLY CHURCH

There is a great deal more emphasis upon prosperity in the history of the early Christian church than many people have realized. Although the first churches have often been depicted as bare and unadorned, this was not so. The early Christian churches were built at a time when the alliance between the Emperor and Christianity placed emphasis upon pomp and ceremony. This was long after the days of clandestine worship. The persecutions were over.

Since the Emperor was considered Christ's vicar, his residence was lavishly decorated as that befitting so great a personage. This was all the more reason why the church as the house of God was not to be poor, lowly or unadorned. Mosaics, frescoes, marble, and other rich materials were used so that the church would appear as a paradise in which the soul might achieve mystical ecstacy. Under the protection of the Emperor, an aristocratic emphasis was placed upon the Christian art surrounding and embodying the first churches.

Certainly the history of art reveals that many of the ancient artists had the early Christian's concept of Jesus as a prosperous Messiah. I was reminded of this recently while viewing an impressive collection of religious paintings at the J. Paul Getty Art Museum in Malibu, California. One could feel a consciousness of the prosperous Messiah that radiated from the elegant paintings found there, which depicted early works of religious art.

WHY YOU SHOULD DARE TO PROSPER

In view of the overwhelming prosperity teachings found not only in the four Gospels, but throughout the Bible and in the early Christian church, why has there been so much talk of sacrifice, persecution and hard times associated with the spiritual way of life? History indicates that the prosperous, inspired teachings of Jesus continued to be observed during the early centuries after Christ.

However, religion later became more secularized, leading to variations and departures from Jesus' original teachings. The feudal systems of the Middle Ages assured wealth only for the privileged few. During this period, the teaching of "poverty and penance" was offered to the masses as the only way to salvation, in order to keep people in poverty, and to make lack and privation a supposed "Christian virtue." Unsuspecting millions were led to believe that it was "pious to be poor," a belief which was useful in forestalling revolution among the masses. This belief had a political, not a spiritual, foundation.

Even though Jesus was a master teacher of prosperity, some of those old feudal ideas about poverty as a spiritual virtue have persisted until this day. As a child, growing up in the Deep South, I often heard people say, "I am poor, but I'm a *good* Christian.'' That statement made it sound as if all the rich folks were bound for hell just because they were prosperous. This attitude always bothered me. My silent reaction was, ''Why should Christians, or any other group, have to be poor? God is our loving Father and He isn't poor. Neither is He stingy.'' People have sometimes assumed that Jesus approved of poverty because he spent so much time with the poor. Through his teachings and presence, Jesus was trying to lift up the poor of his time into a consciousness of universal abundance.

By Jesus' standards, you are not a very ''good Christian'' if you are poor. Poverty is a form of hell caused by man's blindness to God's universal abundance for him. A loving Father's desire for you is unlimited good, not merely the means of a meager existence. You cannot be very happy if you are poor, and nobody needs to be poor. It is a sin to be poor. It is your Father's good pleasure to give you the kingdom of abundance, and it should be your good pleasure to receive it. As stated previously, the word ''wealth'' means ''grand living.'' That is what Jesus stood for and taught: a philosophy of abundance that could lead to grander living than ever before. No one should go through life a beggar when he can be a king. So dare to prosper!

HOW A BUSINESSMAN ATTRACTED
MILLIONAIRE-CUSTOMERS

As related by a California businessman, when you decide to prosper here's how it can work:

''I began studying your book, *The Dynamic Laws of Prosperity,*[2] more than fifteen years ago at a time when I was conducting my business out of the back of a pickup truck. This

---

2. Catherine Ponder, *The Dynamic Laws of Prosperity* (Marina del Rey, CA: DeVorss & Co., rev. ed. 1985).

took place in a poverty-stricken area of Los Angeles. Through my diligent study of the power of prosperous thinking, I have had outstanding business success over the years. I now live and work in a famous desert resort area of Southern California known as the 'playground of the rich.'

"In spite of my earlier success, when the first book in your new series on 'the millionaires of the Bible' was published, entitled *The Millionaires of Genesis,* I devoured it. Those millionaires of Genesis had a dramatic effect upon my life. They revolutionized my already prosperous thinking. They subtly injected within me the realization that *unlimited abundance*—not just 'prosperity'—should be mine. They enabled me to see, sense, and feel the unlimited wealth available to me and around me. All at once I felt bonds of limitation drop and fall away from me, as I realized that the vast wealth of the universe was available to me *right now,* just as in olden times. With that realization came satisfying results!

"A number of literal millionaires became my customers soon after I began keeping company with the millionaires of Genesis. One new customer's 'take-home pay' is reported to be a cool 50 million dollars a year. He is one of the richest oil men in this country. He asked me to work on an 'expense-is-no-object' financial arrangement—the only stipulation being that he and his wife would receive 'the very best in services and goods.' On one party alone, his wife spent $6,500 with my firm. This account could never have come to me until I first broke my own chains of limited thinking, which those ancient millionaires helped me to do.

"My study of the millionaires of the Bible has also brought glamour, flair and excitement into my life. Recently, I was the honored guest of the famed Liberace (another customer) at the opening of his Las Vegas show.

"*I find it pays to keep mental company with the millionaires of the Bible because theirs was a stable, satisfying wealth with a spiritual basis.* They knew that God was the Source of their supply, so they turned to Him constantly for guidance. They praised and thanked Him often for their multiplying blessings, which just continued to grow and grow. By putting God first financially through sharing so lavishly of their tithes and offerings, they kept attuned to His guidance and supply for them.

"From the dramatic rise in my own success, I am convinced that anyone can prosper exceedingly who keeps mental company with the millionaires of the Bible, and applies the methods they used to one's own life and financial affairs."

HOW THE CARPENTER FROM
NAZARETH CAN PROSPER YOU

Jesus' early life has prosperous significance. Nazareth, his boyhood hometown, was a village in Galilee. That thriving area of Galilee symbolizes the energy, life, and activity of the *outer* man, which must work in conjunction with the substance, or foundation of all wealth, of the *inner* man, in order to produce prosperity.

Nazareth was considered a commonplace community, yet in this ordinary village, Jesus grew to manhood. This should give you hope, because Nazareth typifies the commonplace mind of man. It is in that ordinary place of development, or those ordinary circumstances, that the prosperous Truth is born: first in your thinking, then in your life. (I first became aware of the prosperous Truth while working in ordinary circumstances as a secretary in the business world.) The word "Nazareth" means "branch, offshoot, sprout, watched, guarded." Often it is that first prosperous Truth that you watch, guard, and secretly think about which, in turn, grows, expands and leads you into far greater good than you have previously known.

Yet it may all have begun in your commonplace Nazareth-experiences. Historically, Nazareth was considered a despised place. "Can any good thing come out of

Nazareth?'' was the standard attitude of that day. (John 1:46) Can anything good come out of your despised experiences of the past or present? Yes! Because that carpenter from Nazareth came to open the way for you to become attuned to a universal prosperity consciousness. A carpenter is a workman who builds or repairs; one who converts ideas or thoughts into visible form. As you learn to use the prosperity methods Jesus applied, you can make repairs upon your life, or build anew, converting ideas and thoughts into visible forms as the need arises. When you do this you feel like a millionaire, since you experience increased abundance and happiness. (Remember that the word ''millionaire'' in its root means ''abundance and happiness.'')

YOUR FIRST SUCCESS SECRET FROM
THE MILLIONAIRE OF NAZARETH

Here is your first success secret from that carpenter from Nazareth who became Lord of Plenty—a secret that can help you make repairs upon your life, or build it anew:

No person's name ever stood for such colossal achievement as the name ''Jesus Christ.'' There is power for colossal achievement along all lines to those who dwell upon that Name today. The mightiest vibration is set up by speaking the name ''Jesus Christ.'' It is the Name that has power to mold the rich substance of the universe into definite, visible good for you. When spoken, it sets forces into activity that can bring prosperous results to you!

HOW OTHERS HAVE BEEN HELPED BY THIS
MYSTICAL PROSPERITY METHOD

You are prosperous to the degree that you are experiencing peace, health and plenty in your world. By dwelling upon the name "Jesus Christ," you can experience the increased peace, health and plenty you desire in your life. Here is how others have done so:

1. *Prosperity as Peace*. How Peace and Harmony Were Restored to an Office Worker in California:

> "About a month ago I wrote your Prayer Ministry requesting prayers about the many changes and conflicts of personality that were in our office. You suggested that I declare daily that 'JESUS CHRIST IS IN CHARGE AND ON THE JOB EIGHT HOURS A DAY IN THIS OFFICE.'

> "I am happy to report that it worked! Peace and harmony have been restored. Needed changes are being worked out quietly and effectively. Those previously uncooperative workers have either become silent and peaceful, or have moved on elsewhere. It has been gratifying to learn how to handle this situation (and others that may arise) successfully."

2. *Prosperity as Health*. How a Healing Occurred in New York. A minister wrote:

> "A gentleman came to our church's healing service. The congregation chanted 'JESUS CHRIST HEALS YOU NOW, SO ARISE AND WALK.' This man arose from his wheelchair and walked out of the church all the way to his house chanting these healing words."

3. *a) Prosperity as Plenty*. The Prospering Power Found in the Name "Jesus Christ" by a Housewife from Pennsylvania:

> "By dwelling on the name 'Jesus Christ,' my mother finally received $150 for damages done to her car. Also, the rear blinkers in the car were repaired for only $2.12—after

several mechanics had said it would cost $50 or more. *As I continue to daily meditate on the name 'Jesus Christ,' life is taking on a more secure and peaceful tone.* I am grateful to have learned of the prospering power that can be released by dwelling upon that Name.''

b) Prosperity as Plenty. How an Out-of-Work Professor Prospered in Real Estate in Texas:

''Thanks to my study of *The Dynamic Laws of Prosperity,* I am a school teacher who went back to college, got another degree, and became a college professor. Then came a surprise: After seven years in that job, I was fired, or so it seemed. Later, I realized that a job I had outgrown simply released me to do something better. I had bought 57 acres just prior to this. That was quite a prosperity demonstration because I had saved only $2,500, but was able to borrow the rest for a downpayment. Altogether I went into debt $60,000.

''Although I knew nothing about developing land, I decided that was what I was supposed to do at that point in my life. So I began to declare daily: 'JESUS CHRIST IS IN CHARGE OF ALL MY REAL ESTATE DEALINGS, AND THEY PROSPER ME MIGHTILY NOW. THANK GOD.'

''The results? I felt guided to begin subdividing the land to sell for mobile homes. Help came from everywhere about surveying, legal procedures, building roads, piping utilities, and selling. That same prayer statement showed me how to collect back payments, how to carry my own notes, and how to write sales contracts. I have never lost a cent in the process!

''The land has now paid for itself. I kept 17 acres on a bluff overlooking a picturesque river, and have built a nice home. It's paid for, furnished and I don't owe anybody anything. Furthermore, I am still living well from the income of the sale of the mobile home property. Of course, through all of this I have tithed. Now I am taking drama

preparation for becoming a playwright—thanks to
ering power that can be released by speaking forth
name 'Jesus Christ.' "

HOW YOU, TOO, CAN BECOME
LORD OF PLENTY

When he turned within, recognized and called forth his
divinity, Jesus, that humble carpenter from Nazareth,
became the powerful Lord of Plenty known as "Jesus
Christ." You can also call forth that divine "Lord of
Plenty" nature within you, and reap its vast benefits, as you
begin to:

First: Dwell often upon the words "Jesus Christ,"
meditating inwardly, and affirming outwardly, this name.

Second: Follow through in studying and using the same
prosperity formulas that Jesus used, many of which are explained in the coming pages.

Now, before going on to Chapter Two to learn one of
Jesus' most famous prosperity formulas, you will enjoy
meditating upon, and declaring often, these words:

"NO PERSON'S NAME EVER STOOD FOR SUCH COLOSSAL
ACHIEVEMENT AS THE NAME 'JESUS CHRIST.' THERE IS POWER
FOR COLOSSAL ACHIEVEMENT ALONG ALL LINES FOR ME AS I
DWELL UPON THIS NAME TODAY.

"THE MIGHTIEST VIBRATION CAN BE SET UP BY SPEAKING THE
NAME 'JESUS CHRIST.' IT IS THE NAME THAT HAS THE POWER TO
MOLD THE RICH SUBSTANCE OF THE UNIVERSE INTO DEFINITE
VISIBLE GOOD FOR ME. AS I SPEAK THE NAME 'JESUS CHRIST'
OFTEN, IT SETS FORCES INTO ACTIVITY THAT BRING PROSPEROUS
RESULTS.

"YES, I REJOICE THAT CHRIST IN ME IS MY PROSPERING
POWER, AND THAT CHRIST IN ME IS LORD OF PLENTY, NOW AND
FOREVER."

SUMMARY

1. Jesus was not poor. He was one of the most prosperous thinkers who ever lived, a master teacher of prosperity. He became Lord of Plenty.

2. The Christ nature in Jesus symbolizes the Divinity in you that is never poor, so that you can become Lord of Plenty, too.

3. Jesus' interest in prosperity began at birth, continued throughout his life, and was shown even after his resurrection.

4. Jesus' ministry began at the fishing port of Capernaum. Since fish symbolize ideas of increase, Capernaum was a place of both physical and metaphysical prosperity.

5. In Jesus' time, the poor were despised. Poverty was considered a curse and wealth was considered a spiritual blessing.

6. Jesus endorsed wealth attained by honorable methods. He did not hesitate to use his deeper powers to promote earthly prosperity.

7. Through his various prosperity teachings, Jesus emphasized the good news about plenty: that we do not have to wait until some future life for it; we can have it now.

8. There was a great deal of emphasis upon prosperity in the early Christian church. Only in later centuries and for political reasons, was the false belief instilled in the masses that it was pious to be poor.

9. Jesus was born in Nazareth, which typifies the commonplace mind of man, in which the prosperous Truth is born. Jesus as a carpenter symbolizes one who converts ideas and thoughts into visible form as the need arises. When you learn to do this, you can experience increased abundance and happiness—which is what the word "millionaire" means.

10. Here is one of the first prosperity secrets from the millionaire of Nazareth: The name "Jesus Christ" has the power to mold universal substance into definite, visible good for you. When spoken, that name sets forces into activity that can bring prosperous results to you.

THE PROSPERITY LAW OF ADAPTABILITY

THE WEDDING FEAST MIRACLE

— Chapter 2 —

We have often been led to believe that most of the miracles performed by Jesus were miracles of healing. I find it exciting to realize that *two of his earliest miracles were prosperity miracles in which he turned lack into abundance!*

As mentioned in Chapter One, Jesus' first *private* prosperity miracle occurred just before he called Peter, James, and John to be his disciples. After they had fished all night without success, he manifested fish for them in such abundance that they had to ask fishermen in a second boat to help them bring in the catch. Both boats nearly sank with the abundance of it! As a result of this demonstration of increase, Peter, James, and John were so impressed with Jesus' prosperity consciousness that they unhesitatingly left their boats—bulging with a super-abundance of fish—and went off to become Jesus' disciples. (Luke 5:1–11) They soon witnessed a number of his healing miracles.

JESUS' FIRST PUBLIC PROSPERITY
MIRACLE AT CANA

A "law" is a principle that works. It is a rule of action. An early explorer of nature's laws was the brilliant scientist, Sir Isaac Newton, who said there is one set of natural laws for the physical world. There are also higher mental and spiritual laws than those usually used on the physical plane of life. *The higher mental and spiritual laws are so powerful that they can be used to either multiply, neutralize, or even reverse natural laws. It is when these higher mental and spiritual laws are invoked, through the mind of man, that they often produce results that seem miraculous on the physical plane. Jesus understood the higher laws of the mind and used them constantly to meet the needs of the moment.*

The word "adapt" means "to make suitable by changing," "to change without difficulty," "to adapt to change," or "to bring into harmony." Jesus invoked the prosperity law of adaptability when he performed his first *public* prosperity miracle at the wedding feast in Cana. There he turned ordinary water into the finest of wine. (John 2:1–11)

When you study his first *public* prosperity miracle from that standpoint, you become aware of the mental attitudes Jesus invoked, which you can use, too. As you take those same *steps in mental action,* you experience suitable changes without difficulty that bring you into harmony with greater good in your life than you have ever known before. Thus, when you use the prosperity law of adaptability, and a satisfying result then occurs, some people might regard it as a "miracle." In order to invoke the prosperity law of adaptability, you will enjoy using the following simple steps in mental action:

STEP ONE: WHEN A NEED ARISES, DON'T PANIC

Cana had a prosperous setting. It was located about seven miles from Nazareth in the midst of abundant pomegranate and olive groves. It is fitting that Jesus' first *public* prosperity miracle occurred at a wedding, because a wedding was an experience in abundance. In the Oriental countries, a wedding was an event of great importance and it was lavishly celebrated. In wealthy families the wedding festivities could last for as long as seven days. The Jewish people were known for their profuse hospitality, and even among the poorer classes, a wedding celebration could last one or two days. At this wedding feast in Cana, it was very embarrassing when the wine was suddenly exhausted. Jesus' mother pointed this out to him by saying, "They have no wine." Jesus answered her, "Mine hour is not yet come." (John 2:4)

In using the prosperity law of adaptability, here is the first step in mental action that you should take: When there is a need to be met in your life, it will be immediately brought to your attention: either through people or circumstances outside yourself, or through your own awareness. Yet, like Jesus, *you should not rush forth to try to make it right in an outer way.* You should work it out on the *inner* planes of consciousness—in your thought and feeling nature—first.

Jesus knew it would take a little time for him to turn ordinary water into fine wine. *Rush, force and coercion have no place in the realm of prosperous thinking. They never demonstrate abundance.* Instead rush, force, and coercion only dissipate your good. "There is no rush in the inner realm of mind and Spirit," is a mystical saying that is *so* true. To human senses it may seem to take longer when you are working things out on the mental and spiritual levels. Yet when the result comes, it will be satisfying and enduring.

HOW HEALING CAME WHEN SHE REFUSED TO BE RUSHED

True prosperity includes health, and here is how a housewife in New York was healed when she refused to be rushed into taking action:

"God has been good and answered my prayers. I had a serious health problem, and my own doctor had been disturbed because I had delayed so long. But I told him I was praying about the matter and had to do as I felt led. The specialist he sent me to see was the nicest person. I had prayed that this second doctor would see only the good in my condition and he did.

"He has now told me that no operation is necessary! *I feel that the additional time spent in prayer and inspirational study led to this healing. If people would pray first—instead of rushing forth—how much more often their prayers would be answered.* They, too, would often find that 'no operation was necessary.' "

Not only was this woman saved much pain and suffering from her use of these *inner* methods, she also demonstrated prosperity through being saved considerable medical expense.

WHAT TO DO WHEN YOU ARE BEING PRESSURED BY NEGATIVE APPEARANCES

You cannot force your good, and you cannot force anyone else's good. When Jesus' mother said, "They have no wine," he replied, "Mine hour is not yet come." His refusal meant that *when one is praying for divine guidance, he does not go into action until he is directed to do so from within*— regardless of what people about him are saying or doing. *There is a divine fulfillment for every need, but it cannot be coerced.* Even though he recognized the lack, Jesus was not yet prompted to act. He knew one's good cannot be forced; *zeal that is not tempered with wisdom only leads to confusion.* (See Chapter 11 on "Zeal" in my book, *The Healing Secrets of the Ages.*[1])

When a need appears, take note of it. Then begin to work within your thoughts and feelings to meet it there first. If you immediately rush forth to try to fix things up in an outer way, you will only meet with confusion and defeat. There is a famous and true saying, "There must be an inworking before there can be an outworking."

When you are being pressured by negative appearances, you might respond: "I am listening to the voice of Truth, which does not yet bid me act," or, "It is not my guidance to do anything yet," or, "I feel it is best to wait for a further sign." Even though he recognized the lack, Jesus was not immediately prompted to act. Neither should you allow yourself to be pressured by appearances of lack. Instead declare: "THERE IS NO RUSH IN SPIRIT, SO I WILL NOT ACT UN-TIL I AM PROMPTED TO DO SO FROM WITHIN."

HOW THE AUTHOR'S NEED WAS SUPPLIED

More than twenty years ago at the time I became a minis-ter, I received none of the financial benefits that ministers

---

1. Catherine Ponder, *The Healing Secrets of the Ages* (Marina del Rey, CA: DeVorss & Co., rev. ed. 1985).

should and sometimes do receive today, such as a guaranteed salary, a manse allowance, an annual paid vacation, a health insurance program, or retirement benefits. Being dependent upon receiving "love offerings" to meet my daily needs, and those of my young son, we lived from day to day on an invisible means of supply. I now regard that stringent period as a necessary initiation in the development of my *inner* consciousness of prosperity. Over the years I have grown accustomed to the "love offering" method of supply, since it is a customary means of compensation even today for many ministers. But during that lean period, it seemed an especially harsh method of survival for me.

Once, after having worked a long, full day, there had been no "love offerings" given for the spiritual counseling or other work I had done that day, and there was no money available for food that night. At the end of the day, when my son mentioned how hungry he was, I replied, "Let me rest and pray about this. Then we will know what to do." As I relaxed, I declared over and over in meditation, "GOD IS NEVER TOO LATE. GOD IS ALWAYS ON TIME WITH OUR GOOD."

Within the hour, my son appeared and said, "Mother, I heard a knock at the door and it was a lady who had ridden the bus all the way across town. She said you had prayed for her some time ago, and things had worked out. In appreciation she wanted you to have this 'thank offering.' " At that moment, the two dollars he handed me seemed like two million! The simple meal we ate that night certainly was not lavish, but it tasted especially good to us because, like the priceless manna from heaven enjoyed by the Hebrews in the wilderness, that meal had come in answer to prayer. (See the chapter, "How to Gather Your Prosperous Manna," in my book, *The Millionaire Moses*.) God *had* been on time with our good! A loving Father has continued to provide for me over the years through countless experiences that have seemed just as amazing as that one.

When a need arises, if you immediately rush forth to try to fix things up in an outer way, you will only meet with confusion, defeat and more limitation. Instead, when a need arises, take note of it, but then begin to work *within* your own thoughts and feelings to meet the need there first. *Even though he recognized the lack, Jesus was not immediately prompted to act. Under similar circumstances, neither should we.*

STEP TWO: TO HANDLE THE POSSIBILITY OF NEW GOOD, PREPARE INWARDLY

Sometimes it is not a need that appears on the scene to be met. It may be the possibility of new good trying to come into your life that gets your attention. Again, if you immediately rush forth and try to force that good into expression, you experience an "abortion." Your desired good dissipates because your zeal scared it away.

Remember this: *There is no hope that ever stirs within you, but that God has the actual fulfillment of that hope for you—but in His own time and way.*

In his book, *The Prophet,*[2] Kahlil Gibran wrote:

"You are like an ocean, and though grounded ships await the tides upon your shores; yet even like an ocean, *you cannot hasten your tides.*"

---

2. Reprinted from *The Prophet,* by Kahlil Gibran, with permission of the publisher, Alfred A. Knopf, Inc., New York. Copyright 1923 by Kahlil Gibran; renewal copyright 1951 by Administrators C.T.A. of Kahlil Gibran Estate, and Mary G. Gibran. (Page 86.)

Even if your good is there for you lying quietly in the distance like heavy grounded ships that await the tide, you cannot hasten that good. Instead, you have only to get ready *inwardly* and *outwardly* for that good in order for it to come into your life under divine timing.

But there is a way you can get ready for the good that lies quietly in the distance watching every move you make. As described in the next segment, Jesus used that simple method at the wedding feast in Cana.

STEP THREE: GO TO CANA BY
SPEAKING WORDS OF ABUNDANCE

It was appropriate that Jesus' first *public* prosperity miracle took place at a wedding. As stated previously, attendance at a wedding was considered a prosperous experience, an event of abundance.

There were six waterpots of stone at the wedding in Cana. Jesus told the servants to fill those waterpots with what they had on hand, which was water. Since everything was done on a liberal scale at a wedding, the servants filled those pots *to the brim.*

You get ready for the good that lies at a distance by meeting the situation now at hand with whatever you have to work with. Those six hard, rough, stony waterpots symbolize the hard, rough conditions we sometimes have to meet in life. *However, you already have on hand what is needed to meet the hard, rough conditions of life. Whatever you have at hand to meet a problem is all you need to begin meeting that problem.* Jesus had nothing but ordinary, common water to pour into those rough, stony waterpots. Yet he instructed the servants to pour forth that water abundantly.

The transformation of water into wine symbolized the rich gifts that a loving father has for those who are willing to draw forth that abundance out of the realm of universal substance—or from the invisible store of unlimited supply—through the action of the mind.

The extent to which nature is prepared to make the transformation from lack to abundance is indicated by the pots being filled "to the brim" with water by the servants, after Jesus *spoke* to them. It is significant that Jesus performed this prosperity miracle at Cana, because the word "Cana" symbolizes the power center in the larynx which is released through the voice as spoken words. *You, too, can perform your first public prosperity miracle for all to see when you go to Cana, and use your power center to "speak the word" of abundance. To do so can overcome all lack in your life.*

The six jars would hold an abundant amount, about one hundred gallons. Your thoughts are your servants. The water poured into the pots by the servants is symbolic of the thoughts and *words* of light, Truth and abundance that you can pour forth on hard conditions of lack and limitation, thereby transforming them into conditions of abundance. *You must pour something into the appearance of lack before you can get anything out of it.*

HOW SHE BECAME A SUCCESSFUL
UNION NEGOTIATOR

Here is how one businesswoman poured forth thoughts and *words* of light, Truth and abundance on conditions of lack—both for herself and others—and transformed them into conditions of abundance.

From the State of Nevada she wrote:

"So many wonderful things have happened to me and mine since I began studying your book, *The Prosperity Secrets of the Ages.*[3] I can only list the use of prosperous thinking as described in that book:

1. "At the time I began to study that book, I was unemployed. I spoke forth a prosperity statement every day that 'A GOOD POSITION WITH A SALARY OF $15,000 OR MORE PER YEAR IS COMING TO ME NOW IN GOD'S OWN WONDERFUL WAY.' The results? My total income last year as an employer consultant and negotiator of labor contracts for employees' associations was in excess of $20,000!

2. "I gave a copy of *The Prosperity Secrets of the Ages* to a friend who was not only unemployed, but also unhappily involved with a married man. I suggested that she declare daily: 'I AM NOW GUIDED INTO MY TRUE PLACE WITH THE TRUE PEOPLE AND WITH THE TRUE PROSPERITY, QUICKLY AND IN PEACE.' A few months later she married a fine, successful businessman, and they are presently expecting their first child. She no longer has to work.

3. "I began to daily speak forth this prosperity statement for my company: 'I GIVE THANKS FOR AN ANNUAL $50,000 INCREASE IN REVENUE FOR THE ORGANIZATION FOR WHOM I WORK.' The results? $20,000 has been replaced in lost membership, and an additional $30,000 revenue has been scheduled.

4. "Part of my responsibility in my job is that of labor negotiator. It is an unusual job for a woman. It fell my lot to go up against the largest and most powerful union leader in this state, and one of the most powerful in the United States. I had never negotiated on my own before. No one believed I had a chance. My own board of directors was about to desert me. In the middle of my negotiations, the director gave notice of quitting and the whole staff also threatened to quit. (This was not related to my negotiations, however.) In addition, the attorneys retained by my organization (because of imagined wrongs) notified the board president they would withdraw their services if I were retained.

---

3. Catherine Ponder, *The Prosperity Secrets of the Ages* (Marina del Rey, CA: DeVorss & Co., rev. ed. 1985).

"I spoke forth appropriate affirmations daily throughout that two-month period. One of my favorites was: 'ALL THINGS CONFORM TO THE RIGHT THING NOW, QUICKLY AND IN PEACE.' Here are the amazing results that came from those spoken words:

a) "Complete success in my negotiations! I have become famous for my courage and skill at handling the whole transaction.

b) "The president of the board gave me his complete confidence. He stood between me and the forces who were threatening me. He fired the attorneys.

c) "Two more attorneys came to my assistance at no cost to our organization.

d) "The whole board of directors now agree that my negotiations have established a precedent that has improved the labor relations climate for the entire state.

e) "More beneficial results are happening daily. We have a new managing director who is very compatible with the staff and me.

5. "My sixteen-year-old daughter has learned the value of speaking forth prosperity affirmations daily, and she is on her way to a wonderful way of life. *She has quadrupled her income* since she began to declare, 'I AM BEAUTIFULLY AND APPROPRIATELY SUPPLIED WITH THE RICH SUBSTANCE OF THE UNIVERSE NOW.'

6. "The employers whom I represented have individually given me very generous gifts. I have started one employer on the way to success through giving him a copy of *The Prosperity Secrets of the Ages* to study.

7. "I owned a second deed of trust that had been delinquent for two years. I affirmed 'light' and 'prosperity' for the person who owed me. He paid me off in full just before Christmas.

8. "For a dear friend who needed a job, I spoke this affirmation: 'YOU NOW MOVE FORWARD INTO YOUR EXPANDED GOOD, DIVINELY DIRECTED AND LAVISHLY PROSPERED.' He phoned me tonight to say he has landed the job he wanted.

9. "Lost objects have been found.

10. "After affirming I would soon be a size ten again, one of my clients made me a present of a weight-reducing program which begins tomorrow.

11. "Since I took up the practice of prosperous thinking, *my income seems to buy more and last longer!* It is a good feeling to have a balance left over after paying the tithe and bills on time. *My tithes are now ten times what they were only a short time ago!"*

STEP FOUR: BY TREATING THE AVAILABLE SUPPLY AS THE DESIRED SUPPLY, WATER BECOMES WINE

You already have on hand what you need to meet the demands that are made upon you. Your good is adaptable. This is one of the great secrets we learn from Jesus' prosperity miracle at Cana. By treating the available supply as the *desired* supply, water became wine.

Here is how to invoke the law of adaptability: *The good you have on hand becomes adaptable and will meet your needs, if you begin appreciating it and using it.* The good you have on hand may be nothing more than the use of constructive thoughts and words. Yet those are the only financial assets you need, if you will begin to use them.

In Jesus' prosperity miracles, he always took the materials at hand, such as they were, and used them. You, too, already have what is needed to begin meeting the needs of your life. God will help you when once you make the start in faith. It has been proven down through the ages that faith moves on substance to prosper and bless the one using it. When it is put into action there is prospering power in faith!

STEP FIVE: HOW TO POUR FORTH SPECIFIC
PROSPERITY INTO THE STONY WATERPOTS

Jesus took what was on hand: the hard, stony waterpots, and common, ordinary water. *These two ingredients were all with which he had to work. Yet with them he produced a miracle of abundance.* He told the servants (symbolizing one's thoughts) to pour the water into the hard, stony pots. They did not pour meagerly, but "to the brim."

You can take your rough circumstances, your bodily conditions, your human affairs, just as they are and hold them in your mind. Then begin to praise them, bless them, and give thanks to the all-providing God that within them is the wine of peace, health and success that is yours by divine right.

If hard, stony conditions are all you have to work with, then they are all you need with which to perform a miracle! Treat the available supply as the desired supply, and it will become so.

You may be thinking, "But there is nothing on hand with which to meet this need." Oh, yes there is! There *always* is. Take the thought, the idea, the Bible verse, the prayer statement, or the passage in an inspirational book that appeals to you. Begin meditating upon it and declaring it. Bless and praise what you have, regarding it as "abundance," instead of condemning it and regarding it as "lack."

Take the circumstances of your life just as they are. Take the people in your life just as you find them. Take the home conditions just as they are. Take your bodily health just as it is. Take your business affairs and financial matters just as they are. Take your personal dreams and your professional hopes just as they are. Take this period of life, whether you regard yourself as young, old, or somewhere in between, just as it is. *All* of these are your rough, stony waterpots.

Then begin pouring into them the highest and best ideas you can hold about them. *Begin to praise and bless that which you have previously condemned. There is a multiplying power for good that can be released through use of this simple process.*

HOW A WIFE TRANSFORMED HER ROCKY
MARRIAGE INTO A HAPPY ONE

There once was a housewife whose husband had left her and their three children for another woman. He was gone for three months. Then he returned and wanted her forgiveness and help in straightening out their marriage.

She went to her minister and said, "How can I ever forget that he left me and the children for another woman?" The minister replied, "By remembering that he came back, confessed his error, and asked to try again."

The minister advised, "Go home, take your husband back, and begin at once to show the love you have always had for him, but may have seldom expressed. See his good qualities. Refuse to think of the past. Live one day at a time in the highest way you know, and things will work out for the best."

This wife faithfully followed her minister's instructions. Today she has a very happy home life. How did it come about? Only as she took the rough, stony, hard conditions of her marriage and began pouring forth the thoughts of love and blessing into them. Then the ordinary became extraordinary; the water became wine.

STEP SIX: HOW NOT TO REJECT YOUR GOOD

Do not reject your good just because it is not in the form you would like it to be. Treat the available marriage as though it were the desired marriage. Treat the available people in your life as though they were the desired people. Treat the available circumstances as though they were the desired circumstances. Treat the available supply as though it were the desired supply. As you adapt in this way to both the seen and unseen good at hand, the desires of your heart begin to materialize more and more as results. This is the prosperity law of adaptability.

Concerning those supposedly unwanted cares and responsibilities that life seems to thrust upon us, Kahlil Gibran wrote in *The Prophet:*[4]

"If it is a care you would cast off, that care has been chosen by *you,* rather than imposed upon you."

You may say, "But it is unjust to have to deal with these people, or these circumstances in my life which cause me so much worry and concern."

Kahlil Gibran further advised:[5]

"If it is an unjust law you would abolish, that law was written with *your* own hand upon your forehead."

HOW A FARMER USED UNUSUAL
AVAILABLE SUPPLY TO PROSPER

One of the most unique ways I've heard of anyone using the available supply to prosper is found in the story of the farmer in French West Africa who had lost everything he owned.[6] Because of a drought, his rich farm land became a desert.

---

4. Gibran, (New York, Alfred A. Knopf) p. 49.

5. Ibid, p. 48.

6. From the book by Alexander Lake, *Your Prayers Are Always Answered* (Reprinted by permission of Simon & Schuster, a Division of Gulf & Western Corp., NY: 1956), p. 13.

When this happened, all of his neighbors left. But this man felt guided to stay on his land. As he continued to pray about how he was to make a living, a strange thing happened: poisonous snakes swarmed onto his farm. For a time it looked as though he and his family would be forced to flee for their lives. But, as he continued to pray for guidance, he learned how to safely handle those cobras. Within two years, he was earning a comfortable income by selling venom used in making anti-snakebite serum. Here is an unusual example of how one person treated the available supply as though it were the desired form of supply, and it became so.

In taking stock of your *inner* abilities and of your *outer* supply, you may be inclined to say, "There is not enough to go around." Not enough of you, perhaps. But there is enough of God to go around, and since substance is the body of God, there is enough divine substance to go around, too. *So do not turn away from your good just because it does not appear in the form you think it should.* Instead, as you treat the available supply as though it were the desired supply, it will become so.

HIS LAST MINUTE RESCUE
FROM EAST AFRICA

Here is an amusing incident which shows how the available supply became the desired supply in a surprising way:

A member of the film industry wrote from Hollywood, California:

"Some years ago, I began to practice your suggestion for a visual aid to prosperity by carrying 'play money' in my wallet. As you had explained in *The Dynamic Laws of Prosperi-*

ty, doing this could create a feeling of financial abundance. Yet I was unprepared for the practical way that play money worked to literally extricate me from a difficult situation at a time when I was traveling in East Africa.

"I was in the troubled Republic of Uganda, producing a motion picture documentary on Kenya, Tanzania and Uganda. As I completed the last segments of my film, the capital city of Kampala in Uganda was in a state of jitters. President Idi Amin's decree expelling thousands of Asians from Uganda had created an atmosphere of fear and uncertainty. Not only Asians, but all non-Africans, were feeling the sting of official harassment, ranging from petty to violent.

"It was with considerable relief that I finished my film assignment and arrived at the Kampala-Entebbe airport at midnight to board a flight to London. I had already disposed of all local currency which is without exchange value outside Uganda. When I entered Customs, I was appalled to find that a 'new tax' had suddenly been levied on foreigners leaving Uganda. To my consternation, the tax had to be paid in Ugandan currency, of which I had none left. The only alternative was to cash my last traveler's check of a large denomination and get change in Uganda currency, which would be worthless the moment I was in the air.

"In an attempt to convince the sullen young Customs official that I was without Ugandan currency, I spread open my billfold. 'What is that?' he asked—pointing to the play money in my wallet. 'Oh, that is not real money,' I innocently replied. 'It is only play money.'

"Then came the first Ugandan smile of the evening when he said, 'I'd like some and we will forget the tax.' As I boarded the airplane, I watched the grinning young officer flash my play money before the dazzled eyes of his co-workers. He looked almost as happy as I was, to have been delivered in such an unusual way. That experience convinced me that there *is* literal prospering power in carrying play money in one's wallet, and I will never be without it again!''

STEP SEVEN: TO PERSIST IN FILLING "TO
THE BRIM" CAN PRODUCE HEALING AND ABUNDANCE

At the wedding in Cana, it was of great importance that when the servants poured water into those hard, stony waterpots, they filled them—not halfway, or toward the top—but all the way up "to the brim." (John 2:7)

When you are pouring forth good words—such as those of healing, abundance, or love—into hard, stony conditions in an attempt to produce good results (or when you are using some other invisible method in an effort to produce visible results), remember that *you must persist in the use of your method until you fill the situation "to the brim."* Don't give up and stop halfway (as many people do), and then erroneously say, "It doesn't work." The method works beautifully if you work it. So persist until you fill "to the brim" and see the breaking forth of good in the situation. This is what it takes to produce miracles.

A lady in Southern California had suffered from great personal misfortune. Her home had been broken up through death. She had a severe heart condition and major surgery. Not only was she suddenly without family or funds, but she was left helpless in a weakened condition from the surgery. What could have seemed more hopeless than that?

Yet within three years, her life had been completely transformed: She had regained her health, and was perfectly beautiful. She had established a thriving business, and she was living in a charming hotel apartment.

During that three year period, when this miracle occurred, she had no physical or financial assistance, no windfall of any kind, and no instantaneous healing. Instead, *she had only the ordinary materials of life with which to work—and very few of those.* After her surgery, while she was still bedridden and at her lowest ebb, a friend sent her an inspirational book. By applying the simple, uplifting ideas which she found in that book, she began to make a comeback.

For the first time in years she found peace of mind as she gave up bitterness and resentment toward her hard experiences, including the death of loved ones. From the depths of despair and physical weakness, she began to declare this affirmative prayer daily: "GOD WORKS IN ME TO WILL AND TO DO WHATSOEVER HE WISHES ME TO DO. GOD CANNOT FAIL, THEREFORE I CANNOT FAIL." She began to trust in God for daily guidance, health and supply. She blessed her mind, body and financial affairs. She praised and gave thanks for her life: "I PRAISE MY WORLD AS THE PERFECT CREATION OF DIVINE SUBSTANCE. I NOW SEE MORE HEALTH, WEALTH AND HAPPINESS IN MY WORLD THAN I HAVE EVER SEEN BEFORE."

When she finally was able to work again, she took a small room and with her few personal belongings, converted it into a home, which also became her studio for dress designing. As she assembled the tools and materials of her craft, she blessed them. Then she blessed her potential customers, and while she waited, she prayed for business.

Her prayers were answered, and her first customer spread the word. This dress designer was soon busy. Beginning with the receipt of her very first income check, she began to put God first financially by tithing ten percent to His work at the point from which she had received spiritual help and inspiration. Three years later, she was working in a lovely new studio, enjoying the best health and success ever. She even had to employ an assistant designer! Yet at one point in her life, the only help she had had was that inspirational book and the ideas she found in it.

Nevertheless, when she had treated the available supply of ideas as the desired supply—filling the hard conditions of her life *to the brim* with them—those ideas went to work for her, and she was gradually healed and prospered. She was finally led into a far better life than she had ever known before.

STEP EIGHT: HOW TO DRAW OUT OF YOUR ABUNDANT GOOD FROM THE HARD EXPERIENCES OF LIFE

When those hard, stony waterpots had been filled to the brim, Jesus then instructed the servants to "draw out" what they found in the waterpots and take it to the steward of the feast. Upon tasting the delicious substance, the steward was pleasantly surprised to discover that ordinary water had become fine wine.

After you have patiently poured something into the hard, stony waterpots that you find in life's experiences, you must then patiently draw something out of them. Many people stop their good at this point. They become impatient as they rush forth, turn the hard, stony waterpots in their life circumstances upside down, and impatiently ask, "Where is my good?" Because they become impatient for results, they miss their good.

People sometimes fill the waterpots with their thoughts of abundance, but they do not complete the miracle. They do not then *draw out* the formless substance as specific results, because *they do not get definite.* They have no specific plans, no definite pictures of the good they desire. They do not use explicit affirmations, nor do they dare to take precise action in faith. *At this point, it is the definite, specific thought, word or action that turns ordinary water into the finest of wine.*

You should begin now to express explicitly, in words, what you desire. Your words will then begin to bring into your life that which you have put into them. You can make yourself into a new creature and rebuild your world to your highest ideals through your definite words of Truth. Then follow through on these definite words with specific plans that are acted upon in faith. For most of us it is a degree by degree process. Nevertheless, *this is how you "draw out" of ordinary circumstances extraordinary results.*

HOW SHE DREW HEALTH OUT OF ILLNESS

There was once a lady who was suffering from arthritis. She kept thinking that *when* her arthritis got better, she would improve her appearance and that of her home; she would begin to work in her flower garden again; she would prepare some of her husband's favorite dishes. But as long as she maintained this attitude, her arthritis just never got any better.

One day she realized that she must "draw out" the health she desired by: (1) getting specific and expecting health, (2) planning on the return of her health, (3) acting upon her faith that this would happen, (4) making the most of the health she already had.

She stopped criticizing her body. She stopped talking about her arthritis. She decided to get specific by acting as though she were already healed. Even though it was painful for her, she went out into her flower garden and began pulling up weeds. Although she did not feel like it, she went into the kitchen and made her husband's favorite pie. She also made the effort to improve her personal appearance and that of their home, although this effort was also difficult for her.

She realized *she could not just sit down and wait for her problems to be solved,* and for her health to return. *God would help her when once she made the start toward a normal life again;* that this was the way to "draw out" health where previously there had been only pain and illness. Her method worked. Gradually she began to feel better and better, until finally she was leading an entirely normal life again!

STEP NINE: WHY THE GOOD THAT
COMES LAST IS SATISFYING AND ENDURING

The steward of the feast exclaimed with delight, "Thou hast kept the good wine until now." (John 2:10) He was pleasantly surprised by this turn of events, since it was the custom to serve the good wine first. Then, as the guests drank fully, a less desirable wine was usually served.

Like the steward of the feast—when your demonstration comes—you may find that the good wine has been kept until the last. *The good that comes to you as a result of prayer, inspirational study, affirmations, meditation, and the constructive use of your mind powers is always the best. It is soul-satisfying and enduring.* You may wonder why the good wine was kept until last, instead of being made available to you earlier in your life experiences.

"The longer your good is in coming, the greater it will be when it comes, so hold on " This statement has helped me (and countless others) over the years. Perhaps the truth of that statement is why this first *public* prosperity miracle of Jesus is one of my favorites. I, too, have so often had to pour forth *to the brim* thoughts and words of abundance on the hard, stony conditions I have encountered in life. Then I have had to slowly and patiently draw out greater good from those conditions by getting specific, and taking action in faith. This process has always led the way to an inner strength and a deeper understanding in my soul growth. The outer results that have followed have always been soul-satisfying and enduring.

Do not miss your good by overlooking the last step in this prosperity miracle. Even though the best seems to be kept until the last, when it appears you will find yourself declaring with the well-known comedian, "How sweet it is." And you will not lose it. It cannot be taken from you. Instead, your life will begin to be "filled to the brim" with life's ever-expanding blessings.

HOW A BUSINESSMAN
TURNED HIS LIFE AROUND

A businessman from Maryland wrote:

"A year ago my wife left me, taking our daughter with her. My heart was broken, but I began daily to practice forgiving my wife, releasing the situation, and declaring that something good would come out of that experience.

"Now I am stronger than ever. I found out that I am not such a bad guy after all, and that is good news. I also found it helpful to take some definite outer action. So I joined the Parents Without Partners organization, and I now have a whole new family of friends. I have danced more this year than in the past twenty-five. I have also played lots of golf, which I love. *By declaring that something good would come out of hard experiences of the past, then acting as though it had happened, a miracle has taken place.*"

STEP TEN: HOW TO FILL YOUR LIFE TO
THE BRIM WITH ABUNDANT GOOD

As you see the simple steps given in Jesus' first *public* prosperity miracle at Cana, MAY YOUR LIFE BE FILLED TO THE

BRIM WITH ABUNDANT GOOD! To help you experience this, you will enjoy meditating upon, and declaring often, these words:

"I TRUST THE AVAILABLE SUPPLY AS THE DESIRED SUPPLY, AND IT BECOMES SO. WHATEVER I HAVE AT HAND WITH WHICH TO MEET LIFE'S PROBLEMS, IS ALL THAT I NEED TO BEGIN MEETING THOSE PROBLEMS VICTORIOUSLY. I PRAISE AND BLESS WHAT I HAVE, AND THE GOOD MULTIPLIES. I PRAISE AND BLESS MY PERSONAL DREAMS. I PRAISE AND BLESS THE PEOPLE IN MY LIFE. I PRAISE AND BLESS THE CIRCUMSTANCES OF MY LIFE. I PRAISE AND BLESS MY FINANCIAL INCOME AND BUSINESS AFFAIRS. I PRAISE AND BLESS MY HEALTH. I BLESS THE GOOD I HAVE, AND I LOOK WITH WONDER AT ITS BOUNTIFUL INCREASE NOW. I PRAISE GOD THAT MY GOOD IS ADAPTABLE. AS I SPEAK WORDS OF ABUNDANCE, I OVERCOME ALL LACK IN MY LIFE. SO I REJOICE THAT MY LIFE IS NOW FILLED TO THE BRIM WITH ABUNDANT GOOD!"

SUMMARY

1. Two of Jesus' earliest miracles were prosperity miracles in which he turned lack into abundance.

   a) His first *private* prosperity miracle occurred when he manifested fish for Peter, James and John in such abundance that they left their fish-laden boats to become his disciples.

   b) His first *public* prosperity miracle occurred at the wedding feast in Cana when he turned ordinary water into fine wine.

2. The word "adapt" means "to make suitable by changing." Jesus took certain steps in mental action which made the water suitable for the occasion by changing it into fine wine.

3. The steps in mental action you can take to invoke the prosperity law of adaptability are:

    a) "They have no wine." *When a need arises, don't panic.* To rush forth to try to make it right in an outer way only dissipates your good.

    b) "Mine hour is not yet come." *To handle the possibility of new good, prepare inwardly.* Pray for guidance, then act only when directed to do so from within.

    c) You can perform your first public prosperity miracle for all to see when you *go to Cana, and use your power center to "speak the word" of abundance.* You must pour something into the appearance of lack before you can get anything out of it.

    d) "Fill the waterpots with water." Do not reject your good just because it is not in the form you thought it should be. *By treating the available supply (water) as the desired supply, water becomes wine.* The good you have on hand becomes adaptable and will meet your needs, if you begin appreciating it and pouring it into the situation.

    e) "They filled them to the brim." If hard, stony conditions are all you have to work with, then they are all you need with which to perform a miracle. Begin to praise and bless that which you have previously condemned. As you persist in filling the hard conditions of your life "to the brim" with thoughts and words of good, this multiplies your good.

    f) "Draw out now and bear unto the steward of the feast." Then patiently draw your good out of those hard, stony experiences by getting definite in thoughts, words and actions. To do so draws out of ordinary circumstances extraordinary results.

    g) "Thou hast kept the good wine until last." To take these steps in mental action can fill your life "to the brim" with permanent, sastisfying abundance.

THE PROSPEROUS SETTING FOR JESUS' FAMOUS SUCCESS TEACHINGS

— Chapter 3 —

Palestine is a little country about the size of the State of Vermont. Often called "the Holy Land," it is an oasis that is located between the sea on one side and the desert on the other. One can drive through it in a day. *Yet no other area of the world has held more fascination for mankind.*

For the past twenty centuries the world has thought, spoken and written about Palestine's most famous citizen, Jesus, more than about any other individual in history. He has been described as history's supreme personality, yet his mystic fascination remains.

In spite of all that has been said and written about him, nowhere in my research do I find Jesus sufficiently described by religious writers outside the Bible as a prosperous individual, or as a prosperity teacher.

Yet *some of Jesus' most famous teachings are filled with powerful prosperity formulas.* These would include the Beatitudes (Chapter 4) and the Lord's Prayer (Chapter 5). Jesus shared both of these well-known treatises on prosperity with his followers soon after completing his early, obscure Judean ministry. He gave the success formulas in the Beatitudes and Lord's Prayer during a year of great popularity in his Galilean ministry—at a time *before* he had performed many of his miracles of prosperity or healing.[1] And this is significant.

When the inner nature of man is fed, outer suppy comes far more easily. This is why Jesus wisely gave some of his most powerful teachings early in his ministry; then he showed the results of those teachings. Just as he did not rush forth headlong to achieve *outer* results first, neither should we. Some experts have estimated that success may be the result of as much as 98% *inner* preparation and only 2% *outer* action. In some of Jesus' most famous success teachings found in both the Beatitudes and the Lord's Prayer, *one is first prepared inwardly for outer success.*

It is significant that soon after calling his twelve disciples, Jesus shared with his followers the prosperity teachings that were found in the Beatitudes and the Lord's Prayer. The people of Jesus' time spoke in the Oriental fashion of allegory, parable and fable, all of which were filled with inner, hidden meanings. Learning the inner meanings of the Beatitudes and the Lord's Prayer was doubtless a part of the disciples' prosperity indoctrination, and a foundation for their later accomplishments.

Before considering the prosperous meaning of the individual Beatitudes, and his famous statements made in the Lord's Prayer, let us first review the background in which they were presented.

---

1. Although some historians believe that Jesus gave the Lord's Prayer from the Mount of Olives, Luke's version states only that "he was praying in a certain place." (Luke 11:1) Matthew's more popular version of the prayer indicates that it was probably given in Galilee immediately following the Beatitudes. (Matthew 6)

THE PROSPEROUS MATTHEW

It is fitting that some of the Bible's finest prosperity teachings are found in the Gospel according to Matthew, because Matthew was a prosperous businessman. Although he could have remained in the position of Chief Tax Collector, where he would have become very wealthy, he preferred to become one of Jesus' disciples. Matthew learned from Jesus the *inner* truth about prosperity, and how to manifest his supply from *within* outwardly. When he met the master teacher of prosperity, Matthew was ready in his soul-growth to expand from an *outer* competitive, hard-work consciousness of supply into an *inner* creative level of abundance. Matthew realized that in that *inner* consciousness of supply, prosperity would come as the need arose, but he would not be encumbered with the *outer* burdens so often associated with a strictly material wealth.

Matthew was considered an educated man. In order to hold such an important position as Chief Tax Collector, one had to be able to read and write. His fine education was to become the foundation for his life's work. His Gospel is the first record of Jesus' teachings, and it is considered by many to be the most popular gospel—probably because it was written in a simple straightforward style. In any event, some of Jesus' most powerful success teachings, including the Beatitudes and the Lord's Prayer, are found in the prosperous Matthew's Gospel.

JESUS WAS AN EDUCATED MYSTIC

Contrary to what many of us have been led to believe, Jesus was not an illiterate carpenter, but an educated man. He was called "Rabbi," not only by his disciples but also by his enemies. The word "Rabbi" means "doctor" or "professor." It was a title given only to learned men of higher education of that era, even as it is today among members of the Jewish faith.

Jesus may have spent as much as eighteen years of his early life studying the Scriptures. Nearly all of his teaching is quoted from the Mosaic law and the prophets, which he knew by heart. He was an authoritative teacher of the Law. When he went to the synagogue, he was given the scroll of Isaiah to read to the congregation. It is generally believed that he attained a thorough knowledge of the Jewish law through his studies at home as well as at the synagogue.

From the time he returned with his parents, after visiting the Temple at the age of twelve, to the beginning of his active ministry eighteen years later, there is nothing told of his life in the New Testament. The Gospel relates only that "Jesus advanced in wisdom and stature, and in favor with God and men." (Luke 2:52)

However, he may have been a student of the noted rabbi, Hillel, who was a brother in spirit to the patriarch, Gamaliel. It was Gamaliel who later instructed Paul against the excessive strictness of the Law. The illustrious Gamaliel endeavored to give Paul a sensible, human interpretation of the Law. In any event, many of the sayings attributed to Jesus apparently had been current in the Jewish teachings for many years, but were first written down after Jesus' time. His uniqueness lay in the fact that *he gave these familiar sayings a practical, prosperous interpretation not commonly given by other rabbis of his time.*

JESUS WAS A MASTER AND
A GREAT INITIATE

Jesus was also addressed as "master," which indicates he may have been a master of the teachings of the East. By some he was called "the Great Initiate." Although there is nothing to historically substantiate it, there are those who believe that after he was presented at the Temple at the age of twelve, he left his parents' household to study abroad in Egypt, India, and Persia. There is a mystical belief that he may have studied in the ancient city of Heliopolis, a center of learning noted for its school of philosophy. It was located near Cairo, not far from the Great Pyramid of Gizeh, which legend states was built to become the Hall of the Initiates of the White Brotherhood. Theirs was a mystical stream of thought to which Jesus may have been exposed.

Others feel that he probably studied extensively at the famous "school of philosophy" in Alexandria. This school was established about 30 B.C. and continued for several centuries. The world-renowned library located there contained the literature of many countries including Egypt, India, Greece, Rome and Asia Minor. That library may have contained as many as seven hundred thousand handwritten manuscripts which were used for study by those who visited it from near and far. Alexandria was the center of philosophical study in Jesus' time and the greatest center of learning in all history.

Since the teachings of many lands were brought together in Egyptian culture, the universality of Jesus' teachings indicates that he may have been influenced by Egypt as well as by Galilee. If so, there would have been nothing unusual about it. According to mystical lore, other great Biblical leaders may have been exposed to a similar education.

THE MYSTICAL TRAINING OF THE
BIBLE'S EARLIER MILLIONAIRES

According to ancient legend, the elegant High Priest, Melchizedek, conducted a "wisdom school" in wealthy

Babylon, which Abraham attended during the first period of his life spent there.

The word "Moses," in an esoteric Egyptian sense, meant "One who has been admitted into the mystery schools of wisdom." Whether Moses ever served as a priest in the mystical temples of Egypt has been debated. But, as a member of the royal family, he was instructed in all the secrets of the Egyptian priesthood. This included secret instruction in metaphysics, as well as instruction in the little-known teaching that "substance" was the key to all wealth. The Bible's first literal millionaire, Abraham, learned this same secret prosperity teaching from the wealthy Babylonians. When Abraham passed it on to his followers, they became millionaires.

The prosperity secrets which Moses may have learned while attending the mystery schools in Egypt were powerful enough to: (1) help him free the Hebrews from the feared, materialistic Pharaoh; (2) help them survive in the barren wilderness for forty years; and (3) help them travel to the edge of their fabled Promised Land.

Legend states that while in the wilderness, Moses had established a mystery school which his student, Joshua, attended. It is believed that Moses gave a few chosen initiates certain oral teachings, which were never written, but were passed on from one generation to the next by word of mouth. These instructions were in the form of philosophical keys based upon metaphysical interpretation, some of which are still known and taught today. Joshua learned well these secret teachings from Moses as shown in the daring way he led the Hebrews into the Land of Canaan, when he became their leader. There the Hebrews went on to experience unprecedented wealth.

The same secret success philosophy, passed down from Abraham, Moses and Joshua to the Hebrews of the Old Testament era, was reportedly taught at the time of Jesus at the school of philosophy in Alexandria. It may also have been part of the secret teachings that were quietly passed on to a select few among the Jews of Jesus' era.

Whether Jesus studied outside Israel will always remain debatable. As the Son of God, he had been sufficiently endowed with the inner powers of mind and Spirit to know and to achieve all that he did; and to show his followers how to do likewise. "He that believeth on me, the works that I do shall he do also; and greater works than these shall he do; because I go unto the Father," had been his promise. (John 14:12)

Regardless of how he gained his mystic knowledge, Jesus' understanding of the metaphysical keys to prosperous living are reflected in both his literal and allegorical teachings. *The most prominent of his prosperity teachings began with the Beatitudes.* (Chapter 4)

NOTHING NEW ABOUT THE
BIBLE'S PROSPERITY SYMBOLOGY

Even after the time of Jesus, there was nothing new about the prosperity symbology in which the Bible is cloaked. *Mystical minds have always searched out the success and prosperity symbology of the Bible, which was often given in allegory and symbols.*

It was a common method used by spiritual teachers throughout the history of the early church—both Catholic and Protestant—including Bernard of Clairvaux, St. John of the Cross, Jeremy Taylor, and John Wesley. As early as 180 A.D., Pantaenus, Clement, and Origen taught this success symbology, based upon metaphysical Bible interpretation, in the excellent Christian university at Alexandria.

They derived the metaphysical meaning of the Bible teachings by tracing significant Biblical words and names back to their root meaning, based on the original Hebrew, Greek, and Aramaic words, from which they were translated. By doing the same thing in this book, the prosperity secrets of Jesus become obvious.

Metaphysical interpretation has been secretly taught down through the ages, but it has not been generally shared with the masses. *The great people of the Bible were master psychologists and metaphysicians who strove constantly to teach the power of mental attitudes for success or failure.*

In this age of metaphysical enlightenment which we are entering, the prosperity symbology of the Bible is coming into its own! The time is ripe to teach all, instead of a select few, how the power of thought can produce either abundance or financial limitation in their lives.

WHY GALILEE WAS A PROPER
SETTING FOR THE BEATITUDES

Dr. Emmet Fox has explained in *The Sermon on the Mount:*

"Jesus is the most revolutionary of all teachers. He turns the world upside down for those who accept his teaching. When once you have accepted the Jesus Christ message, nothing is ever the same again. All values change radically."[2]

Nowhere is this more true than in studying the prosperity teachings of Jesus. Perhaps the early disciples knew best. They did not argue or reason overmuch about what they heard and observed. Instead, they gratefully accepted what Jesus taught, and left the rest to faith.

---

2. Emmet Fox, *The Sermon on the Mount* (New York: Harper & Row, Publishers, Inc., 1938), p. 79.

There were political and religious reasons for their intense desire to believe Jesus' revolutionary teaching. Life was harsh and difficult. The Jews lived in a police state manned by the hated King Herod and the heathen Romans. The rigid teachings of the Sadducees, Pharisees and Essenes were hardly of any practical help. Leaders in the traditional church made no effort to heal the sick or help the downtrodden. Instead, they sought out those who were in power. *No wonder a strong excitement ran through the masses when Jesus appeared, and began to prosper and heal his followers!*

It was significant that Jesus first taught his prosperity philosophy from the Beatitudes in Galilee, and that he began the most prominent phases of his ministry there. The Galileans were freethinkers. For many centuries they had lived in a land that had been in the path of attacking armies. They had suffered much from foreign invasions, so they were eager for the prosperous truth which Jesus taught. Galilee was a melting pot for diverse races, cultures and religions. This caused Galileans to be far more open and receptive to Jesus' teachings than were the people to the south in Judea, where religion had become narrow and stereotyped. Galilee seemed far away from Jerusalem, where most of the Jews appeared to be happier and more prosperous.

In Jerusalem the Jewish religion was respected by the Roman conquerors, and the Temple was functioning as it had for many years. The priests and Pharisees were satisfied with things as they were, and opposed even the slightest change. It is easy to see why the people far to the north, in Galilee, welcomed Jesus' teachings of prosperity, peace, health and harmony as one's spiritual heritage, while such bold ideas were resisted in Jerusalem.

THE ABUNDANCE AND BEAUTY
OF PROSPEROUS GALILEE

A businessman on a trip to the Holy Land sent me a card from the Sea of Galilee. His message read:

"I love Galilee. It is still relatively unspoiled. I can feel Jesus' prosperous presence here. He obviously radiated a consciousness of wealth, moving freely in and through such a rich land. What a fitting setting in which to have taught the prosperous Truth!"

It was appropriate that Jesus taught the Beatitudes on a hillside in Galilee, high above the jewel-like lake of Galilee. This was a picturesque land, surrounded by historic mountains and proud hills. It contained brooks, streams and fertile fields, graced with shrubs and flowers. There were luxuriant pastures in which sheep and goats grazed.

There are still more specimens of flowers in bloom upon the hills of Galilee in the spring of the year than anywhere else in the world! Colorful poppies, phlox, lupine, and oleanders are just some of the varieties that blossom there annually in brilliant profusion.

When compared with the arid hills of Judea, or the adjacent lands of Moab, Galilee was a beautiful, fertile, fruitful land; a thriving area of prosperous economic life. In a part of the world where water was precious, nature had given Galilee an abundance of it. This provided the area with much scenic beauty. There was something mysterious about the region surrounding the Lake of Galilee—a land bountiful in walnut, palm, fig, and olive trees; an area whose Lake was famous for its fish that were both different in taste and appearance from those found elsewhere.

THE SIGNIFICANCE OF THE
"BEAUTIFUL ATTITUDES"

A noted psychiatrist once said:

"If you were to take the sum total of all the authoritative articles ever written on the subject of mental hygiene by the most qualified of psychologists and psychiatrists; if you were to combine and refine them; and if you were to have these unadulterated bits of pure scientific knowledge concisely expressed by the most capable of living poets—you would have an awkward and incomplete summation of the Sermon on the Mount! *It is an outstanding blueprint for successful living, with optimum mental health and contentment.*"

The Beatitudes are a group of "beautiful attitudes" or happy sayings, which are among Jesus' most famous, and taken from the more lengthy Sermon on the Mount. It was after giving his basic prosperity philosophy in the Beatitudes, that Jesus then proceeded with a more detailed account of it in the rest of the Sermon on the Mount.[3] Metaphysically interpreted, the Beatitudes describe the ideal *inner* thoughts and feelings of the prosperous thinker who knows that, like Jesus, he is also the rich child of a loving Father— an heir to unlimited good.

However, it is generally believed that the Beatitudes were not an original contribution by Jesus. They brought together various utterances contained in the literature of the Old Testament, particularly those found in the Psalms and Proverbs. Whereas the teachings of the Psalms and Proverbs had rebuked the greed, injustice and violence of the wealthy, they had promised the poor that their sufferings

---

3. The author looks forward to covering the prosperity teachings of the entire Sermon on the Mount in a later book.

would end and that they would enjoy all the good things of the earth. Jesus' "beautiful attitudes" reiterated this.

In any event, there was a close connection between the teachings of Jesus and the traditional Jewish religion. Some authors feel that Jesus' teachings in the Beatitudes had first existed in the writings of prominent rabbis of his time, based upon Old Testament teachings.

Whereas the Law that Moses received on Mount Sinai is the heart of Judaism, the Sermon on the Mount, beginning with the Beatitudes, is the heart of the glad tidings of Christianity. The "thou shalt not" of the Ten Commandments is replaced by the words "blessed are ye" in the Beatitudes. In order to live an ordinary life at the time of Jesus, a person had to abide by over six hundred laws daily. The people had become so bound by *outer,* human laws that they did not know how to live and enjoy life according to the *inner* laws of mind and Spirit. This explains why the followers of Jesus welcomed so gladly his teachings, which emphasized these *inner* powers of mind and Spirit.

There may be periods in your own growth when you are still in such a negative state of mind, and in such limited circumstances, that the only way to get out of them into happier, more prosperous experiences is by rigid adherence to both the physical and metaphysical laws of life. However, as you become more positive in your outlook, you will find yourself going from the "thou shalt not" attitudes of the Ten Commandments to the "blessed are ye" attitudes of the Beatitudes. And you will reap happy results accordingly!

HE EXPERIENCED A NEW VENTURE IN PROSPEROUS LIVING, AND YOU CAN, TOO

Before launching forth into Chapters Four and Five on a specific study of the prosperous thinking contained in the

Beatitudes and the Lord's Prayer, you will find assurance in this letter written by a businessman from the State of Washington.

> *"Prosperous thinking really works if you persist in using it.* Since I took up this study, I have bought a business, and the building to house it. This is quite a prosperity deomonstration for me. I started out working for the man who now works for me! I will be sixty-two this year, and had thought by this age I would be rocking away placidly. But I am able and God is willing—so *here we go* into a new venture in prosperous living!"

I trust that as you now take the study of the prosperous truths found in each of the Beatitudes and in the Lord's Prayer, you will also find yourself launching forth into new ventures in prosperous living. As you turn to Chapter Four and begin, *here we go!*

SUMMARY

1. Some of Jesus' most famous teachings—the Beatitudes and the Lord's Prayer—contain powerful prosperity formulas.

2. The reason that Jesus gave these at a time *before* he had performed many of his miracles of prosperity and healing was this: When the *inner* nature of man is fed, *outer* results then come far more easily.

3. It has been estimated that success may be the result of as much as 98% *inner* preparation and only 2% outer action. In both the Beatitudes and the Lord's Prayer, one is first prepared *inwardly* for *outer* success.

4. The reason some of Jesus' most powerful success teachings, including the Beatitudes and the Lord's Prayer,

are found in the prosperous Matthew's Gospel is because: the successful Matthew learned from Jesus the *inner* truth about prosperity, and how to manifest his supply from *within* outwardly.

5. As Chief Tax Collector, Matthew was ready in his soul-growth to expand from an *outer,* competitive, hard-work consciousness of supply into an *inner,* creative level of abundance, which he did as a disciple of Jesus.

6. Matthew realized that by learning from Jesus how to develop an *inner* consciousness of supply, his prosperity would come as the need arose, but he would not be encumbered with the outer burdens so often associated with a strictly material wealth.

7. Jesus was not an illiterate carpenter, but an educated man, often called "Rabbi," which meant "doctor" or "professor." Not only did he have great knowledge of the Hebrew law, but he was also considered by some to be a master and great initiate of the teachings of the East. In any event, he gave a practical, prosperous interpretation of the teachings of his time, one not commonly given by other rabbis.

8. Whether Jesus ever studied outside Israel will always be debatable. As the Son of God, he had been sufficiently endowed with the *inner* powers of mind and Spirit to know and to achieve all that he did; and to show his followers how to do likewise.

9. Mystical minds have always searched out the success and prosperity symbology of the Bible, which was often given in allegory and symbols. The great people of the Bible were master psychologists and metaphysicians who strove constantly to teach the power of mental attitudes for success or failure.

10. No wonder a strong excitement ran through the masses when Jesus appeared, began to prosper and heal, and gave his followers hope for a better way of life. For political reasons, life had become harsh and difficult for the Jews.

11. Beautiful Galilee was a proper setting for Jesus' early prosperity teachings, beginning with the Beatitudes. Located far from conservative Jerusalem, the free-thinking Galileans accepted his revolutionary success teachings gladly, starting with ''the beautiful attitudes'' from the Sermon on the Mount, or ''the bountiful attitudes.''

PROSPERITY FROM THE BEATITUDES

THE BOUNTIFUL ATTITUDES

— Chapter 4 —

Some of Jesus' most famous success teachings are contained in the Beatitudes. In fact, *his "beautiful attitudes," which might also be described as "bountiful attitudes," point out some of the most important "dynamic laws of prosperity" ever offered mankind!* Remember that the word "dynamic" in its root means "spiritual," and the word "prosperity" in its root means "wholeness." So his "beautiful attitudes" are filled with the spiritual laws which will lead to wholeness in your life, when you use them.

Although the Gospel according to Luke gives only four Beatitudes, most people prefer to study the eight more detailed Beatitudes given by the prosperous Matthew. (Matthew 5:1-12) These are followed by two separate sayings that are also significant to the student of prosperous thinking. In addition, there are other beatitudes scattered

77

throughout most of the Gospels. Yet, those cited by Matthew, as a prelude to the Sermon on the Mount, seem to have had the most impact. His account begins by pointing out *the first thing you should do when a financial need confronts you.*

HOW TO HANDLE A FINANCIAL NEED

"And seeing the multitudes, he went up into the mountain; and when he had sat down, his disciples came unto him; and he opened his mouth and taught them, saying," (Matthew 5:1,2)

When Jesus saw the multitude, he did not sigh, complain, or talk financial lack. Instead he: (1) went up into the mountain; (2) called his disciples; and (3) taught them in words.

When you have a financial need or any problem, instead of talking negatively about it, you, too, should "go up into the mountain" by reading, studying, and meditating along prosperous lines. This lifts you up into a prosperous state of mind where you should then call your disciples (your thoughts and feelings), and you should teach them with prosperous ideas and words. *You can multiply and increase what you have by doing this. Thoughts and words of abundance will more quickly and surely bring what is yours by divine right to you than any other method!*

A businesswoman from the State of Washington wrote:

"I have just returned from a lovely holiday in Hawaii with my husband. *We had hoped to make this trip for two years, to no avail.* Then I began to spend some time daily reading along prosperous lines, and speaking forth prosperity statements. Soon after I began this practice, the trip to Hawaii suddenly materialized! The prosperity decree I used

was: 'I AM BEAUTIFULLY AND APPROPRIATELY SUPPLIED WITH
THE RICH SUBSTANCE OF THE UNIVERSE NOW.'

"There have been other prosperous results from my use of
those words. Just before we left for Hawaii, my employer informed me that I would receive a well-deserved raise when I
returned. This was a surprise since it was not due—but is
most appreciated. The week of our departure, my daughter
obtained a job which was just perfect to keep her occupied,
and away from certain undesirable influences. I have even
been told by friends that I am becoming more beautiful
every day and radiating an inner glow. It's all the result of
my study of prosperous thinking, and my use of prosperity
statements. I am now traveling a new path of illumination
that is outwardly exciting and inwardly satisfying."

THE FIRST PROSPEROUS BEATITUDE:
A SUMMARY OF THE POWER OF PROSPEROUS THINKING

1. "BE TEACHABLE AND WILLING TO LEARN AND PRACTICE
PROSPEROUS THINKING."

"Blessed are the poor in spirit; for theirs is the kingdom of
heaven." (Matthew 5:3)

Some scholars believe that this Beatitude is the root from
which the others grew; that it summarizes *all* of them. People who interpret the Bible literally sometimes use this
Beatitude to try to prove that Jesus did not believe in prosperity; that he favored the poor.

The Literal Poor: In Jesus' time the "poor" were the
group who were open and receptive to new ideas, and willing to learn. The Jewish religion was respected by the
Roman conquerors, so the Temple in Jerusalem was functioning as usual. Under Roman rule, the high priests were
granted even more power than they had enjoyed under the
Jewish kings of Old Testament times; they were a part of the

favored wealthy class. As such, they were exempt from taxes and other heavy financial burdens borne by the poor. So the priests wished no changes in their traditional teaching which emphasized the daily observance of six hundred laws. They despised the poor who were forced to search elsewhere for a practical teaching that would help solve their daily problems. The poor were considered outcasts by the official class because they looked to God for help, rather than to their own traditional church, or to the Roman government.

The Metaphysical Poor: To be "poor in spirit" means to be humble, receptive, teachable, and willing to learn and to accept higher, more prosperous ideas. The illustrious Solomon had been "poor in spirit" when he quietly prayed, "Give thy servant therefore an understanding heart . . . that I may discern between good and evil." (I Kings 3:9) Because of his humble receptivity to higher ideas, he became not only one of the world's wisest men, but also a billionaire upon whom both riches and honor were lavished.

To be "poor in spirit" is to surrender your doubts, fears, and failure-thinking. Instead of saying, "I cannot do it," "I don't know how," "I cannot see the way," or "I will never make it"—*humbly declare to yourself often that you are a winner.* In your daily quiet times of prosperous study and reflection, meditate upon, and verbally declare statements such as these: "NOTHING SUCCEEDS LIKE SUCCESS. MY SUCCESS IS BIG, POWERFUL AND IRRESISTIBLE NOW." Or "MY CUP RUNNETH OVER." Or "VAST IMPROVEMENT COMES QUICKLY IN EVERY PHASE OF MY LIFE NOW. EVERY DAY IN EVERY WAY, THINGS ARE GETTING BETTER AND BETTER FOR ME NOW. THE MARK OF SUCCESS IS UPON ME."

HOW A TEXAS BUSINESSMAN PROSPERED

A Texas businessman had some office space on his used car lot that he had been unable to rent. Because of mounting financial pressures, this had concerned him. He decided, however, to surrender his doubts and fears, and to humbly pray for guidance about the matter. Soon afterwards he was introduced to the power of prosperous thinking by a friend. He learned that *successful results could be obtained by dwelling upon thoughts of abundance and success, instead of continuing to dwell upon the multitude of financial needs in his life.* "THE SPIRIT OF SUCCESS IS NOW WORKING WITH ME, AND I AM IN ALL WAYS GUIDED, PROSPERED AND BLESSED," was the prosperity statement he began to declare daily.

Within a few days, another businessman appeared, unprompted by anyone, and rented the available office space on the spot, paying cash. As the used car dealer continued to humbly invite the Spirit of Success to work with him, he was guided, prospered and blessed in numerous ways. A whole new way of life opened to him.

THE SECOND PROSPEROUS BEATITUDE: THE BASIC PROSPERITY LAW IS THAT MAN SHOULD LOOK TO GOD AS THE SOURCE OF HIS SUPPLY

2. "TROUBLE (MOURNING) CAN BE A BLESSING IN DISGUISE BECAUSE IT CAUSES MANY TO TURN TO GOD FOR GUIDANCE AND SUPPLY."

"Blessed are they that mourn; for they shall be comforted." (Matthew 5:4)

Literal Mourning: Because of the frequent wars, revolutions and persecutions in the East, mourning was common. Those who interpret the Bible literally often point to this passage as a reason why people should deliberately mourn and be sad, especially at the passing of a loved one from this earthly plane. A certain amount of mourning is considered mentally healthy as well as a necessary emotional release. A loving Father *does* comfort those who turn to Him at such times.

However, a person who deliberately mourns, thinking it is expected of him, can delay the healing and release process that transition demands. It is good at such times to declare release for the departed soul, as well as for your own emotional ties with them: "I FULLY AND FREELY RELEASE YOU, (calling their name). I LOOSE YOU AND LET YOU GO. I LET GO AND LET GOD DO HIS PERFECT WORK IN THIS EXPERIENCE FOR THE GOOD OF ALL CONCERNED." This attitude blesses the departed one, and it makes your own adjustment to change easier.

Metaphysical Mourning: Trials and tribulations can be for good when they cause you to turn to God for help. *Blessed are they who experience sorrow with a resolve to learn from it.* Our instinct is to rebel against it; yet *sorrow expands us as it shakes us up and causes us to grow.* Through the process of growth into greater good, which can be painful, we are comforted!

From a prosperity standpoint, *you experience a form of mourning when financial troubles cause you to look to God for guidance and supply. Financial trials and tribulations can be blessings in disguise when they cause you to turn to God seeking greater understanding. Troubles and suffering are often extremely useful, because many people do not bother to learn the prosperous Truth until driven to do so through such experiences.*

HOW THEY WERE FORCED FROM MOURNING INTO PROSPERITY

A DESERTED WIFE DEVELOPED HER OWN BUSINESS IN COLORADO: "My husband left me without child support. I did not seek any because I felt he must be free to build his own life. My children and I released him to find his highest good elsewhere.

"We began to declare daily that 'GOD IS THE SOURCE OF OUR SUPPLY, AND HE IS PROVIDING ABUNDANTLY FOR US NOW.' It has been a real adventure! We had no visible funds to work with, but as we prayed for prosperity, I felt led to go into the mail-order business. I enjoy this work and the children enjoy helping me. *As we have continued to declare that God is the Source of our supply, we have prospered daily.* What a wonderful, free way to live!"

A PENNILESS DIVORCEE PROSPERED IN CALIFORNIA: "More than four years ago, I made a decision that involved a relationship with a sick man, my former husband. That problem caused me to continuously stay in prayer and meditation, and really practice loving as God loves. *I came out of that experience with thanksgiving for having experienced so many blessings where previously there had seemed to be nothing but problems.* As a result of that experience, I grew spiritually and became more wise.

"In our separation, which became one of peace and harmony thanks to my prayer work, I was left completely without financial funds. Instead of panicking, I began to declare daily that: 'GOD IS THE SOURCE OF MY SUPPLY, AND HE IS SHOWING ME THE WAY TO PROSPER NOW.' *There is a prospering power in that prayer!* I now have an income that sustains me at the level at which I had lived previously. This income is a gift from God, and comes without my having to laboriously work for it.

"I am also a recipient of many other blessings in material goods and services. I know that I am loved by my family and others. Therefore, I have no feeling of any of the problems that plagued me for years. In the past, I had taken on other people's responsibilities. This had caused me to put myself and my goals aside. *Now I know that I have no personal obligations to anyone or anything, except my own higher Godself.* These experiences have convinced me that *God is a rich, loving Father who pours out His blessings upon those who open their minds to receive.*"

A BUSINESSMAN IN UTAH TURNED SORROW INTO BLESSINGS: "My soul continues to soar when I use this prayer, 'GOD IS THE SOURCE OF MY SUPPLY, AND MY

UNLIMITED ABUNDANCE OF EVERY GOOD THING NOW.' Although I have an excellent job, more job offers keep coming in. *If more people recognized God as the source of their supply, and entertained thoughts of abundance—not only for themselves, but also for others—they would never have to worry about money again.* What you wish for someone else comes to you. I have proved in my own life that this method is an excellent way to turn sorrow into blessings.''

THE THIRD PROSPEROUS BEATITUDE:
THE PROSPERING POWER OF
FORGIVENESS AND RELEASE

3. ''THE MEEK ARE NOT WEAK WHEN THEY DARE TO FORGIVE AND RELEASE THE HURTS OF THE PAST; THEREBY OPENING THE WAY TO RECEIVE FAR GREATER GOOD IN THE PRESENT.''

''Blessed are the meek: for they shall inherit the earth.'' (Matthew 5:5)

The people of Jesus' time had relied upon the sword, believing that only force could destroy force. Yet their use of force had always brought on more suffering. *Since it describes the secret for overcoming all kinds of difficulties, this Beatitude contains one of the most important success formulas in the Bible!*

When Jesus promised that the meek should inherit the earth, he was not speaking of the weak, negative states of mind that retaliate or fight back. He was referring to the positive, teachable, prosperous states of mind that become a magnet for every blessing.

Jesus' statement was probably startling to most of his followers, since they had considered the ''meek'' to be ''weak'' and defenseless. Jesus, however, knew that to be ''meek'' was to be quietly but firmly positive. A meek person is adaptable, flexible, teachable. So to be ''meek'' is to be positive to the good, and nonresistant to all else, knowing that ''this, too, shall pass.''

HOW MEEKNESS PROSPERED
A FORMERLY BITTER DIVORCEE

To be "meek" is to deny, forget, dismiss, and release thoughts of previous hurt, loss or failure. The meek state of mind knows that the divine law of compensation can produce so much good in the present that it dissolves and blots out the bitterness, disappointment, and failure of the past.

There are many people who suffer financial difficulties because their minds are so filled with memories of loss, hurt and failure of the past, that there is no room for entertaining prosperous ideas in the present. To dwell upon losses or failures of the past not only assures us of more losses of money and other financial blessings in the present, but it also prepares the way for loss of health, family, friends, and many other blessings we hold dear.[1]

A businesswoman worked hard, yet she constantly suffered from financial reverses and ill health. This divorcee constantly spoke in bitter, critical terms of her former husband who had deserted her twenty years earlier. Although she had often taken court action against him, he never consistently helped in the support of their children. It was easy for her to dwell often upon life's apparent injustices to her.

It was only after she learned to stop blaming her former husband for all of her troubles, and began to meekly declare often, "THE DIVINE LAW OF LOVE AND JUSTICE IS WORKING PERFECTLY THROUGH ME TOWARD ALL PEOPLE, AND THROUGH ALL PEOPLE TOWARD ME," that her health and finances began to improve. As she became forgiving toward the past, adaptable and flexible in the present, and persevered in the

---

1. See the chapter on "Divine Restoration" in the book *Open Your Mind to Prosperity* by Catherine Ponder (Marina del Rey, CA: DeVorss & Co., rev. ed. 1983) pp. 154–173.

thought of "divine love and justice" doing their perfect work in her life, many new blessings appeared. Meekness did its perfect, prospering work!

HOW THEY EXPERIENCED THE VAST
BENEFITS OF FORGIVENESS AND RELEASE

Remember that to be "meek" is to deny, forget, dismiss, forgive, and release thoughts of previous hurt, loss or failure. One of the best ways to do this is through the daily practice of forgiveness and release.

A CHANGED ATTITUDE TOWARD HER INVALID HUSBAND BROUGHT OTHER IMPROVEMENTS: "My husband has been an invalid for ten years. He has improved a great deal recently. But more than that, my attitude toward his illness has changed. In an unconscious way, I had blamed him for getting sick and leaving me to carry the burden of his illness. I had also blamed him for thrusting upon me the financial burden of trying to make a living for us.

"I discovered this—much to my surprise—while practicing forgiveness. *Since I have been making a daily Forgiveness List, I have had a lighter, freer attitude about everything.* After forty years of marriage, this is a great step forward. My own life is also improving. I am enjoying my new job and the pay is far better than I had expected."

A SENIOR CITIZEN IN OREGON IS WELCOMED BACK INTO THE FAMILY: "Amazing things have happened since I began the daily practice of forgiving and releasing hurts, losses, failures, and unhappy memories of the past. I received a telephone call from my nephew inviting me over to his house for a family celebration. This was the first one I had been allowed to attend in twelve years! (The family felt I had previously done a poor job in handling the sale of my mother's estate.) What a blessing to finally be welcomed back into the family—thanks to the miracle power of forgiveness—practiced by me to which the family subconsciously responded.''

A PRAYER GROUP IN TEXAS WITNESSED HEALINGS AND PROSPERITY DEMONSTRATIONS: ''I have a prayer group that has met once a week for the past five years. It continues to grow spiritually and in numbers. We've had many reports of healings, including those of cancer and heart conditions. Most of the healings have resulted from our joint verbal use of these prayer statements: 'I NOW FORGIVE AND RELEASE EVERYTHING AND EVERYBODY OF THE PAST OR PRESENT WHO NEEDS FORGIVENESS AND RELEASE. I LOOSE THEM AND LET THEM GO. THEY ARE FREE, AND I AM FREE, TOO. ALL THINGS ARE CLEARED UP BETWEEN US NOW AND FOREVER.' We've had prosperity demonstrations including the inheritance of money, the winning of money, and several promotions and raises in pay. *We never cease to be amazed at the miracle power of forgiveness.* ''

A BUSINESSMAN IN AUSTRALIA WENT FROM DEPRESSION TO PROSPERITY: ''I felt so depressed and neglected last year when everything seemed to go wrong in business. Some new employees became very negative and failed to keep their promises to me. My whole future seemed in jeopardy until I remembered to speak words of release daily: 'I NOW LAY DOWN EVERY WEIGHT. I LET GO ALL EXCESS, ALL BURDENS. I LET GO AND LET GOD SHOW ME THE WAY.'

''When I practiced release in this way, I was able to watch the drama of life go by as if it did not concern me. It was like watching a film. Now I have learned that the firm I work for will soon be taken over by one of this country's largest corporations. This means my future position is assured, and that it will be a very prosperous one.''

HOW YOU CAN INHERIT THE EARTH

In Jesus' time the meek *did* sometimes literally inherit the earth, or the lands of those who had taken up the sword and gone off to meet force with more force. While some of the meek inherited the lands of their masters who had perished in wars, others received inheritances from those who had died without leaving heirs.

To "inherit the earth" means to claim the dominion that is your spiritual heritage over the limiting experiences of life, such as ill health, insufficient supply, indebtedness, inharmony, or loneliness; and to bring your life into harmony with true success. When you do this, the "earth" or your outer world shows forth happy results. For this purpose declare often: "MY LIFE (HEALTH, WEALTH, HAPPINESS) CANNOT BE LIMITED. CHRIST IN ME NOW FREES ME FROM ALL LIMITATION. I AM UNFETTERED AND UNBOUND. I RECEIVE THE ABUNDANT GOOD THAT IS MINE BY DIVINE RIGHT NOW."

THE FOURTH PROSPEROUS BEATITUDE:
THE WILL OF GOD FOR MAN IS WEALTH

4. "THOSE WHO HUNGER AND THIRST AFTER THE RIGHT USE OF PROSPEROUS IDEAS SHALL FIND THEIR LIVES FILLED WITH ABUNDANT BLESSINGS."

"Blessed are they that hunger and thirst after righteousness: for they shall be filled." (Matthew 5:6)

The Galileans, with whom Jesus shared these Beatitudes, were a warlike people. Galilee had been a center of many insurrections. They had made numerous attempts to free Palestine from the Roman yoke, but had failed. Corruption and graft were rampant in the land, and some of the Jewish leaders had even turned from their own people in an effort to receive special favors from the Roman officials. It was natural that Jesus' followers complained of the injustice and dishonesty of the times, while intensely desiring a better way of life.

In this "beautiful attitude," Jesus was reminding his followers of an age-old teaching embraced by ancient philosophers. The word "righteous" has sometimes been translated to mean "goodness," yet righteousness is more than right conduct. To be righteous does not mean to be "goody-goody," self-righteous, or pious in an outer way. It means to think and act in a just, upright, harmonious manner. *It is right thinking on all subjects of life! What you think in your mind, you will produce in your life—that is the great law of life.*

In Jesus' time, water was a matter of life and death, so "hunger and thirst" indicated *an intense longing for greater good. For most of us, life is a dominant hunger, an intense urge to experience far more good than ever before. Those who hunger and thirst after uplifting, prosperous ideas, find their lives filled with the blessings of health, wealth, and happiness.* That was what Jesus was promising.

HOW SHE WAS HEALED AND PROSPERED

Here is how it works: A woman attended a prosperity class. Her mind became filled with the exciting ideas about successful living that she heard in class. The very next day, she discovered that she had been healed of a health condition of long standing. As she continued to hunger and thirst after prosperous ideas, through her daily study and use of prosperity decrees, many new blessings filled her life.

In one instance, she had long sought to obtain financing from a bank for the construction of a commercial building on some ground she owned. Each time the bank had informed her that she did not have sufficient collateral. After meditating upon prosperous ideas and decreeing often, "EVERYTHING AND EVERYBODY PROSPERS ME NOW, AND I

PROSPER EVERYTHING AND EVERYBODY NOW,'' she was able to get the financial assistance needed. The building was constructed, and it became the scene of a profitable business.

A MAID IN COLORADO BECAME A
MUSEUM EXECUTIVE IN CALIFORNIA

A businesswoman wrote:

"I learned about and began to study the power of prosperous thinking at a time when I was working in a small town in Colorado near a beautiful ski resort. Though a college graduate, I was working as a maid. *I had told myself I was non-materialistic, that living for beauty, nature and peace were enough.* I had the erroneous idea that it was wrong to prosper. This ski area was one in which it was not uncommon to find Ph.D.'s washing dishes in order just to survive and ski.

"My thinking began to change and expand just as soon as I started filling my mind with prosperous thoughts, such as 'THE WILL OF GOD FOR ME IS WEALTH. IT IS SPIRITUALLY RIGHT FOR ME TO PROSPER.' *Troublesome situations began to clear up!* I was surprised when I applied to teach art classes at a local college and was accepted. Next, I got a part-time job as a cashier and that helped.

"As I continued to fill my mind daily with prosperous thoughts, I got up the courage to borrow money from a relative and head for California—a lifetime dream. I found a lovely apartment in San Francisco where I could live with my pets. By the time the money ran out, I had gotten a job as a receptionist in an art museum surrounded by lavish paintings. This was an environment most pleasing to my artistic nature. I then applied for a special administrative assistant's position and came close to getting it, but did not, in spite of my use of prosperity affirmations.

"Instead, three days ago a fellow employee told me she was getting a promotion and that she had recommended me for her old job. Within hours I was hired for a semi-executive job where I will handle large contributions for art charities, organize interesting lectures, gala concerts, dinners, and balls. I now have a private office in one of this area's most prestigious museums!

"Last night I attended a staff meeting in a beautiful home on Nob Hill. One staffer reported on her recent visit with the famed Conrad Hilton. Another reported on a similar visit with well-known philanthropist Norton Simon. I smiled and patted a well-worn copy of Dr. Ponder's book, *Pray and Grow Rich*,[2] which I had carried in my purse for months. It had become my "prosperity Bible." *I am making more money now than I have ever made before, with the promise of another raise in six months!* I can personally attest to the truth that it is God's will for me to prosper. As I continue to 'hunger and thirst' after prosperous ideas, I realize that it is entirely possible for me to 'pray and grow rich.' "

THE FIFTH PROSPEROUS BEATITUDE: THE PROSPERING POWER OF LOVE

5. "BLESSED ARE THOSE WHO HOLD MERCIFUL, LOVING ATTITUDES TOWARD OTHERS. IN TURN, THEY, TOO SHALL BE PROSPERED AND LOVINGLY BLESSED."

"Blessed are the merciful: for they shall obtain mercy." (Matthew 5:7)

This was a revolutionary statement when Jesus made it. The Romans considered it weak to be merciful. In their self-righteousness, the Pharisees also showed little mercy. And Jesus' followers were very critical of both their Roman and Pharisee neighbors.

---

2. Catherine Ponder, *The Dynamic Laws of Prayer* (formerly *Pray and Grow Rich*) (Marina del Rey, CA: DeVorss & Co., rev. ed. 1986).

In this Beatitude, Jesus was trying to remind his followers of an Old Testament custom: The people of the East had long been noted for their merciful kindness to friend and foe alike. Surrounded by the harshness of nature, those simple desert people lived in arid places, and had to depend upon the merciful kindness of others for water, grass for their cattle, and the bare necessities of life that they needed just to survive.

Jesus was trying to remind his followers that *instead of dwelling upon the appearance of persecution and injustice all about them, they could again release great power for good in their lives by dwelling upon thoughts of mercy and acts of kindness.*

Unmerciful attitudes are those of criticism, condemnation, hate, revenge, and the desire to get even. *Unmerciful attitudes cause more indebtedness and financial worry than any other state of mind.* "The arrogant never escape" is a true statement. *Criticism, condemnation, and unforgiveness of both ourselves and others can cause hard financial conditions that have to be broken up and dissolved before we can be permanently prospered.*

There is no ill will or revenge among the merciful. *The most merciful attitude you can have toward others is to remember that when their weakness comes to your attention, they are unconsciously calling out for your blessing, so be merciful. You will ultimately receive the same merciful treatment from others just when you need it most!*

The thought of "love" is the most powerful and merciful healing balm for all ills. You can begin to develop loving, merciful attitudes toward yourself, as well as toward others, by declaring often, "THERE IS NO CONDEMNATION IN ME, FOR ME, OR AROUND ME. DIVINE LOVE NOW HEALS ALL MY CRITICAL ATTITUDES TOWARD OTHERS. DIVINE LOVE NOW HEALS ALL OTHERS' CRITICAL ATTITUDES TOWARD ME." Yes, loving thoughts and loving actions are the most kind, merciful ones, and they reap accordingly for both the giver and the receiver. Everyone involved benefits from the use of this "beautiful attitude."

HE CONVERTED A RAGING
CUSTOMER INTO A GOOD ONE

The owner of a furniture store in Alabama had a customer who refused to pay for a washing machine purchased from his store. The finance company finally reclaimed it. Soon afterwards, the customer came rushing into the furniture store and started screaming at the proprietor in vile language. This raging man weighed about two hundred and forty pounds. He was six feet, three inches tall, whereas the store owner was of much smaller stature. As the customer made his abusive accusations, the furniture dealer listened quietly. Whenever possible, he declared, between accusations, "But (name of the customer), I love you!" He repeated this statement dozens of times until the enraged customer finally left in utter disgust.

Thirty minutes later, this customer returned to apologize for his behavior, and to thank the furniture dealer for the merciful way he had dealt with the situation. The customer then explained that he had lost his last job because his temper had caused him to assault a man who had to be hospitalized.

He stated that the way this merchant had handled the situation turned the tide of his temper and made him see how foolish he had been. He promised that as soon as he found another job he would pay for the washing machine—and he did. He became a fine, stable customer. This merchant said it had not been easy to say to another man—especially a raging 6-foot, 3-inch one—"I love you." But the results had been well worth the effort.

HOW A LAWYER COLLECTED
TWO LARGE ACCOUNTS

In going over his books at the end of the year, a lawyer found two large accounts still due. He reasoned that as long as he resented those unpaid accounts and the clients involved, they would not be paid. Instead, he began to deliberately praise and bless the names of those two clients each day. He would also declare: "DIVINE LOVE IS DOING ITS PERFECT WORK THROUGH ME TOWARD ALL PEOPLE, AND THROUGH ALL PEOPLE TOWARD ME. SO DIVINE LOVE IS DOING ITS PERFECT WORK IN THESE ACCOUNTS, AND ALL IS WELL."

Within a short time, both clients paid their accounts *on the same day!* One even mailed his check for the full amount from a distant state. This lawyer felt he would never have been able to collect these large amounts had he not released merciful thoughts of love and good will to those involved.

HOW MERCY SAVED A MARRIAGE
AND BROUGHT PROSPERITY

A housewife in Florida wrote:

"As a 56-year-old Jewess, it is comfortable to finally be able to release burdens and to know that God approves of me. A neighbor introduced me to the merciful power of love at a time when the problems in my life were almost beyond belief. I began to declare daily: 'DIVINE LOVE IS DOING ITS PERFECT WORK HERE AND NOW, AND ALL IS WELL.'

"Divine Love *has* certainly done its perfect work! That statement, declared thousands of times by me for my own life and for the lives of others involved, has saved my sanity. It has also saved my 34-year-old marriage, and helped my husband to prosper in business. Becoming more merciful in my attitudes, and more loving in my words, has helped me to stop calling my husband 'cantankerous' and to become more understanding of his needs. *A computer couldn't count all the ways I have been helped by merciful, loving attitudes.*"

THE SIXTH PROSPEROUS BEATITUDE:
THE PROSPERING POWER OF PICTURES

6. "BLESSED ARE THE PURE IN HEART, WHO ALWAYS PICTURE SUCCESS FOR EACH EXPERIENCE. THROUGH PICTURING GOD'S GOODNESS, THEY SHALL EXPERIENCE THE PEACE, HEALTH AND PLENTY OF TRUE ABUNDANCE."

"Blessed are the pure in heart: for they shall see God." (Matthew 5:8)

In Jesus' time, as today, people often dwelled upon one another's shortcomings instead of observing each person's good qualities. Because of their resentment toward foreign rule, there were many people in Palestine who could not "see God" or His goodness in their daily lives. Their minds were so poisoned with hatred toward their enemies that they saw nothing but a dark, hopeless future.

In this Beatitude Jesus was pointing out that *the secret for freedom from all kinds of trouble—sickness, inharmony, poverty and limitation of every type—is to release resentment, hate and condemnation of others; and to deliberately begin to see God's goodness everywhere.*

Since God is the sum total of all good, to "see God" is to "see good" in all phases of life. The "pure in heart" would never think of harming other people. They think, feel, speak, and expect only the good from each experience. "I

PRONOUNCE THIS GOOD, KNOWING THAT ONLY GOOD SHALL COME FROM THIS." As the pure in heart stand firm in this conviction, they help to bring it to pass.

"Purity" in the New Testament always included the idea of singleness of purpose. To be "pure in heart" meant to be "pure in mind." The way to be pure in mind and to see only God's goodness is to do it literally through the picturing power of the mind: (1) to picture only success for any situation or endeavor; (2) to get definite in one's goals about the good one wishes to experience in his life; (3) to behold greater good being outpictured in the lives of others.

HOW THEY PROSPERED THROUGH PICTURES

HE PUT HIMSELF THROUGH COLLEGE AND BECAME A TELEVISION WRITER IN CALIFORNIA: "I came to a formal study of spiritual thinking several years ago and discovered that *a strong desire, and the daily visualization of that desire, always works.* When I became 'pure in heart' through deliberately picturing the goals I wished to reach, that process got me into college, helped me to become a writer, and led me to the house where I wanted to live. As I continued to 'see God' by picturing only the good I desired, it happened. I have now achieved a long-standing goal of writing for television."

A WIDOW WENT FROM 2¢ TO $200: "Because of a long bout with ill health, I got to the point where I didn't have enough to eat. Then I remembered the fantastic power there is in picturing the good that you want. At the time, I had only two cents in my wallet and exactly $1 left in my bank account.

"I took those two cents in my hand, blessed them with words of increase, pictured them multiplying, and gave thanks for immediate results. Three hours later I had $110 in my wallet and a debt of $179 had been cancelled! Then another $100 came, making more than $200 in cash. Evidently *I needed this prosperity lesson at this point in my spiritual growth.* It has encouraged me to realize how quickly the picturing power of the mind can produce results—even to the point of providing ready cash!''

AN AROUND-THE-WORLD CRUISE FOR AN ARIZONA HOUSEWIFE: ''In her book, *The Dynamic Laws of Prosperity,* Dr. Ponder relates the story of the lady who wore a dress with pictures of maps and travel on it. As a result of those pictures, she later traveled abroad. I decided to try it. I made a dress with 'around-the-world' pictures on it, and I wore it often. My husband and I just returned from a South American cruise, which was delightful. The way has now opened for us to take a cruise around the world!''

THE SEVENTH PROSPEROUS BEATITUDE:
THE PROSPERING POWER OF PEACE AND BLESSING

7. ''BLESSED ARE THE PEACEMAKERS, FOR TRUE SUCCESS IS ALWAYS ACCOMPANIED BY PEACE OF MIND. THE PEACEMAKERS SHALL BE CALLED THE SONS OF GOD, THE 'SONS OF GOOD,' SINCE THEIR PRESENCE ALWAYS BRINGS HARMONY AND BLESSINGS.''

''Blessed are the peacemakers: for they shall be called the sons of God.'' (Matthew 5:9)

Jesus' age was so torn by animosities that elderly men sat in public places in order to settle disputes and act as peacemakers. Even today there is no word in the vocabulary of any language that is sweeter than the word ''peace.'' *Prophets and philosophers have long felt that the peaceful state of mind was the remedy for healing the world's ills*—from banishing poverty and disease, to causing treaties and agreements to be kept, and wars to cease.

The attitudes described in the first six Beatitudes are essential prerequisites for the prosperous peacemaker. They emphasize (1) the power of prosperous thinking; (2) that

God is the Source of man's supply; (3) the prospering power of forgiveness and release; (4) that the will of God for man is wealth; (5) the prospering power of love; and (6) the prospering power of deliberate picturing. Thus, it is appropriate that this seventh "beautiful attitude" on peace should be given toward the close of Jesus' teachings on the subject.

HER SUCCESS SECRET WAS "PEACE"

True success is always accompanied by peace of mind. The peacemakers are those who "make peace." They seek peace, and pursue it. The Psalmist advised, "Depart from evil, and do good. Seek peace, and pursue it." (Psalms 34:14) *"Peace" in the Bible meant more than an absence of strife. It was that which brought harmony and blessing.*

A businessman had one employee who always produced a peaceful effect upon those around her. When there was office inharmony, this employee had only to walk into the room in order for bickering to stop. This man finally discovered his employee's secret: As a student of the power of thought, she knew how to silently bless people, atmospheres, and conditions with the thought of peace.

The Psalmist promised: "They shall prosper that love thee. Peace be within thy walls, and prosperity within thy palaces." He also advised, "For my brethren and companions' sakes, I will now say, Peace be *within* thee." (Psalms 122:6-8)

As long as you express fear, resentment, criticism and other negative emotions—which result in a lack of peace—it is not possible to attain very much in life. The act of blessing brings peace within and without. You can be a peacemaker to any situation by blessing it, rather than condemning it. So bless pain, financial problems, troublesome personalities, or worrisome conditions with the thought, "Peace. Be still."

HOW THE ACT OF BLESSING
BROUGHT PEACE AND PROSPERITY

A housewife in California wrote:

"Since our home is located out in the desert near Yucca Valley, we have to go into town about once a month on business and to shop. There are two sweet sisters who are maids at the motel where we stay. We got acquainted with them on our December visit. In April the motel was sold. There was a lot of unhappiness between the new owners and the workers. We loved the workers, and we soon got to know the new owners and their dear little girls.

"We told the maids about the power of prosperous, peaceful thinking. My husband suggested that they bless the motel rooms as they made them up each day with the thought of 'peace and prosperity.' We also talked with the owners about the power of blessing the rooms each morning, seeing them abundantly filled with just the right, paying guests. They had been worried about business. When we arrived on our last visit, business was very good.

"Both maids are now blessing their purses with the thought of abundant increase. One told me *her pay check goes much further, since she began blessing it.* The other maid had wanted to fix up her kitchen for years, but never had the money. Recently her father (who never has helped his children) said, 'I want to make you a loan of $50 toward redoing your kitchen.' Her mother gave her $100 as a gift. Both maids are now teaching others how to bless people, situations and financial matters as a method for bringing peace and prosperity into their lives.

"We blessed our son, and he has made a wonderful marriage. He is also doing very well in college. The power of blessing has really changed his life. We blessed our daughter, and she has gone back to church, and is taking night courses to better her job status. *Over and over we have used the power of blessing to bring peace to troublesome situations, personalities, and even to inanimate objects—all with amazing results.*"

THE EIGHTH PROSPEROUS BEATITUDE: CHEMICALIZATION IS A HEALING, PROSPERING PROCESS THAT BRINGS JOYOUS RESULTS

8. "BLESSED ARE THEY WHO WILLINGLY EXPERIENCE THE IN-
NER CLEANSING THAT ACCOMPANIES EXPANDED THINKING,
FOR THEY SHALL BE REWARDED WITH HAPPY RESULTS.

"Blessed are they that have been persecuted for righteousness' sake: for theirs is the kingdom ot heaven.

"Blessed are ye when men shall reproach you, and
persecute you, and say all manner of evil against you
falsely for my sake.

"Rejoice and be exceeding glad: for great is your reward
in heaven." (Matthew 5:10–12)

Some scholars regard this last Beatitude as one that may
have been added much later to the original seven. Jesus
probably realized that as his followers attempted to use the
"beautiful attitudes" described in the seven foregoing sayings, they might be persecuted from within by old limited
thoughts; that an inner cleansing, or "chemicalization,"
would take place in their thinking and in their lives.[3]

This Beatitude does not mean you are to be a martyr. *All
persecution comes from within.* The thing you are most
persecuted by is your own fearful thinking. The source of
your persecution is none other than your own limited states
of mind.

Every time you think in a bigger way, it involves a tussle
with your limited beliefs of the past. The great prophets and
enlightened leaders of the race often experienced such inner

---

3. See chapter entitled "Chemicalization, A Healing Process" in *The
Dynamic Laws of Healing* by Catherine Ponder. (Marina del Rey, CA:
DeVorss & Co., rev. ed. 1985) p. 190.

struggles as they progressed. They, too, were being persecuted, but from within. "Evolve or dissolve" is a true saying. *When you are experiencing an initiation into a bigger way of
thinking, you are evolving; but you may feel you are dissolving!*
Growth and expansion are not always comfortable, but are
necessary if we are to go forward.

A California housewife wrote:

> "I thought I knew what chemicalization was until I began
> experiencing this present one. What a commotion! I am
> beginning to get a glimpse of the wonderful results that are
> on the horizon as I complete this inner housecleaning, and
> make way for the desired results. Thanks to the excellent
> chapter on 'Chemicalization, A Healing Process,' in Dr.
> Ponder's book, *The Dynamic Laws of Healing,* I know how to
> meet this cleansing experience victoriously."

When you begin entertaining prosperous thinking, the
old thoughts of lack and limitation that have long been
lodged in your subconscious will rise to the surface of your
conscious mind, and they may even accuse you: "Who do
you think you are that you should expect so much good to
come to you? Why should you expect to prosper when
you've never had enough? Why should you expect to succeed when you have so often failed? Why should you expect
good health when you've experienced so much illness? Why
should you expect miracles when your life has been so
grim?"

Those old attitudes of lack, limitation and failure may try
to insist: "Your expectations are too good to be true. They
are too wonderful to happen. Even if they did happen, they
would be too good to last."

When Jesus said, "Blessed are they that have been
persecuted for righteousness' sake, for theirs is the kingdom
of heaven," he meant: You can know you are in the process

of getting results; that your mind is being cleansed of fear and limitation; that your life is being freed of problems—when you begin to think prosperously and those old attitudes loom up from within and try to persecute you. Do not be discouraged, but rejoice! They are rising to the surface of your mind to fade away forever. *Your steadfastness to the expanded viewpoint shall bring advancement.* This is the time to say, "Peace, be still," to the doubts and fears. This is the time to declare, "AS I MEET THIS EXPERIENCE CONSTRUCTIVELY, I SHALL GO FORWARD TO GREATER GOOD."

CHEMICALIZATION STARTED HIS HEALING

A businessman from Ohio wrote:

"After reading about chemicalization as a cleansing process in *The Dynamic Laws of Healing,* I realized what had been happening to me in several ways. I had not known that the problems and difficulties I had been having recently were a chemicalization taking place, so I had tried to stop that uncomfortable *inner* cleansing—when I should have let it work itself out, so that new good could come.

"Right now I am going through a physical chemicalization in my body, which is trying to right conditions there so that a permanent healing can take place. *This healing has tried to come through for the last three years.* But I did not realize what was happening, and did not cooperate. Now I will."

CHEMICALIZATION BROUGHT
HER A FAR BETTER JOB

Once when I lectured in New Orleans, a lady I met there was going through a chemicalization in her financial affairs, but did not realize it. At the conclusion of my prosperity lecture she said to me rather accusingly, "I just lost my job, which I had had for many years. It happened after I took up the study of prosperous thinking."

My reply startled her, "That's great. You have just been 'kicked upstairs.' "

She did not like that answer, because she felt I should have sympathized with her. Later when I returned to New Orleans for another lecture, the lady again appeared. This time she said, "Now I realize that that difficult period was a chemicalization and cleansing period for me. After I lost that job—which I had never liked anyway—I got the best job of my life. I am now the only woman in a high-placed government position. *My monthly deductions are now more than my entire monthly paycheck used to be!* You were right. I *did* get 'kicked upstairs'—but only after an *inner* cleansing took place. I am doing so well financially that I am now putting three children through college on my expanded income. *Thank God for chemicalization!*"

HOW HE ATTRACTED AN
$800,000 BUSINESS TRANSACTION

When Jesus said, "Blessed are ye when men shall reproach you and persecute you and say all manner of evil against you falsely for my sake," he was giving a prosperity formula. He meant that *when words of lack, limitation and hard times are being spoken by others as the truth about economic conditions, that is the time for you to think, speak and act prosperously.*

A young man in the investments business proved this. During a recessional period, he attended a prosperity class and began speaking in prosperous terms. His business associates reproached him, teased him, and, in a manner, persecuted him for his prosperous outlook. They said, "Your prosperous thinking will get you nowhere in this present stockmarket recession. You might as well give up and face financial failure like the rest of us are having to do." Instead, this man declared to himself daily, "I GIVE THANKS FOR PROSPEROUS FINANCIAL TRANSACTIONS NOW IN WHICH ALL CONCERNED ARE SATISFIED, PROSPERED, AND BLESSED."

A client with whom he had not done business for several years, soon telephoned. The result was that this client invested $800,000 through this stockbroker—during a severe recessional period! It was one of the biggest single investments ever made with that company in that state. The broker not only received much acclaim from his fellow investment counselors, but they never again taunted him for his use of prosperous thinking.

IN CONCLUSION, THE MOST "BEAUTIFUL ATTITUDE" OF ALL: USE OFTEN THE PROSPERING POWER OF JOY

Perhaps the last verse in Jesus' "beautiful attitudes" contains the greatest prosperity teaching of all: "Rejoice and be exceeding glad, for great is your reward in heaven."

Heaven symbolized those prosperous, uplifted states of mind that can be so rewarding in both *inner* and *outer* ways. *Jesus knew that such joyous states of mind are a magnet to which the riches of both heaven and earth rush.*

A Texas businessman wrote:

"I write with gratitude because of the great changes for good that have taken place in my parents and in my daughter since I have been meditating upon 'joy.' It has

become a pleasure to telephone my parents and talk with
them. They are so pleasant now. It was not always so. My
daughter is finally adjusting to her marriage, too. There is
also prospering power in the use of joy. I am finally making
progress in getting my bills paid. This is a real victory for
me."

As you joyously give thanks for perfect results in all that
concerns you, your reward from such heavenly thinking can
lead to more rewarding experiences in every phase of your
life. On this happy note, Jesus concluded his "beautiful attitudes."

SUMMARY

1. Jesus' "beautiful attitudes" point out some of the most
   important "dynamic laws of prosperity" ever offered
   mankind! The use of these basic "bountiful attitudes"
   can always bring worthwhile results.

2. When you are being confronted by a multitude of
   needs, like Jesus who was confronted by the multitudes—instead of talking negatively about them, "go
   up into the mountain" by reading, studying, and
   meditating along prosperous lines. Then "call" your
   disciples, your thoughts and feelings, and teach them
   with prosperous ideas and words. You can multiply
   your good by doing this, since thoughts and words of
   abundance will more surely bring what is yours to you
   by divine right than any other method!

3. The prosperous "beautiful attitudes" were these:

   a) Be teachable and willing to learn and practice pros-
      perous thinking.

   b) The basic law of prosperity is that man should look
      to God as the Source of his supply.

c) When the meek practice the prospering power of forgiveness and release, they experience vast good.

d) The will of God for man is wealth.

e) Practice the prospering power of love.

f) Practice the prospering power of picturing.

g) Practice the prospering power of peace and blessing.

h) Chemicalization is a healing, prospering process that brings joyous results.

i) On this happy note, Jesus concluded with the most ''beautiful attitude'' of all: Use often the prospering power of joy.

PROSPERITY FROM THE LORD'S PRAYER

— Chapter 5 —

People sometimes say, "I know prayer works, but I am not very good at it. I do not really know how to pray." *If you know the Lord's Prayer, that's all you need to begin to develop a miracle prayer consciousness—provided you know how to pray it: over and over, slowly with authority, feeling its meaning, calling alive its power, stirring up its miraculous energy.*

The Lord's Prayer has been described as among the shortest and clearest prayers of all religions. You can say the Lord's Prayer in only fifteen seconds. Even a large congregation declaring it together slowly can pray the Lord's Prayer in just thirty seconds. Yet, in spite of its conciseness, *the Lord's Prayer contains one of the greatest series of success formulas ever offered mankind!* Although the Lord's Prayer has often been used, it has seldom been understood from this standpoint.

It is considered to be a brief summary of the "good news" that Jesus gave in the Gospels. It has been regarded by some to be a Gospel in itself, filled with healing, harmonizing, prospering power. "It is your Father's good pleasure to give you the kingdom, and it should be your good pleasure to receive it" seems to be the basic message of the Lord's Prayer. *The success formulas it contains then proceed to show you how to receive those blessings.*

THE SECRET OF HER HEALTH, YOUTH AND SUCCESS

People have often made a practice of parroting the Lord's Prayer one time automatically, instead of declaring it over and over slowly. So they have not realized its healing, prospering power. *The repeated declaration of the Lord's Prayer has a certain energizing effect, like eating and drinking.*

When you meditate upon, verbally declare, or even write out the Lord's Prayer over and over, you bring alive, tune in on, and tap that same healing consciousness that Jesus used to restore the blind, the lame, and the incurables. When you declare over and over the Lord's Prayer, you become attuned to the same prospering power that Jesus used to feed the five thousand, to turn mere water into fine wine, and to manifest tax money from the fish's mouth. Yes, *the Lord's Prayer is filled with tremendous power that can be successfully released into your daily life here and now! To declare the Lord's Prayer over and over can fire your whole being with new energy, power and substance.*

I once talked with a businesswoman who had many demands made upon her time and energy. Yet she never seemed to tire. I finally inquired as to her success secret. She replied that for half an hour every day she rested, relaxed, and meditated over and over upon each line of the Lord's Prayer. As she reflected upon it—sometimes silently and sometimes aloud—the Lord's Prayer filled her with new energy and power. New ways to solve old problems would be revealed, and new good would manifest.

She felt this method was the most practical, yet the most powerful way she had found to solve her problems, to insure her health, and to remain filled with energy, free from fatigue. This businesswoman worked long hours. She also enjoyed many evening activities with friends and business associates. People often commented upon her extremely youthful appearance and great vitality. She stated that declaring the Lord's Prayer over and over had an energizing effect that filled her whole being with uplift. *She said that to let a day pass without spending at least a half hour meditating upon and declaring the Lord's Prayer would have had the same effect upon her as missing a day's meals.*

THE EARLY CHRISTIANS' SUCCESS SECRETS CAN BE YOURS

About the year 40 A.D., a school was formed in Jerusalem whose whole purpose was to understand the sayings of Jesus. The early Christians who studied in that school went forth repeating his words, parables, promises, and teachings with such power that they led transformed lives. Whereas they had previously been common, ordinary disciples, they became bold, illumined apostles. This handful of ordinary men were then able to spread the Gospel's extraordinary message filled with "good news" to the entire ancient world—a colossal achievement for those times. *And they transformed the lives of those to whom they ministered.* One had only to be in touch with their consciousness to be healed and prospered. Some historians claim that they performed far more miracles than did Jesus. Why did they have such extraordinary power? In addition to other methods used, they prayed the Lord's Prayer over and over.

Here is one of the first success secrets you can learn from the Lord's Prayer: Instead of ripping through it just one time in fifteen seconds, begin to speak it over and over with authority. This can open the way for you to witness its electrifying, energizing, transforming effect upon your life. Through this daily practice, the Lord's Prayer may literally shock you into greater good than you have ever known before!

AN INCURABLE CONDITION WAS HEALED

There once was a lady whose condition had been diagnosed as "incurable." In desperation she traveled halfway across the United States to visit a noted spiritual healer. When she arrived, she expected the healer to do something highly spiritual, or perhaps mystical, to help effect her healing. She was very surprised when the noted healer did nothing more than pray the Lord's Prayer over and over aloud with her. The healer then sent this woman back to her home with the simple instruction to declare many times each day the Lord's Prayer. In a few weeks her formerly "incurable" condition was permanently gone.

THE SECRET FOR OVERCOMING HARD CONDITIONS

It has been reported in the past that some of those seeking help at the healing shrine at Lourdes were taught to declare over and over at least fifteen times the Lord's Prayer while entering the healing waters.

The ancients believed that fifteen was the mystical

number that would dissolve hard conditions of mind, body or affairs. When you seem to have a hard financial problem, or any great need, that is the time to declare over and over the Lord's Prayer at least fifteen times each day, preferably in a loud voice. This can cause such hard conditions to break up and to be dissolved forever. If your life circumstances do not allow you the freedom to declare the prayer aloud, then write it out at least fifteen times a day.

Not only have spiritual authorities realized the healing power to be found in the Lord's Prayer, but it has also been noted by medical authorities. In the sixteenth century, the physician, Paracelsus, who was recognized as a miraculous healer in Zurich, Switzerland, spoke of the healing power to be found in the Lord's Prayer. This German doctor also said he caught flashes of genius through declaring it over and over.

A BUSINESSWOMAN DISSOLVED HARD CONDITIONS

A businesswoman heard of the power that the Lord's Prayer had to dissolve hard conditions. Because she had a problem that long years of spiritual study had not helped her to solve, she decided to try this prayer method.

Every day she went alone to her room and declared the Lord's Prayer aloud at least fifteen times. She prayed it slowly, reflecting upon how each line of the prayer related to her problem. Not only did she receive very strong guidance about how to solve her problem, but flashes of genius came to her concerning various other phases of her life, especially her work. One day while loudly declaring the Lord's Prayer, she heard and felt the old bondage begin to break up and dissolve in her consciousness. Within a few weeks, the tide of her affairs had taken a new direction, all barriers were gone, and the good she had long sought appeared. Her associates called it "a miracle," but she knew she had simply witnessed the miracle power of the Lord's Prayer.

WHY THE LORD'S PRAYER HAS PROSPERING POWER

A California businessman wrote:

"Through my study of *The Dynamic Laws of Prosperity*, I began to prosper. Then, after having attained a high level of consciousness and having demonstrated abundance, I got careless. I decided I did not need to use those simple prosperity laws anymore, that I had 'advanced' past them and could just 'be.' I assumed abundance would keep flowing. I'll bet you already know what happened. Over a three-year period of just 'being,' I went from a net worth of $500,000 back down to only $50,000.

"Now I am wondering how I could have ever been so foolish. I am again busy opening my mind to prosperity through the practice of cleansing, forgiveness, and release. I am busy getting definite through list-making, speaking forth prosperity decrees, and picturing. And I am again putting God first financially through tithing.

"Yes, I have learned the hard way that *it pays to get definite about prosperity, if you want prosperity to get definite about you.* And that once you do prosper, you shouldn't take it for granted. That old saying, 'What you don't use, you lose,' is true. When I stopped using the *inner* laws of prosperity, I lost their *outer* results. *I will never again stop getting definite about* prosperity."

The Lord's Prayer is one of the most important spiritual documents of all times because it shows man how to get definite about prosperity, and how to attain true prosperity through spiritual methods. In the sixth chapter of the Gospel according to Matthew, *the Lord's*

Prayer contains some of the finest prosperity secrets offered mankind. They are "secrets" simply because the average person has not studied and applied the Lord's Prayer from a prosperous standpoint. Yet, it was from a prosperous state of mind that Jesus spoke when he gave the success formulas contained in the Lord's Prayer.

In the American Version of the Bible, the Lord's Prayer sounds more like a petition, but in other versions of the Bible—particularly in the Fenton translation—the Lord's Prayer is a series of determined affirmations. In them we find definite prosperity formulas. This is not unusual in the teachings of Jesus, because he was very positive and determined. He made big claims on God and demonstrated them. His prayers were made of one strong affirmation after another. Nowhere is this more evident than in studying the series of success formulas he gave in the Lord's Prayer.

One reason the Lord's Prayer is so filled with prospering power is because *Jesus passed through the trials, tribulations and temptations that most of us have to meet on the road of life.* In the world in which he grew up, Jesus witnessed the bitterness and privation of the poor. He was aware that the accumulation of wealth by the rich was often done at the expense of the poor. He was aware of the wretched, poverty-stricken existence led by the people of Palestine in his time. Both the Jews and Herodians were constantly bargaining with the Romans over the kingdom of Israel. In turn, the Romans appointed rulers from among those Jews who pledged higher taxes and who paid higher prices for political positions. Tyranny and high taxation, especially for the poor, were the results. These were just some of the reasons why Jesus dedicated his life to teaching the gospel of abundance to his followers, and why they heard it so gladly.

THE INNER AND OUTER BENEFITS

The basic reason that the Lord's Prayer is so powerful is because both the *inner* and *outer* needs of man are covered in this short, concise prayer, which is divided into two parts:

Part One, The Inner Benefits: Of the fifty-four words in the Lord's Prayer, the first twenty-four are concerned with the nature of God, both within man and universally. When man recognizes God as the Source of his supply, this knowledge satisfies his *inner* needs. Daily use of this portion of the Lord's Prayer can provide rapid spiritual development. You will find a new and finer side of your being coming into expression. You will experience peace of mind. You will feel a love for God and for your fellowman not previously realized. It can also open the way to receive God's goodness as vast benefits in every phase of your life.

Part Two, The Outer Benefits: The second half of the Lord's Prayer takes up man's *outer* needs for guidance, forgiveness, prosperity, protection, and completed results. When you take its practical power seriously, this second half of the Lord's Prayer can supply your daily needs. It is an invitation to inaugurate God's blessings in your day-to-day existence. By following the advice Jesus gave in the last half of the Lord's Prayer, you will develop a capacity to accomplish far beyond your previous expectations; and you will demonstrate over life's problems.

In an overall way, as you learn to take the *inner* and *outer* steps that Jesus taught in this famous series of success formulas, you will find yourself living a happier, richer, and more useful life than ever before. Just as in the Beatitudes, you will discover that *the success formulas found in the Lord's Prayer point out some of the most important "dynamic laws of prosperity" ever offered mankind!*

PROSPERITY: PART I

THE PROSPERING POWER OF GOD'S NATURE, BOTH UNIVERSALLY AND WITHIN MAN

THE FIRST PROSPERITY SECRET FROM THE LORD'S PRAYER: THE BASIC LAW OF PROSPERITY

1. "TRUE PROSPERITY HAS A SPIRITUAL BASIS."

"Our Father which art in heaven. (Matthew 6:9)[1]

In this, among the most powerful of all prayers, Jesus began by directing our attention to God as a loving Father. It makes God personal and loving to call Him "Father." I like to use that term, "Father," often in communicating with God: "Father, what is the Truth about this situation?" "Father, help me." "Father, show me the way." "Father, I am trusting."

A fellow minister had to release his son to return to war in Viet Nam *for the third time.* In his anguish, this parent said the only prayer that came to him was, "I release you to the Father." He released his son not to cruel warlike conditions, but to a loving Father. Praying in this way made it easier for all involved to survive the experience. Later the son safely returned from war.

Jesus begins the Lord's Prayer by laying down once and for all the true relationship between God and man as that of Father and child. In this first phrase, we find a succinct description of the fatherhood of God and the brotherhood of

---

1. The Lord's Prayer, as quoted in this chapter, is taken from the King James Version of the Holy Bible, except for: (1) verse 12, which is quoted from the American Standard Version of the Holy Bible; (2) the first portion of verse 13, which quotes a common early translation.

man. *If your prayers have not been answered, it may be because you have not thought of God as a loving Father. Most of your difficulties in mind, body and financial affairs would disappear, if you would begin to meditate often upon God as a loving Father. It is only natural that you must be in harmony with God's love, if the things you have asked for and desired are to be granted. Thinking of God in this way attunes you to His unlimited blessings.*

FROM A JOB LAYOFF TO A
BIGGER COMPANY WITHIN ONE WEEK

Heaven is symbolically described as a rich state of mind in the Revelation of John, where it is depicted as a city of pure gold, surrounded by a wall of jasper, of which the foundation was precious stones and the gates were pearl. (Revelation 21) When Jesus affirmed, "Our Father which art in heaven," he was emphasizing that God's abundance is found in heavenly, prosperous states of mind.

In this first prosperity affirmation from the Lord's Prayer, Jesus was pointing out that *if you try to beg, plead, coerce, force or bargain with God for prosperity in the realm of human thinking, you get nowhere.* If you try through worry and fear to cheat or scheme to produce prosperity, you get nowhere. The first prosperity secret is to recognize that God is the Source of your supply, and that you can first contact that rich Source, and tap its supply through your heavenly, prosperous thinking.

A California housewife wrote:

"On November 1st, my husband was laid off work. He received a sizeable check which included vacation and severance pay. We used it to catch up on late financial obligations. From it we also tithed. We did not panic over his being out of work. Instead, we affirmed daily these words: 'WE DO NOT DEPEND UPON PERSONS OR CONDITIONS FOR OUR PROSPERITY. GOD IS THE SOURCE OF OUR SUPPLY, AND GOD PROVIDES HIS OWN AMAZING CHANNELS OF SUPPLY TO US NOW. WE ARE NOW GUIDED INTO OUR TRUE PLACE WITH THE TRUE PEOPLE AND WITH THE TRUE PROSPERITY, QUICKLY AND IN PEACE.'

"The next week my husband got a *better* job with a *bigger* company. It includes more benefits and job opportunities. He was even asked to work overtime his first week on the job! We are still praising God as the Source of all our blessings."

The word "heaven" is derived from a Greek root meaning "expansion." As you begin to think of God as a rich, loving, Father, this will bring you into a heavenly realm of expanded thinking where you will demonstrate abundance as you have never demonstrated it before!

THE SECOND PROSPERITY SECRET FROM THE LORD'S PRAYER: HOW TO BECOME ATTUNED TO THE PROSPEROUS NATURE OF GOD

2. "TO DWELL UPON GOD'S GOODNESS BRINGS PROSPERITY."

"Hallowed be thy name." (Matthew 6:9)

The Lord's Prayer was first given in the Aramaic language, and the more common version was in Latin. The Greek version of the Lord's Prayer, however, was in the form of a chant. The ancient Greeks were so well aware of the tremendous power released through chanting, intoning, or affirming one's good, that even their common speech was chanted. They knew that by affirming the sacred name of God, it could bring an entire change on the physical, mental and spiritual planes of life. They found that chanting the Lord's Prayer not only had a certain energizing effect upon them, like eating and drinking; but that to do so also quickened their ability to produce successful results in their daily lives.

After declaring "Our Father which art in heaven," Jesus went a step further and explained why he dared to claim God as the rich Source of his supply: "Hallowed be thy name." The word "hallowed" means "whole and perfect." Jesus understood that the name and nature of God was that of unchanging, perfect, whole good; that God is the sum total of all good. Thus, he was affirming, "Whole and perfect is thy good."

By chanting, intoning, or affirming the sacred name of God through declaring over and over His goodness, you, too, can bring about an entire change on the physical, mental and spiritual planes of your life. By declaring daily the goodness of God in your life and affairs—regardless of appearances—you can produce miracles!

A prosperous businessman said his success secret had been to declare for every situation in his life: "I PRONOUNCE THIS GOOD, REGARDLESS." A happy career woman said her miracle formula had been to declare: "WHEREVER I AM, GOOD THINGS ALWAYS HAPPEN."

TWO BUSINESSMEN PROSPERED FROM THIS METHOD

People of all ages have known of God's transcendence or universal power. But for many centuries God's immanence —the divinity within man—was a secret teaching. The sages of the past felt that had the suppressed masses learned they had a divine power within them, they would have used it to free themselves from cruel bondage. In this first segment from the Lord's Prayer, Jesus was trying to again reveal this age-old success secret to his followers.

Many of man's problems are solved when he understands the nature of God both within him (immanent) and universally (transcendent) as good, whole, perfect and available to him! Thus, you can be prospered just by meditating upon, and decreeing a belief in God's whole, unchanging, perfect good for you.

A businessman, who has become independently wealthy, said that he constantly affirms the goodness of God for every experience. He keeps these words where he can see them daily: "I REJOICE IN THE GOODNESS OF GOD, CONSTANTLY MANIFESTING TO MEET MY EVERY NEED NOW. I PRAISE GOD FOR HIS ABUNDANT GOODNESS TO ME NOW."

When you dwell upon the nature of God within and around you as good, whole and perfect, any good thing can happen! Another businessman meditated upon and declared often: "WHOLE AND PERFECT IS GOD'S GOOD FOR ME HERE AND NOW." The result was that $30,000 came to him in one business deal where such a result had previously seemed impossible.

Thousands of people have been helped when they turned their attention away from their problems, and thought instead of God's goodness within (God-immanent) and all around them (God-transcendent). This method can be the answer for you, too, since it helps you to contact the abundance of the universe both in *inner* and *outer* ways.

THE THIRD PROSPERITY SECRET FROM THE LORD'S PRAYER: THE PROSPERING POWER OF GOD'S KINGDOM

3. "TO ASK THAT GOD'S KINGDOM COME IS THE COVER-ALL PRAYER FOR SUCCESS."

"Thy kingdom come." (Matthew 6:10)

It has been observed that the most successful people are either praying people, or acquaintances of praying people. Some authorities estimate that *what usually takes a person six hours to do could easily be accomplished in only one by a person who knew how to pray and meditate first!* Especially if his prayer was "Thy kingdom come."

In the first two phrases of the Lord's Prayer, our attention has been centered on the nature of God: Our Father (universal, transcendent, everywhere present); Who art in heaven (immanent, within); Hallowed be thy name (whole and perfect is God's goodness for me, both within and without.)

In this next phrase, you can begin to bring the nature of God and His goodness into your life and affairs. *When you catch a glimpse of the nature of God's goodness within and around you, it seems natural to demand, "Thy kingdom come." It is one of the greatest affirmations you can ever pray.*

Since the nature of God is supreme good, then His kingdom manifesting in any situation is bound to be the highest good for all concerned. In the Greek translation to affirm "thy kingdom come" meant "thy realm returned" or "thy realm restored." Of course, for God's good to be returned or restored in any situation brings success of the highest kind. *You can never go wrong by praying, "Thy kingdom come." It is a cover-all prayer for success.*

HOW THIS PRAYER BROUGHT A BETTER JOB

God's kingdom is one of rich ideas and rich results. When a situation seems to be static and no results have appeared, that is the time to decree, "Thy kingdom come." This is a prayer for fulfillment and for visible, satisfying results.

A businesswoman had longed for a change in jobs. She had used every inner and outer method she knew to produce results, but still she had remained in a job she felt she had outgrown. When she had applied to her superiors for a transfer, they had refused, replying that she was doing so well in her present position they hesitated making a change.

She learned of the success power of the Lord's Prayer and began to declare daily: "THY KINGDOM COME." With almost breathtaking speed, a new job opened to her in a distant area. This time instead of refusing this employee a transfer, her superiors *insisted* she take the new job! It proved to be the answer to her prayers.

ARE YOU WILLING TO RECEIVE THE SURPRISES AND CHANGES THIS PRAYER MAY BRING?

When you pray "thy kingdom come," get ready for these surprises:

First: You are not praying for something to be imposed *upon* you, but for something to be released *within* you, because the kingdom of God begins *within* your own thought and feeling nature. To pray this prayer may mean that first great changes must come *within* your own thoughts and feelings.

Second: Also the use of this prayer may bring *outer* changes, because *you are asking God to strip your life of everything that is not for your highest good.*

Third: This prayer also means that God's kingdom of good can come into your life only when you are equally willing for it to come into the lives of others. *Your own prayers may not be answered until you are willing to pray that God's kingdom of good comes even into the lives of those people who have oppressed, hurt, disappointed, pained or tormented you.* One of the easiest ways to pray for such people is to declare, "LET GOD'S KINGDOM COME FOR THIS PERSON OR SITUATION NOW." This is the finest prayer you can pray for your enemies as well as for your friends. When you are uncertain how to pray about any situation, either for yourself or others, the most powerful prayer method you can use is simply to declare, "THY KINGDOM COME."

THE FOURTH PROSPERITY SECRET FROM THE LORD'S PRAYER: THE PROSPERING POWER OF GOD'S WILL

4. "THE GOOD THINGS IN LIFE ARE GOD'S WILL FOR YOU."

"Thy will be done in earth, as it is in heaven." (Matthew 6: 1 0)

Every moment of your life, your good is seeking you! All things needful for your progress and success are moving toward you, trying to find you. When you begin to declare this magic line from the Lord's Prayer, "Thy will be done," you open the way for your good to manifest.

When Jesus affirmed, "Thy will be done on earth as it is in heaven," he was asking for definite results to appear. "Earth" symbolizes *visible* results, whereas "heaven" symbolizes *invisible* states of mind.

One of the most prominent of all the saints was St. Gregory, and this was his success formula:

"I never prayed the set prayers of the church, but always when the opportunity for praying was offered, I turned obediently to God with these words, 'Thy will be done.' These words formed my only thought in prayer."

If that prayer, "Thy will be done," could make a saint out of a lowly parish priest, think what it can do for you and me. Yes, *the good things in life are God's will for you!*

HOW THIS PRAYER BROUGHT
HEALING AND PROSPERITY

A businessman had been told that the disease from which he had suffered for twenty years, tuberculosis of the spine, was incurable. Yet when he began to pray, "Thy will be done," he was healed in just six months. After that he not only lived a long life, but enjoyed a successful career.

Another businessman had been successful until he was injured and had to have five operations. Finally his health began to slowly return, but he was unable to get steady work. During the next five years he led a hand-to-mouth existence on an income of less than two hundred dollars a month. Finally he prayed, "Father, I have done all I know to do to be prospered again. Thy will be done in me now."

As he spoke that prayer, a sense of peace overcame all former feelings of anxiety and worry. Instead of continuing to study the want ads for work, he felt guided to write the editor of the local newspaper and submit a sample newspaper column that he had been thinking about for a long time.

When he did not receive an immediate reply, he continued to pray: "THY WILL BE DONE." Finally word came that they would allow him to write a column on a trial basis. He rejoiced and continued to affirm: "THY WILL BE DONE." The reader reaction from his column was so great that he was soon given a permanent column and worked at it happily. His column was later syndicated and ran in almost one thousand newspapers, with mail coming to him from all parts of the world. This man proved that when you dare to pray, "Thy will be done," you open the way to the perfect solution.

That prayer can bring amazing results into every phase of your life, too. However, don't forget the last phrase of this prayer, "In earth as it is in heaven." These words open the way for heavenly results to appear in your earthly conditions. "Heaven" comes from a Greek word meaning "expansion," so the faithful use of this prayer can bring results of expanded good, not just mere improvement.

PROSPERITY: PART II

HOW MAN'S SPECIFIC DAILY
NEEDS CAN BE MET

THE FIFTH PROSPERITY SECRET FROM
THE LORD'S PRAYER:
THE POWER OF SPECIFIC PROSPERITY DECREES

5. "ASK DAILY FOR 'MORE THAN ENOUGH.' "

"Give us this day our daily bread." (Matthew 6:11)

The people of the East thought in terms of food on a daily basis, because there was no refrigeration. No matter what else was served, a good host would not think of feeding guests without having plenty of bread on the table. It was considered a basic food. *An abundance of bread also indicated an abundance of prosperity.*

In the Greek translation, the phrase "daily bread" meant "super-substantial bread" or "more than enough." Jesus' prayer meant, "Give us this day our super-substantial bread, or *more than enough.*" Jesus knew that *a rich, loving Father, who made our physical bodies, is also concerned with our physical needs.* The body is the temple of the living God and as such, it should be so honored.

Metaphysically, the word "bread" symbolizes the rich substance of the universe. "Give us this day our daily bread" was a decree to "give us this day our daily supply of the unlimited substance of the universe in rich, appropriate form."

And why not? *The abundance of the earth is staggering.* If you considered the amount of food that is consumed each day by the birds of the air, and how much it would cost if we personally had to purchase that food, the figure would be astronomical. No country in the world could afford to feed the birds of the air. Yet, they are well-fed by the lavish abundance of the universe. *God is extravagant supply. It is man who is miserly in his limited acceptance of God's universal abundance for him.*

So think of God in the grandest possible terms. Then think of your own spiritual nature in equally large terms. God is tremendous, magnificent, unlimited, and *all* of His blessings are meant for you!

JESUS' SECRET FOR MANIFESTING RICH SUPPLY

Jesus had spent the first half of the Lord's Prayer reminding himself and his followers of the nature of God as lavish good, and of man's availability to that abundant goodness. Now, in this last half of the Lord's Prayer, Jesus spoke of man's daily, practical needs, and of a loving Father's desire to meet those needs *when man asks His help.* Prosperity, forgiveness, protection, and deliverance were all promised.

Jesus' prosperity formula from the Lord's Prayer had been this: In the *first* half, he had recognized God as the

Source of man's supply, and had assured man of his availability to it. In the *second* half, he got specific and described how man's daily needs could be met by this rich Source.

Here is the secret for manifesting unlimited supply: It is not enough just to recognize God as the Source of your supply. That leaves your desired good in the realm of invisible substance. After recognizing God as the Source of your supply, then *claim* that supply in definite, specific form. To do so opens the way for it to manifest for you. "Give us this day our daily bread" is a powerful prosperity prayer because it opens your mind to receive *specifically* the wealth of the universe *now*.

HOW A HOUSEWIFE MANIFESTED AN
ABUNDANCE OF FOOD DURING A JOB LAYOFF

The Aramaic word for *bread* also meant "food." It is reassuring to realize that right in the middle of the Lord's Prayer, Jesus was concerned about his followers daily struggle to make ends meet, and that he recognized a rich Father's power to meet man's earthly needs with "more than enough."

Here is how a housewife from Arizona used this success formula to prosper at a crucial time in her life:

"My husband was temporarily unemployed. My sister, her husband and baby had also moved in with us. Including our children, there were eight of us and no jobs or money. The cupboard was bare. One day my sister and I affirmed together, 'Give us this day our daily bread.' The next day a neighbor brought us $20 worth of *bread*. Another neighbor sent over raisin *bread*. Our prayer had been answered literally! This was great, but we had no butter to spread the bread, so this time my sister and I affirmed, 'GIVE US OUR DAILY BREAD, BUTTER AND MEAT.' I then cleaned my empty freezer to get ready to receive as I boldly decreed, 'FOOD MANIFEST NOW!'

"Within the next two days, things started to happen. Our former pastor heard my husband wasn't working, so he graciously paid us a visit, gave us $10 and a turkey that was a gift from one of his members. I began declaring, 'I PRAISE GOD FROM WHOM ALL BLESSINGS FLOW.' And the *flow* began: One neighbor gave us two turkeys, a large box filled with canned goods, and another sack filled to overflowing with groceries. My mother gave us $20. We were given three boxes of food from the Moose Lodge. The Elks gave us a $25 food certificate. The Sunday School class from our former church chipped in. When one of their members arrived in a truck, I counted twenty-seven sacks of groceries containing oil, ten pounds of sausage, ten pounds of corn meal, thirty pounds of fresh potatoes, and forty pounds of flour. There was also an abundance of powdered milk and sixteen pounds of margerine. Our freezer was soon filled to overflowing with meat, vegetables and juices. Next, a lady arrived with twenty-five loaves of *bread.* That Sunday School class also gave us $30, and on Christmas Eve, their minister brought another gift of $30; also an abundance of toys. Between Thanksgiving and Christmas, we were given sixty pounds of turkey alone, plus roasts, steaks, chickens, bacon and chops. It was the most prosperous holiday season we had ever had!

"Things are back to normal in our financial affairs now, but *I shall never forget how that prosperity affirmation from the Lord's Prayer brought abundance to us just when we needed it most.*"

As this housewife proved, that simple prayer, "Give us this day our daily bread," is a powerful prayer of faith and trust. Your use of faith and trust can move on the rich substance of the universe to produce prosperous results, even "more than enough" for you, too!

THE SIXTH PROSPERITY SECRET FROM
THE LORD'S PRAYER:
THE RESULT-GETTING POWER OF FORGIVENESS

6. "FORGIVENESS IS THE TURNING POINT TO RESULTS."

"Forgive us our debts as we also have forgiven our debtors." (Matthew 6:12)

When we think in terms of our needs, we have rarely thought of forgiveness as one of them. Yet Jesus knew that forgiveness is such a great and constant need in the life of man, that he made it the second decree among those concerning man's specific needs. Immediately after the prayer for prosperity came the forgiveness prayer. This is one of the least understood, yet one of the most powerful, of all the prayer statements given in the Lord's Prayer.

Perhaps the reason that Jesus listed forgiveness as one of the tangible needs of man is because forgiveness is more than a spiritual, mental, emotional or psychological action. *In order to be successful on all levels of life, forgiveness should become not just an occasional act, but one that is practiced daily as a way of life.* You should declare prayers of forgiveness, not just when someone has wronged or upset you, but every day. When this is done, successful results invariably appear.

Most of us are confronted with the negative emotions that arise within us from dealing with people and situations that do not act or react as we think they should. When they do not, it builds up resentments within us of which we are often unaware. Nevertheless, those resentments block our good.

"Forgive us our debts as we also have forgiven our debtors" (the Greek version) implies that you should not wait for others to do the forgiving. You should forgive first and often. Why? Because God, as a loving Father, has already forgiven you and all concerned. So by your mental acts of forgiveness, you open the way for God's forgiving power to move in and through situations and events, freeing all negative emotions that have blocked results. Such a daily practice of forgiveness can lead to dramatic good.

THE HEALING POWER OF
FORGIVENESS HELPED HER RETURN TO WORK

An instructor was due to teach a special month-long course; yet only a few days before the course began she learned that she had pneumonia. She sought healing through the use of drugs and medical aids, but the pneumonia persisted. On Friday before the course was to begin on Monday, she was informed that people were arriving from all over the United States and from abroad to study with her. She was also told that no substitute teacher was available for that specialized course.

As she faced the diagnosis of pneumonia that Friday, she prayed for guidance. Even though she was suffering from a high fever, which medication had been unable to lower, her guidance was to begin declaring over and over the Lord's Prayer; and to continue until the turning point came. She did so, night and day, and by Sunday the fever, which she had battled for days, was gone. Even though she was very weak, she began her month-long course on Monday morning as scheduled.

This teacher later realized why she may have contracted the pneumonia in the first place: She had gotten upset and angry about something someone had said about her. When she had prayed over and over, "Forgive us our debts as we also have forgiven our debtors," she had been able to forgive, be healed, and return to work.

A rich and loving Father has every blessing for you, too. But your mind may have been so filled with hurts, disappointments and criticisms that there has been no room to receive that abundance. Forgiveness opens the way to receive the lavish good that God has for you. As you loosen up in your thinking through the daily practice of forgiveness, you loosen up to receive your own God-given abundance, which often comes to you in unforeseen ways.

THE SEVENTH PROSPERITY SECRET FROM THE LORD'S PRAYER: THERE IS PROSPERING POWER IN CLAIMING DIVINE PROTECTION

7. "YOU CAN BE PROTECTED FROM LIFE'S PROBLEMS, AND DIVINELY DELIVERED INTO GREATER GOOD, WHEN YOU CLAIM IT."

"And leave us not in temptation, but deliver us from evil. (Matthew 6:13)

A loving Father does not "lead" you into temptation, nor does He "leave" you there. According to the common root meaning, "*Leave* us not in temptation" means "to test." Jesus was praying "Leave us not in times of testing." It was a prayer for protection.

As you begin to expand your thinking and your world, you may have testing periods, but they are for good. Periods of testing may sometimes seem a necessity for your soul growth and expansion. They cause you to gain insight and inner strength that you may gain in no other way. Trials and tests come not to hurt, harm, or destroy you, but to make you wiser, stronger, more sure of your *inner* mind powers, and better able to use them to meet life's experiences victoriously.

However, this passage also has another meaning: "Leave us not in temptation but deliver us from evil" means just that. Because of what you learn and the strength you gain from times of testing, they can be a blessing. But once you have learned the lesson the test period provides, you should be freed from it. Pruning periods are for the purpose of bearing much fruit. But once the pruning period has completed its purpose, you should be freed from it so that you can bear the fruitful results you desire.

Too many people get into periods of testing and just stay there fighting them, so that such periods become destructive, negative experiences, rather than the constructive periods in soul growth and expanded good that they were meant to be. *Many negative conditions in life would clear up quickly if those involved would:* (1) stop fighting them; (2) ask that the lesson to be learned be revealed; (3) ask for deliverance from the experience.

You may have suffered needlessly when your life could have been transformed if only you would have declared: "LEAVE ME NOT IN TEMPTATION, BUT DELIVER ME FROM EVIL."

A "WOMAN DRIVER" WAS DIVINELY DELIVERED

This can work in a practical way. A woman who was driving in a strange city in heavy afternoon traffic was arrested. Her actions had seemed the only safe ones she could have undertaken under the circumstances, so she did not understand the charges against her.

Upon relating the events to her husband later, neither could he determine what mistakes she had made. Nevertheless, she was scheduled to appear in court within a few days to face the possibility of a penalty and heavy fine.

At first, the thought of great injustice welled up within her. Not only did she feel that the charge was unwarranted, but neither did she have the required money for the fine. When she remembered this phrase from the Lord's Prayer,

she declared over and over: "LEAVE ME NOT IN THIS TIME OF
TESTING, BUT DELIVER ME FROM EVIL." She also declared a
favorite prayer for protection: "GOD IS MY DEFENSE AND MY
DELIVERANCE NOW."

On the day of her court appearance, after the judge listened sympathetically to the facts of the case, he quickly
dismissed the violation against her. He said there was insufficient evidence that she had broken the law. Her
deliverance from evil *had* come after *she asked for it.*

THE PROSPERING POWER OF INITIATION PERIODS

That periods of testing are a part of one's expansion into
greater good has been a universal teaching. As long as
history has been recorded, there have been secret
brotherhoods which felt that before an initiate could be admitted to brotherhood, he must first go through certain
trials, tests, and proving periods. There are many kinds of
testings described in the Bible.

In a sense we are all "initiates." Your "initiations" may
come in the form of ill health, emotional strain, loss, disappointment, or as financial limitation. Those experiences are
your testing periods. As you prove through your use of *inner*
mind powers that you can produce satisfying *outer* results,
you then find yourself moving forward to greater good than
ever before. After such "initiation" periods, you are then
able to accomplish great things with ease and joy.

THE EIGHTH PROSPERITY SECRET FROM
THE LORD'S PRAYER:
THE PROSPERITY POWER OF PRAISE

8. "PRAISE GOD AS THE SOURCE OF ALL YOUR BLESSINGS.
THEN DARE TO THINK BIG!"

"For thine is the kingdom and the power and the glory forever." (Matthew 6:13)

This last phrase was not a part of the original Lord's Prayer as given by Jesus. Before the end of the first century, the Syrian Christians added this doxology of praise as a final statement, perhaps patterning it after David's famous prosperity doxology: "Thine, O Lord, is the greatness, and the power, and the glory, and the victory, and the majesty . . . for all that is in the heavens and in the earth is thine . . . Both riches and honor come of thee." (I Chronicles 29:11–12)

Perhaps you question the rightness of the early Christians to add this "phrase of praise" plus an "Amen" to the original Lord's Prayer, but I think they did the wise thing. The phrase they added sums up the power of prayer, and again reminds us of the power of God's goodness to help us: "For thine is the kingdom and the power and the glory forever." This is a reaffirmation of the *first half* of the Lord's Prayer, which described God's nature as good, both within man (immanent) and universally (transcendent).

It is significant that the Lord's Prayer begins and ends with a description of the nature of God and His goodness to man. This last phrase ends the prayer, not on a problem note, but by again reminding man of the availability of God's goodness to him. Realizing this helps man to mentally accept the answers to his prayers. *Strength for overcoming life's problems is gathered through repetition of God's goodness. If you could realize the importance of this last phrase from the Lord's Prayer, suffering, problems, and burdens would all disappear like a morning mist from your life!*

The Persian philosopher, Kahlil Gibran, wrote in *The Prophet:*[2]

---

2. Gibran, New York, (Alfred A. Knopf) p.67.

"You pray in your distress and in your need. Would that you might also pray in the fullness of your joy, and in your days of sunshine."

To dwell upon this last "phrase of praise" from the Lord's Prayer can increase the fullness of your joy and your days of abundance!

A MILLIONAIRE'S SUCCESS SECRET

It is important that the Lord's Prayer ended as it had begun: by recognizing God as the Source of man's supply. This last "phrase of praise" also points out the necessity for thinking big in order to prosper.

A millionaire, who was asked the secret of his success, obviously understood this passage, "For thine is the kingdom and the power and the glory forever," because he replied.

"Prosperity comes as a result of thinking big. You should not hesitate to ask largely, for God can give much as easily as He can give a little. Most people think in terms of hundreds of dollars. It is a crowded field. Still others think in terms of thousands of dollars. It is a less crowded field. But few people think in terms of millions of dollars. The less crowded the area of thought, the less competition, and the more room there is for experiencing prosperity in bigger terms."

When you are trying to expand your prosperity consciousness, declare often: "FOR THINE IS THE KINGDOM AND THE POWER AND THE GLORY FOREVER." You are thereby claiming God as the Source of your inexhaustible supply. You are affirming that you have a rich Father, and that *all* that the Father has is yours!

THE NINTH PROSPERITY SECRET FROM THE LORD'S PRAYER: THE PROSPERING POWER OF COMPLETION

9. "MIRACLES OFTEN HAPPEN WHEN YOU SPEAK WORDS OF COMPLETION."

"Amen." (Matthew 6:13)

The series of eight bold affirmations in the Lord's Prayer were concluded with the word "Amen," which meant, "SO BE IT," or "ACCORDING TO THY FAITH IN THESE RICH IDEAS, IT WILL BE DONE UNTO THEE." The word "Amen" means simply, "LET THE GOOD MANIFEST NOW." It signifies completion. *It is an assurance that God can bring great things to pass.*

The reason the early Christians ended the Lord's Prayer with the word "Amen," was because they were declaring that their prayers would be answered. They knew a secret: *A situation can drag on endlessly just because it is waiting for someone to declare "Amen." Whereas, when you speak the word of completion, it speeds up results. Miracles often happen.* So here is your last success secret from the Lord's Prayer: *You, too, can work miracles in your* life by declaring "completion." Amen!

SUMMARY

1. The Lord's Prayer is considered to be a brief summary of the "good news" that Jesus gave in the Gospels. It has been regarded by some to be a Gospel in itself, filled with healing, harmonizing, prospering power.

2. People have often made a practice of parroting the Lord's Prayer one time automatically, instead of declaring it over and over slowly, and with authority. So they

have not realized its healing, prospering, miracle-producing power.

3. The Lord's Prayer is one of the most important spiritual documents of all times because it shows man how to get definite about prosperity, and how to attain true prosperity through spiritual methods.

4. The success formulas found in the Lord's Prayer point out some of the most important "dynamic laws of prosperity" (spiritual laws of wholeness) ever offered mankind!

5. One reason the Lord's Prayer is so powerful is because both the *inner* and *outer* needs of man are covered.

6. *Prosperity, Part One, The Inner Benefits:* Of the fifty-four words in the Lord's Prayer, the first twenty-four describe the prospering power of God's nature, both universally and within man.

   a) True prosperity has a spiritual basis.

   b) To dwell upon God's goodness brings prosperity.

   c) To ask that God's kingdom come is the cover-all prayer for success.

   d) The good things in life are God's will for you.

7. *Prosperity, Part Two, The Outer Benefits:* The second half of the Lord's Prayer takes up man's *outer* needs for guidance, forgiveness, prosperity, protection and completed results, and it shows how these daily needs can be met.

   e) Ask daily for "more than enough."

   f) Forgiveness is the turning point to results.

   g) There is prospering power in claiming divine protection.

   h) Praise God as the Source of all your blessings; then dare to think big.

   i) Miracles often happen when you speak words of completion.

THE PROSPERITY LAW OF CONTINUATION

FROM THE LOAVES AND FISHES MIRACLE

— Chapter 6 —

Down through the centuries, stories of "miraculous plenty" have abounded in the Holy Land, and are current even until this day. *That there is nothing niggardly about the Lord's provision for man is found in the miracle of the loaves and fishes.* The importance of this popular miracle is shown in the fact that it is the only one of Jesus' prosperity miracles to be mentioned in all four gospels (a total of six times): Matthew 14:13–21; Mark 6:31–44; Luke 9:10–17; Matthew 15:32–39; Mark 8:1–21; John 6:1–14.

It is reassuring to realize that Jesus was concerned about the physical, as well as the spiritual, needs of his followers. Jesus knew that the spiritual leaders and organizations of his time should concern themselves with the economic and material welfare of humanity, if their ministries were to be of real help—just as religious leaders and organizations should do today.

137

The word "continue" means "to go on without interruption" or "to begin again after interruption." All of us are interested in the prosperity law of continuation. You want your good to go on without interruption. If your good has been interrupted, then you want it to begin again. It can and it will, as you learn to use the steps Jesus used in this famous old fish story.

It has been generally assumed that the process of multiplication is almost beyond man's comprehension. *Yet Jesus pointed out the simple steps that each one of us can take to experience the miracle of supply!* Jesus gave those mystic steps for continuing one's supply when he multiplied the loaves and fishes to feed thousands. (Matthew 14:13–21)

THE TWO BASIC STEPS TO DEVELOPING A PROSPERITY CONSCIOUSNESS THAT HAVE HELPED THE AUTHOR

It is important to realize that: (1) Jesus first gave his famous success philosophy in the Beatitudes and Lord's Prayer comparatively early in his ministry. Through these teachings, he shared with his followers some of the most powerful prosperity formulas ever offered mankind! It is equally as significant to realize that: (2) after he set forth these powerful treatises, he then got busy showing his followers how that success philosophy could be put to work in daily living; and he then performed some of his most outstanding works, beginning with his most popular prosperity miracle.[1]

---

1. It is true that Jesus may have performed at least two prosperity miracles and some of his healings *before* giving the Beatitudes and the Lord's Prayer. By so doing, he caused his followers to become open, receptive and interested in the great truths he was yet to impart.

The secret for developing a prosperity consciousness is this: (1) You must learn the philosophy of prosperous thinking and how to apply its specific prosperity principles; (2) Then you must get busy applying and practicing those enchanting formulas over and over. To do so gives you an *inner* hold on the rich substance of the universe, which then produces satisfying, *outer* results for you. It is a fascinating lifetime process. I can assure you from my own experience that this is the only sure process for experiencing true, permanent abundance that you will ever find!

This two-step formula has gradually taken me from a poverty level to a normal income level of supply over the years; from life in one room in the Deep South to a comfortable home in America's foremost desert resort in the Golden West: from an overworked, underpaid level to a lifestyle where I now work for the joy of serving and sharing, more than through sheer necessity. It is a life style that finally includes an adequate staff to help me carry the ever-expanding workload, with which I struggled alone for so many years. My present way of life makes it possible for me to lead a fairly normal life *for the first time,* rather than continuing to try to just survive against almost impossible odds which I was forced to do for so many years.

I continue to use daily some of the prosperity principles taught by the millionaires of the Bible, and I look forward to doing so for the rest of my life. Not only do they meet the needs of my *outer* life, but those prosperity principles richly feed my *inner* soul nature as well. It is only when our deep *inner* needs are met that our *outer* supply can become permanent.

NO PLACE IS BARREN OF GOOD

Jesus' most popular prosperity miracle begins by saying that Jesus withdrew into "a desert place apart." (Matthew

14:13) It was in this desert setting that he had to meet the great needs of the multitude.

There is nothing wrong with desert places. The desert's peace passes all understanding. It was on the peaceful deserts of the world that the great religions were born. Moses, Elijah, and Paul all spent long periods in the desert. Mohammed lived all of his life in the desert. Even today common folk, as well as world leaders and religious seekers, take refuge in isolated places in order to become renewed within and without, and to make important decisions.

At times most of us find ourselves in "a desert place apart," either literally or through the circumstances of our lives. *Such desert experiences can produce vast good.* We need to go alone on occasion to pray and meditate, to think things through, and to get our perspective. We need to get free of other peoples' opinions and the pressure of personality at times, so that we can listen to the voice of Truth within us.

If you find yourself in a desert place apart, you can know that you are there for a good reason. In that place apart, you can make your good continue. If it has been interrupted, you can even cause it to begin flowing again.

I now live and work "in the desert" by choice. Yet I shall never forget the dramatic effect it had upon me the first time I saw the desert area surrounding Palm Springs, California. I was fascinated as I viewed flowers and desert plants I had never seen before. I saw a "mirage" on the desert for the first time. I observed the majestic mountain ranges that changed in color from pale pink at dawn to deep purple at dusk. Even the date palms radiated a mysticism all their own. There was a quietness and beauty about the desert that was soul-satisfying. It is little wonder that the beautiful resort area in which I now live is one where so many of the great and near-great in the worlds of industry, politics, and the arts, come to vacation or to enjoy winter retreats. This "great desert empire" surrounding the Palm Springs area radiates an aura of mystic glamour and indescribable peace that is soul-satisfying; and that offers physical renewal as well.

HOW LITERAL RETREAT INTO
THE DESERT BENEFITTED HER

On my first visit to Palm Springs so many years ago, I met a resident who told me that when she had a problem she did not know how to solve, she would go up into "the high desert," where she would pray and meditate until she got the answer. She had just returned from such an experience where she had lived alone in a cave for a number of days. She felt that experience had given her the peace, power, serenity, and spiritual perspective she needed to meet life victoriously.

Do not fear the barren desert places in your life. Instead, welcome them! They are for good. If you find yourself in a "desert place apart" as did Jesus, right in that barren spot you can have a miracle if it is needed. Your good can be made to continue. In the loaves and fishes miracle, Jesus proved that *no place is barren of good.* This knowledge is among his greatest prosperity secrets for you.

THE CASE OF THE PROSPEROUS ANTS

Alexander Lake[2] tells the story of a man who proved that your good can be made to continue, even in a literal desert

---

2. Alexander Lake, *Your Prayers Are Always Answered* (Reprinted by permission of Simon & Schuster, a Division of Gulf & Western Corp., New York: 1956) pp. 23-33.

place. During World War II, a couple in Southern California had to meet what seemed to be a hopeless problem. After having been childless until they were almost fifty, this couple was finally blessed with a little girl.

When this child was three years old, a mysterious illness came upon her. Doctors could find nothing physically wrong with her. Yet she was listless, would not eat or talk much, and grew weaker day by day. Finally the family doctor advised, "Your baby is very ill. If you want her to get well again, get her out of this climate. She needs sunlight. Take her to the Mojave Desert. Another month may be too late. Take this baby to the desert at once, and keep her there until she's well."

The man resigned from his job in a shipyard; he and his wife filled their car with groceries and household effects, and with their daughter, drove into the desert. There they found an old abandoned shack in which to live. For weeks it seemed they had made a mistake. They had no means of livelihood, and their daughter did not get better. But in this "desert place apart," they kept praying for guidance.

One day, after his daughter had shown an interest in them, the father made a little nest to house desert ants. She happily watched for hours, as the busy ants went to and fro in it. Finally she began to talk again—about the ants. That was the turning point. Her parents knew then they had not made a mistake in bringing her to the desert; that she would get well.

As they prayed for supply, an interesting thing happened. A few days after the ant house had been built, a student from the University of Southern California stopped by their well to get water. He explained that he was spending time on the desert studying the bees, ants and other desert insects. When shown the ants' nest the student asked that one be made for him, and even left an advance payment for it.

When he showed the ants' nest to his fellow students and professors at the University, they placed orders for them, too. The result was that the former shipyard worker, with his family, spent the next two years in that ''desert place apart,'' where he made a living building ant houses. Later when they realized their daughter had been healed, this family left the desert and again resumed a normal way of life.

Yet they had proved that *no place is barren of good, not even a desert place. Your good can be made to continue even in the barren areas of your life, too! When you make the most of the good you find there, one day you are then freed to leave that desert experience for ''re-entry'' into a more normal way of life.*

JESUS' FIRST TWO STEPS IN TURNING LACK INTO ABUNDANCE: THROUGH PROSPEROUS THOUGHTS AND WORDS

After Jesus had spent the entire day healing the multitude who had followed him to his desert place apart, his disciples came to him and talked lack: ''The place is desert, and the time is already past. Send the multitudes away, that they may go into the villages, and buy themselves food.'' (Matthew 14:15)

But *Jesus paid no attention to this negative report.* In the face of lack:

First. He invoked a prosperous attitude. He used the ''no'' power of the mind as he refused to believe in or to be hypnotized by the appearance of lack. In effect, he reversed the thought and said, ''I don't believe a word of it. It is not so.''

Second. He spoke prosperous words. *Jesus made an astonishing statement in the face of lack:* ''They have no need to go away: give ye them to eat.'' (Matthew 14:16) In effect he was saying, "We have enough. We have plenty to spare and to share."

If you find yourself in a desert place apart that seems barren of good, you also have what you need to begin meeting that need—provided like Jesus, you also: (1) invoke a prosperous attitude and refuse to be hypnotized by the appearance of lack; (2) speak words of abundance: "I HAVE ENOUGH. I HAVE PLENTY TO SPARE AND SHARE."

HOW A HOUSEWIFE DEMONSTRATED
INSTANT SUPPLY

A housewife was preparing a salad for lunch when she discovered that she was out of oil for the dressing. She could have dropped everything and gone to the store. Instead, she said very forcefully, "The answer to my need is already on the way to me now."

Five minutes later she heard a voice outside the kitchen window calling, "Free sample for you." She opened the door and there on the step was a cellophane bag, its contents clearly visible. It contained a twelve-ounce bottle of a new brand of salad oil that the manufacturer was promoting by means of door-to-door sample deliveries. She *had* received what she needed after she had spoken the words of abundance, and had expected her good to appear.

THE PROSPERITY SYMBOLOGY
OF THE LOAVES AND FISHES

When Jesus said of the multitude of hungry people, "They have no need to go away; give ye them to eat," the reply was, "We have here but five loaves and two fishes." Jesus said, "Bring them hither to me." (Matthew 14:18)

The loaves and fishes have significant prosperity symbology. In the East, bread was the main food, and it was considered sacred. Bread that was baked by pious women, who devoted themselves to prayer and fasting, was considered blessed bread. The people of Jesus' time also believed that the blessings of holy men caused bread to multiply. *When articles of food were handled, God's name was invoked and His abundant blessings were sought. A poor man in the East expected God to bless what he had, and if necessary, to multiply it.* "GOD WILL INCREASE MY SUBSTANCE, GOD WILL BLESS WHAT I HAVE," was a common prayer. They often blessed their bread by commanding, "GOD, INCREASE IT!"

1. The *bread* which Jesus multiplied did not merely mean food. It symbolized all things that man requires for a healthy, free, harmonious life. Those five loaves symbolize *the good you desire* in life, whether it be greater health, wealth, or happiness.

2. The *fish* symbolize the *increase of that desired good* as expanded health, harmony, and prosperity in your life.

Jesus worked essentially in the realm of ideas rather than in the realm of effects. He often used fish to illustrate his prosperity teachings, because fish are the most prolific of all things. The fish was an ancient art symbol; it was a fertility sign denoting the power to increase. Fish symbolize ideas of abundance, which multiply when used.

Furthermore, a fish was a cherished article of diet throughout the East. The two small fish handed Jesus were a type of salted sardine that was considered a delicacy, or "the best" of foods. Jesus believed that God's will for man was "nothing but the best," so he multiplied the substance at hand—a delicacy or "the best" of foods—which he then shared bountifully with the multitudes. This should be a vast reassurance to you and to me to claim "nothing but the best" for our own lives. *Such a bold claim carries divine favor.*

THE THIRD STEP TO ABUNDANCE:
THE PROSPERING POWER OF DIVINE ORDER

After receiving the five loaves and two fishes, Jesus put things in divine order: He told the multitudes to sit down on the grass, to get quiet, and to get ready to receive.

When you begin to get things in order in this way, you can meet the problem of lack victoriously. Jesus was able to turn the tables on lack when he did this.

HOW SHE GOT THINGS IN
ORDER AND MADE A COMEBACK

There once was a lady whose health was broken, whose financial affairs were in complete disorder, and whose courage was gone. She did not feel she could go on. Yet she knew if she could gain control in her thinking of all the challenges that confronted her, somehow she could meet the situation victoriously and survive.

In an effort to get her thinking in order, she sat down one day with her dictionary. She looked up the word "courage," and wrote down all the meanings of that word which she found. These various definitions led her to other words. She looked them up. Soon she had several pages filled with words expressing courage, strength, power, joy, light, kindness, health, harmony, and peace. All those words were uplifting, helpful, and encouraging. In the process something began to happen in her inner nature. She became so interested in that series of constructive words that she found herself uplifted and encouraged by them so that she was able to go on.

Again she faced her health and human relations problems, but from a hopeful new standpoint. As she did so, she found herself regaining her strength and health almost magically. Best of all, for the first time—even in the midst of problems—she felt lighthearted and happy. As she continued in this happier state of mind, both her health and human relations problems straightened out completely.

When this woman had put things in divine order in her thinking, it led to divine order in her outer life as well. She was then shown how to meet a multitude of needs successfully.

DIVINE ORDER BRINGS
INCREASE IN CLIENTS AND INCOME

A businessman from Nevada wrote:

"I first read about the fantastic power that lies in getting things in divine order in your book, *The Healing Secret of the Ages.* Three times a day I began to declare: 'DIVINE ORDER IS BEING ESTABLISHED IN MY LIFE IMMEDIATELY.' So many wonderful things have happened:

"*First.* I had an increase in clients. (I am a therapist.) *Second.* This brought an increase in income. *Third.* I received a $600 bonus from my boss for services performed throughout the fiscal year. This is the first time the company has ever given a bonus to employees! *Fourth.* I have been able to introduce many people to the prospering power of divine order, and this has given me a deep sense of satisfaction."

Yes, when a need arises, like Jesus, you may say to it, "Sit down, get quiet, and get ready to receive your good." *Then do whatever you can in inner and outer ways to take control and bring about order. This will lead to prosperous results.*

THE FOURTH AND FIFTH STEPS TO ABUNDANCE:
LOOK UP, SHARE WHAT YOU HAVE, AND PROSPER

After Jesus brought about divine order, he took the substance at hand (bread) and the idea of increase (fish), and looking up to heaven, he blessed, broke, and gave out the multiplied result. "If you look up, you will always be provided for," is a wise old saying.

So take what you have, then break or divide it. Next, send it forth to meet the needs of the moment. But do so in a certain way. Instead of thinking, "This isn't enough," remember that sharing is the beginning of financial increase. Also remember the astonishing statement of abundance that Jesus had made in the face of lack: "They have no need to go away: give ye them to eat." (Matthew 14:16) In like manner, declare these words of abundance in the face of lack: "THERE IS PLENTY TO MEET THIS NEED. THERE IS ALWAYS ENOUGH."

You, too, can produce a prosperity miracle if you take what you have, look up and bless it, rather than looking down and criticizing it. Many people with tangled business affairs have straightened them out completely by looking straight at them and saying, "I PRAISE GOD FOR PLENTY NOW." With these words of praise and blessings on your lips, a miracle can happen.

HOW TO LOOK UP IN YOUR RELATIONSHIPS

Human relations problems often result when we look down and criticize, rather than looking up to praise and bless. Here is a marvelous formula for looking up and praising the people in your life whom you may have considered difficult, those who perhaps got "under your skin."

Say to them in your daily meditations: "I REFUSE TO THINK OF YOU AS 'ONLY HUMAN.' I BEHOLD YOU AS A CHILD OF GOD, CREATED IN THE IMAGE OF LOVE. I RECOGNIZE THE DIVINITY IN YOU, WHICH IS YOUR TRUE, BEST SELF. YOU ARE A SPIRITUAL BEING, A TEMPLE OF THE LIVING GOD, AND YOU NOW THINK AND ACT ACCORDINGLY."

If you persist in it daily, this prayer method can produce miraculous results, not only for the other person, but also for you. It is impossible to feel depressed, unattractive, unsuccessful, or in any way negative when you realize that you are a child of the living God; that He loves you; and that you live, move and have your being in the midst of His abundant life, which created you. Neither can you feel awkward, backward, self-conscious, or on the defensive while silently blessing other people, and looking for the beauty, kindness and goodness in them.

As you think in this way, watch *yourself* change. The other person may be unconscious of the forces for good at work, but something will compel him to respond in a constructive way, too.

A businessman said, "I have caused the attitude of many persons to change toward me by the simple method of always greeting them with a silent 'God bless you.' I have sent this 'God bless you' to people near me, on trains, in subways, hotel lobbies and at airports. Many times people have responded with a smile and friendly nod, not realizing why they were moved to do so. *You can save yourself needless wear and tear, and untold friction with this 'God bless you' attitude. You can clear up hurt feelings, criticism, self-pity and many other human weaknesses through using this prayer technique.*" Yes, this is a practical way to look up, praise and bless, rather than continuing to look down and criticize.

THE SIXTH STEP TO ABUNDANCE:
THE ACT OF BLESSING HAS MULTIPLYING POWER

Even in barren conditions, there is much that is available to you if you know how to bring it forth. Jesus did this through the act of blessing. There is no doubt that his act of blessing increased the supply on hand to the point of feeding the multitudes.

The word "bless" means "to make whole by spoken words." The ancients felt that a blessing carried great power to accomplish good. Jesus proved that the act of blessing had a mystical, multiplying power. *The act of blessing still carries that same power to produce increase today!*

A businesswoman from Louisiana wrote:

"At a time when there seemed no way to get delivery on a desk I had purchased, I began to use various affirmations for results, but nothing happened. The people I purchased it from had no way of getting the desk to me, nor did I have a truck in which to move it to my house. Since it was a large metal desk, everyone I knew who had trucks refused to deliver it for me.

"Several weeks went by and still the desk had not been delivered. I finally remembered the power there is in the act of blessing to release one's good. Each day, no matter where I was, I began to decree to each pick-up truck that passed by: 'I BLESS YOU AND BLESS YOU FOR THE GOOD THAT IS WORKING IN AND THROUGH YOU.'

"One morning soon afterwards, while at home on my day off, I decided to check on the possibility of hiring a moving van to deliver the desk to me. As I was looking up a local phone number, *my* telephone rang. It was the secretary from my office calling to say that they had put the desk on *her* pick-up truck, and would have it at my house in a few minutes!

"This seemed a miracle for more than one reason: This woman had not liked me and had tried every trick to get me fired from my job. Because of this, I certainly had not mentioned to her that I needed a truck to haul my desk. Nevertheless, the desk was soon sitting in my office at home.

"The power of blessing had also worked out the big problems between us. She called a few days later to apologize about the way she had treated me on the job. She said she was very sorry that she had tried to get me fired, because she did not want my job; nor did she know anyone else who wanted it. Now we are good friends, and she is very nice to me. She even praises me to our boss."

THE STRONGEST POWER THERE IS

A businessman from California wrote:

"It has been said that a pine tree will not grow if it is planted, then replanted. But a friend once blessed a pine tree for me. We replanted it, that friend prayed for it, and I want you to know that there is not a greener, fuller, faster-growing tree in all of this state. That is proof to me that *God's power, released through the act of blessing, is the strongest power there is!"*

THE ACT OF BLESSING BROUGHT
AN ADDITIONAL ROOM DEBT FREE

A housewife proved that the act of blessing has a mystical, multiplying power. She began to praise and bless everything at hand. As she praised and blessed her home, the money on hand, her husband's income, and God as the Source of their supply, it was as though everything and everybody responded to her words of praise and blessing.

New supply began to pour in to her through gifts, as increased income, and as the materials needed to add another room to her house. Within a short time, the room had been completed debt free. In fact, she personally did much of the work. She has used that room as her den and "meditation room" ever since. She said *it all began the day she started to praise and bless everything at hand.*

THE SEVENTH STEP TO ABUNDANCE: DO NOT TAKE YOUR HANDS OFF VISIBLE SUPPLY, BUT POUR FORTH THE INCREASE FEARLESSLY, THEN EXPECT IMMEDIATE RESULTS

One historian claims that when Jesus took the sacred loaves of bread and "the best" of fishes—which were considered a rich delicacy—in his hands, he then looked up, blessed what was on hand, and began to fearlessly pass it out to the multitudes. The historian reports that as Jesus did this, *the bread and fish multiplied on the spot! When a loaf or a fish was broken, it was immediately made entire again.*

In this way, Jesus gained an *inner* control of substance: He never let down. He never gave in to the appearance of lack. *He never took his hands off the visible supply.* Once he began to bless, break, and pass out what he had, he continued to do so, as though it were endless. *The bread and fish that then passed through his hands in a steady flow were able to feed multitudes!*

In this miracle, Jesus proved that man need not live by bread alone. He can develop an *inner* consciousness of supply which feeds and prospers. When one is functioning from this *inner* level of prosperous thinking, *outer* supply appears as needed. That is *true* prosperity at its best!

HE WAS HEALED AFTER
EIGHTEEN YEARS OF SUFFERING

One of Jesus' secrets in manifesting these miraculous riches was that he did not mentally put off his good. He did not expect a delay. He knew that *faith draws on divine resources, so he expected immediate results.*

A man spent his days feeling deprived of his health because eighteen years before, he had suffered an attack of paralysis that left his right leg stiff. As he moved about on crutches, he prayed constantly for healing, but always with his handicap uppermost in his mind, and always with the reservation that his prayers had not been answered. Hence further delay seemed certain. He did not dare to believe that his good was just as instantly available as was the "meal-in-a-minute" he prepared from a package for his bachelor dinner each night.

Then he made two changes in his thinking that brought release from his crippling condition:

First. He *began to give thanks and rejoice in the health he already had.* He praised his fine eyesight and keen hearing, his excellent digestion, and his freedom from colds and infections.

Second. He learned the value of expecting his healing now, not postponing it until he had made more progress in inner or outer ways. He began to declare daily: "NOTHING CAN OBSTRUCT THE INSTANT, CONSTANT, IMMEDIATE FLOW OF PERFECT GOOD TO ME NOW."

What may appear on the surface as a miracle then took place. While sitting in the park one day, a woman on the same bench noticed his crutches and questioned him about his condition. As they talked, she mentioned that she was a physiotherapist connected with a rehabilitation clinic that helped many people who had similar physical handicaps.

She suggested that he consult the experts at the clinic. Today this man walks freely, without crutches or cane. *Once he began to believe it could happen, his good was made instantly available.*

THE SECRET OF A WIDOW'S WEALTH

A widow went into business "on a shoestring." Yet within a twenty-year period, through the use of prosperous thinking, she became very wealthy. She said that during those busy years, she held sales meetings with her employees once a week. She filled those meetings with the thought of increase. She would often tell them, "Never say that 'business is bad.' Business is *always* good. Even a nickel's worth of business is good. To reinforce this idea, she kept a sign in her store which read, "Business is good."

Through such prosperous thinking, this businesswoman went from one store to ownership of four stores. Although she retired after twenty years, she has enjoyed her wealth ever since. Why did she become so successful? Like Jesus with the loaves and fishes, she never let down in her thinking. Instead, she took the situation at hand, fearlessly filled it with the thought of increase, and expected immediate prosperous results. This method for multiplying the loaves and fishes certainly worked in her life.

THE EIGHTH STEP TO ABUNDANCE: WHEN YOU REMAIN RELAXED, AND BREAK ACCORDING TO THE NEED, YOU PROSPER

The rich substance of the universe flows under your hand in an unending stream of plenty. If you keep your hand on that stream of plenty by blessing it and affirming that "it is enough," you can break substance in any form and in any amount as the need arises.

When the mind centers its attention upon "divine substance" (the foundation of all wealth) long enough and strong enough, this mental action (breaking) causes invisible substance to appear as visible results. Thousands or few, the rich substance of the universe is sufficient to provide abundantly. Desert or garden, substance abounds. Neither circumstances nor numbers need dismay you. *If you remain relaxed and casual, you can cause your good to multiply as needed.*

But when you take your hands off the *inner* stream of substance by criticizing it and saying, "It isn't enough," then you lose your *inner* hold on substance. Also, your tension stops your good.

So, if conditions look doubtful, relax; then continue to break in the form that is required. *Break according to the need.* Whatever comes, whatever goes, keep your hands on the stream of *inner* substance and in a relaxed way, break mentally in a fashion that satisfies your need. This *inner* treatment of substance will help you to feed any multitude of needs that may assemble in your life.

If you have only a small amount, yet hoard it, you shut off the possibilities of gaining more. But if you use what you have wisely in a relaxed way—*even* if it is only a small amount—this mental action makes room for vast increase. Jesus broke and kept giving out the supply on hand. He proved the saying, "Spare and ye have enough for one. Share and you have enough for the multitudes."

A SENIOR CITIZEN BROKE
ACCORDING TO THE NEED AND PROSPERED

A senior citizen wrote from Arizona:

"My Social Security check was late. This put me behind financially. But I knew that tension could stop my good, so I relaxed and blessed the situation with perfect results. This method worked, and my check soon arrived.

"I then used these prosperity methods to disburse that check: *First,* I wrote out my tithe check, 'the sacred tenth,' to God's work, and mailed it immediately. As I did so, I declared, 'THERE IS PROSPERING POWER IN FAITH, AND FAITH MOVES ON DIVINE SUBSTANCE TO PROVIDE ABUNDANTLY FOR ME NOW.' *Second,* in a relaxed way I then boldly blessed what was left, and began to fearlessly pay bills. When I finished, I felt peaceful and prosperous, even though there were still some bills left to be paid.

"I feel that: (1) choosing to put God first financially through tithing, (2) blessing the rest, (3) then sending it out in a relaxed, fearless manner, helped produce these prosperous results:

"*First:* The very next morning I was offered a good part-time job, which will be of vast help to me. *Second:* An income tax refund check arrived, which was more than I had expected. With it I was able to pay the rest of the bills, and to get current financially. *It is true that if you break according to the need in a relaxed way, you can cause your good to continue to multiply.*"

HOW THE PROSPERITY LAW OF CONTINUATION BROUGHT HAPPY RESULTS OF LAVISH ABUNDANCE

I feel that I can write with authority about the prosperity formula for multiplying the loaves and fishes as explained in this chapter, because I have had to use it so often over the years to meet both personal and professional needs. My mail indicates that many other people have had to multiply their loaves and fishes countless times, too. Today's economic scene makes it an almost daily necessity for many. Also, there are vast numbers of people working worldwide in various forms of humanitarian endeavors who are forced to live off an invisible means of supply. It has always been so. Yet to me it has proved to be a fascinating process to: (1) bless what was on hand, (2) pass it out in a relaxed way to meet the need, (3) then watch it multiply—often in totally unforeseen ways.

If you follow the prosperity steps given in this loaves and fishes miracle, *there is no numbering of the avenues through which supply may come to you. Your resource is as far-reaching as the universe!*

Of course, this fabulous old story has a happy ending: The need was more than met. Abundance flowed forth. Thousands ate and were filled, and there were twelve baskets left over! The enthusiasm created by this miracle was so intense that the people wanted to make Jesus a king. Instead, he preferred to withdraw into the mountains in order to prepare for further prosperity miracles.

A MODERN PROSPERITY MIRACLE:
HOW THE SALAD MULTIPLIED TO FEED HUNDREDS

In closing, I think you will enjoy the following true account of how one person invoked the prosperity law of continuation with satisfying results. A housewife in Texas first related this incident to me fifteen years ago. When she recently learned I was writing this book, she reminded me of her experience, and felt it would be of inspiration to my readers. She said this experience proved to her that *the prosperity methods used by Jesus are just as available to us today as they were in his famous fish miracle.*

This housewife had been appointed chairman for a church banquet that was to feed four hundred people. Late on the day of the banquet, it was discovered that the cook had underestimated the amount needed, so there was not enough lettuce for the salad. This housewife started blessing the lettuce on hand as she said out loud, "J.C., I invite you and 'the boys' to multiply this lettuce so that there will be enough salad to feed the four hundred."

Although she had been unaware of it, the minister was standing nearby and heard her comment. He asked, "Just *who* are 'J.C. and the boys?' " She explained that that was what the young people in her sunday School class at the church called Jesus Christ and his disciples. The minister seemed startled, then amused.

"J.C. and the boys" *did* multiply that lettuce. In fact, after feeding the four hundred at the banquet, there was so much salad left over that she gave forty people generous portions of it to take home. "J.C. and the boys" worked another prosperity miracle at that banquet. It was soon reported that the church received more financial benefit from that event than it had made from any other single fund-raiser!

A MEDITATION FOR INVOKING THE PROSPERITY LAW OF CONTINUATION

"IN A FINANCIAL DESERT PLACE, I TAKE CONTROL IN CONSCIOUSNESS. I TURN MY BACK ON THE APPEARANCE OF LACK. INSTEAD, I SPEAK WORDS OF ABUNDANCE: *'There is always enough.'* I THEN ESTABLISH DIVINE ORDER BY TELLING THE MULTITUDE OF NEEDS TO GET QUIET, SIT DOWN, AND GET READY TO RECEIVE.

"I TAKE WHATEVER I HAVE ON HAND, LOOK UP, BLESS IT, BREAK IT, AND BEGIN SENDING IT FORTH IN AN ENDLESS STREAM OF PLENTY. 'IF I LOOK UP, I WILL ALWAYS BE PROVIDED FOR.'

"I START BREAKING ACCORDING TO THE NEED. ONCE I START MEETING THE NEED, I DO NOT LET DOWN. I REMAIN RELAXED AS

I KEEP MY HAND ON THE STEADY STREAM OF PLENTY. I KEEP MEETING THE NEED IN AN UPLIFTED STATE OF MIND.

I AM NOT TENSE OR ANXIOUS. INSTEAD I SEND OUT WHAT I HAVE WITH PRAISE AND BLESSING. 'I PRAISE GOD FOR PLENTY.' AS I REMAIN IN CONTROL OF MY THINKING, I AM ABLE TO MEET EVERY DEMAND. THERE MAY EVEN BE AN ABUNDANCE LEFT OVER! THROUGH THIS PROCESS I SHALL FIND THAT NO PLACE IS TRULY BARREN OF GOOD. THERE IS NO NUMBERING OF THE AVENUES THROUGH WHICH MY GOOD CAN COME TO ME. MY GOOD IS AS FAR-REACHING AS THE UNIVERSE, SO MY GOOD NOW CONTINUES TO MULTIPLY IN BOTH EXPECTED AND UNEXPECTED WAYS—EVEN TO THE POINT OF LAVISH ABUNDANCE!''

SUMMARY

1. The famous loaves and fishes story demonstrates that there is nothing niggardly about the Lord's provision for man, and that Jesus was concerned about the physical, as well as the spiritual, needs of his followers.

2. The secret for developing a prosperity consciousness is: (1) learn the philosophy of prosperous thinking; (2) get busy practicing its specific prosperity principles. This gives you an *inner* hold on the rich substance of the universe, which then produces satisfying, *outer* results.

3. The word "continue" means "to go on without interruption" or "to begin again after interruption." Jesus pointed out the simple steps we can take to experience this same miracle of supply. This action took place in a desert, proving that no place is barren of good.

4. How Jesus invoked the prosperity law of continuation:

a) He began turning lack into abundance by paying no attention to these negative reports of lack: "Send the multitudes away . . . that they may . . . buy themselves food."

b) Instead, he made an astonishing prosperity statement in the face of lack, by speaking prosperous words: "They have no need to go away. Give ye them to eat."

Their reply, "We have but five loaves and two fishes" contained significant prosperity symbology: (1) *Bread* symbolized the good you desire in life; (2) *Fish* symbolized the increase of that desired good through *use* of prosperous ideas.

c) After receiving the loaves and fishes ("bring them hither to me"), Jesus put things in divine order by telling the multitude to sit down, get quiet, and get ready to receive. When you gain control *within,* through divine order, you are then able to meet *outer* needs as they arise.

d) Jesus next took the bread (substance) and fish (ideas of increase), and looked up to God as the Source of his supply. "If you look up, you will always be provided for."

e) He then blessed, broke and gave out the multiplied result. He knew that sharing is the beginning of financial increase.

f) He blessed the substance at hand as he broke and passed it out. If you bless and condemn not as you share what is on hand, your act of blessing also has multiplying power.

g) After Jesus gained an *inner* control of substance through the foregoing steps, he never let down. He never took his hands off the visible supply. Once he began to bless, break and pass out what he had, he was able to continue doing so in an endless steam of plenty, thus supplying the multitudes.

h) If you, too, remain in a relaxed state of mind, declaring, ''It is enough,'' you can cause your good to multiply, with an abundance left over!

THE PROSPERITY LAW OF
UNRESTRICTED SUPPLY

FROM THE MONEY MIRACLE

— Chapter 7 —

The prosperity formula for unrestricted supply is found in just three short verses that are recorded in Matthew's gospel. (Matthew 17:24–27) The story has a "touch of magic" about it that can "magically touch" your financial affairs, too! This "money miracle" is not only a remarkable story in itself, but it is even more remarkable because Matthew, a former tax collector was the only one to record it in his gospel. With his practical prosperity consciousness, Matthew realized that:

1. Money is a necessity to one's spiritual growth, since it can give a person the time and means to grow spiritually, while freeing him from material care.

2. Through his account of this "money miracle," Matthew was also emphasizing that money is a necessary requirement for one's daily supply and it should not be held in

disdain by anyone, especially by those who are on the spiritual path.

Jesus and his disciples had returned from their journeys of three or four weeks. When they arrived in Capernaum, they were penniless with not so much as a shekel between them. There they were confronted by the authorities who asked if Jesus paid taxes. Peter unhesitatingly replied that he did.

Jesus then told Peter how to demonstrate the tax money on the spot: (1) go to the sea; (2) cast a hook; (3) take the first fish that came up; (4) open its mouth; (5) take the money found there and pay the taxes—not only for Jesus, but for all his disciples.

The word "unrestricted" means "umlimited, free, not held down, or confined." This is something that every *normal* person intensely desires. Many of our problems in life result from our feelings of limitation, restriction, a sense of being held down, or confined. We should all be interested in the prosperity law of unrestricted supply, and in learning how we can begin to immediately use it to meet the financial needs in our lives.

PART I: PROSPEROUS ATTITUDES FOR TAPPING UNRESTRICTED SUPPLY

THE FIRST STEP IN THE "MONEY MIRACLE": USE THE PROSPERING POWER OF NONRESISTANCE

Some historians discount this "money miracle," attaching little importance to it. Others claim it was not among Jesus' miracles. One writer called the episode nothing more than playful humor on Jesus' part. He claimed that Jesus had Peter fish, then sell the fish to pay the taxes. Another historian discounted the importance of this incident by piously announcing that Jesus never used his powers for his own welfare or that of his disciples.

However, a close study of the Gospel reveals that just the opposite was true: *Jesus did not hesitate to use his mind powers to promote earthly prosperity.* Furthermore, he not only met his own financial obligations, but he generously supported the twelve disciples who traveled with him. *That* would be quite a prosperity demonstration in these times. Jesus felt that worldly riches *should* manifest for those who demonstrate their divinity. Through the use of mind power, Jesus was able to meet in honorable ways both his own financial needs, as well as those of his followers. As a devout Jew, he gladly paid temple taxes for himself and his disciples.

Jesus began this prosperity miracle by using the prospering power of nonresistance. Since people were generally taxed in their home towns, Jesus could have deferred payment until his return to Nazareth on the grounds that he was just traveling through Capernaum. Instead, through the exercise of his mind powers, Jesus made a fish produce sufficient money to pay the temple dues for himself and the twelve disciples.

When using your inner mind powers to prosper you may find that money to meet your needs is provided for you in strange ways, too. (See the chapter, "How to Gather Your Prosperous Manna," in my book, *The Millionaire Moses*). Through this "money miracle," Jesus showed that the Christ in him was Lord of Plenty; that the Christ in him was his prospering power; and that he had supreme dominion over the whole creation, including the material world. As you persist in using the prosperity formula he gave to Peter, *you will also find that you are able to claim dominion over the material world, and to meet your financial needs*—often on the spot.

The tax that Jesus produced in this story was not the hated tax paid to the Roman government, but a tax paid by individuals to the Temple treasury. Called a "sanctuary tax," it was used to defray the Temple expenses. Devout Jews had paid this tax since ancient times. (Exodus 30:11-16; II Chronicles 24:9) Thus the tax gatherer questioned Jesus in a mild manner. Had the tax official been asking for the tribute payable to Caesar, his attitude doubtless would have been harsher.

THE SECOND STEP IN THE "MONEY MIRACLE": SAY "YES" TO THE FINANCIAL DEMAND

It is important to realize that *when the financial need arose, there was no quibbling, grumbling, or talk of lack.* Instead, as instructed by Jesus, Peter immediately said "yes" to the financial demand. He did not fight it. Many people miss their good when a financial need arises, because they spend both their *inner* mind power and their *outer* physical energy negatively criticizing and condemning the financial need. They should, instead, quickly say, "I have faith that I can meet this need. Yes, with God's help I will gladly pay it now."

By saying "yes" to the need, the battle is half won! The forces of the universe are then freed to go into action to help you meet that need. The rich forces of the universe are also freed to multiply the substance that returns to you, in response to that which you sent out. *Every financial expenditure is but an "investment" in universal substance. If you send it forth nonresistantly, your financial expenditure is guaranteed to return to you multiplied somewhere along the way!*

PAY UP AND PROSPER

A businessman from Oklahoma wrote:

"Some money has just been paid me that had been owed for a long time. Everyone kept telling me how dishonest the people were who owed it, but I had a strong urge to trust God and those people. Just three days ago, I remembered to write this matter down on my list of desires: that I wanted the money owed paid in full. Here is the interesting part: For three days those involved had been trying to contact me in order to pay up!

"Another success principle that I learned from this experience is this: *How important it is to pay one's own bills if you want those people owing you to pay.* This morning I promptly sent money in the mail for a bill I owed, and had intended to pay later. Not until I paid that bill, which I had been withholding, did those owing me reach me and pay what was due. Yes, you must pay your own bills if you wish others to pay you. *When you say 'yes' to financial obligations by paying up, you prosper!*"

THE THIRD STEP IN THE "MONEY MIRACLE": DELIBERATELY GET INTO AN UPLIFTED, UNRESTRICTED STATE OF MIND

Jesus and his disciples were faced with the financial challenge of the money miracle while in Capernaum. The prosperity law of unrestricted good begins to work for you when you do something to deliberately get into an unplifted Capernaum state of mind. You will never find your unrestricted supply in a depressed, discouraged state of mind. There is absolutely no healing or prospering power in a low, negative, critical, lack-talking state of mind. If you want unrestricted supply to flow into your life, you have to get into an unrestricted state of mind.

So as to receive unrestricted supply in your life, how do you get to Capernaum, or into an uplifted state of mind? The following experiences of others show you how:

THEY GOT INTO AN UNRESTRICTED STATE OF MIND, AND PROSPERED WHEN THEY SHARED WITH OTHERS

A businesswoman from Maryland wrote:

"I had been very depressed because of a broken engagement, and had developed suicidal tendencies. I had really struggled to pull myself together. I began to hold to the thought, 'LIFE IS TO ENJOY.' This helped me to become active in our church again, where I met many wonderful people.

"I decided that if I wanted to straighten out my life, I should begin to put God first in every way, even financially. Along with taking time daily for meditation, the use of affirmations, and inspirational study, I began to tithe. The week I started tithing, I found $20 in my wallet I didn't know I had! My washer broke down, and when buying a new one, I was given a $20 discount. I also bought books and magazines at discount prices. *It seemed my purse was never empty. When I needed to make a purchase, the money was there.*

"*As I continued to declare,* 'LIFE IS TO ENJOY,' this led to my first trip to Europe, a tour of the Mediterranean covering six countries. It even included an audience with the Pope. Although I am still pinching myself over this happy turn of events, I am no longer having to pinch pennies."

A businesswoman from Texas wrote:

"After studying the chapter on 'Praise,' in the book, *The Dynamic Laws of Healing,*[1] I decided to try it. I found that praise *does* pay the bills! As soon as I began to praise my bills, my cabinets were filled with lovely new dishes, and my freezer overflowed with an abundance of food. The new dishes, pots, pans, and silver did not cost me a cent. A girl at

---

1. See *The Dynamic Laws of Healing,* page 98.

my office kept receiving these items as gifts. Since she had too many, she asked if she might share them with me. *Praise has worked wonders in my financial affairs.* I have found that once one begins to receive abundance, it is wise to release and let go some of it by sharing with others, so that new channels of abundance can continue to flow into your life. Praise and sharing work!''

Yes, when you are trying to get into an uplifted state of mind, which is the realm of unrestricted good, *try doing something for someone else.*

There is the story about the man whose wife had suddenly passed on in the prime of life. It was a shock because theirs had seemed a perfect marriage. This bereaved man felt he could not make a comeback from this loss. Naturally, his work was affected.

Then his boss asked him to help a fellow employee, who had just lost a baby. As this bereaved husband began to try to help the grieving father, he realized that other people had problems and heartaches that were just as great as his was to him; and that he was able to begin overcoming his own bereavement. *One way to get into an uplifted state of mind is to begin helping others.*

THE FOURTH STEP IN THE "MONEY MIRACLE": DELIBERATELY GET INTO A PROSPEROUS, "CAPERNAUM" STATE OF MIND

Jesus and his disciples' deliberate journey to Capernaum not only symbolized getting into an uplifted state of mind generally. It also symbolized getting into a prosperous state of mind specifically. As stated in Chapter One, Capernaum was a thriving port town located on the shores of the Sea of Galilee. Since it lay on the well-traveled highway between

Damascus and Jerusalem, Capernaum tapped the rich commerce of the entire area. That it was engaged in the fishing industry indicated that *Capernaum was also a place of metaphysical prosperity, since fish symbolize the idea of prosperous increase.*

Although there are numerous ways for getting into a specific prosperous state of mind, among the most powerful is that of studying along prosperous lines, either privately or with others.

HOW HE PAID OFF AN $800,000 INDEBTEDNESS
AND BEGAN MAKING $200,000 A YEAR

A businessman in Wyoming described how he got into a prosperous, Capernaum state of mind at a crucial time in his life:

"My first exposure to the power of prosperous thinking goes back to my study of the early Ponder books.[2] I discovered them at a time when I was in the throes of a business failure that totally wiped me out. I left the state in September, 1965 with only $43 in my pocket, and one of those prosperity books. Many mornings I sat on the top of a mountain watching the sun come up after a sleepless night, with sadness and frustration in my heart, and with that prosperity book in my hands.

"My financial problems seemed almost insurmountable. I owed over $800,000. Nevertheless, as I studied that book and diligently applied its methods, I reduced my indebtedness to $126,000 in only six months!

---

2. The ideas he used are found in the Ponder books, *The Dynamic Laws of Prosperity, The Prosperity Secrets of the Ages,* and *Open Your Mind to Prosperity.*

"I returned to my hometown in 1969. I felt an obligation to make right the consequences of my earlier problems. This took courage. Again, I studied that prosperity book on a daily basis and used the prospering methods it described: list-making, forming a vacuum, forgiveness, release, affirmations, picturing, and tithing.

"Since that time, I have enjoyed a growing prosperity, and now make over $200,000 a year! As soon as those prosperity ideas began to work for me, I felt a responsibility to share them with others. So I began conducting a prosperity study class one night a week. Life became an exciting adventure, not only for me, but for everyone in that class. At first those attending said 'Those are great prosperity ideas, but they won't work for me.' I found many of those in attendance had the 'It can't be done' or 'It's too good to be true' attitude. Nevertheless, I insisted that they begin practicing affirmations, picturing, list-making, forgiveness, and the tithing principles of prosperity. We began using some of these methods together in our class periods. The prosperous results they obtained excited and delighted them. *They were soon a group of transformed individuals.* I shall always give thanks for those prosperity ideas and methods which got me into an uplifted, prosperous state of mind during a very bleak period. Prosperous thinking has worked miracles in my life.''

THE FIFTH STEP IN THE "MONEY MIRACLE": USE THE PROSPERING POWER OF FAITH

In the "money miracle," it was not Jesus who demonstrated the unrestricted supply, but Peter, who symbolized faith. Jesus gave Peter the instructions of what to do, in faith, step by step.

When there is a need to be met, it is always your faith that is first tested. Since there is prospering power in faith, there is always something that you can do in faith in order to bring forth the unrestricted supply.

Peter had to take one step at a time in order to manifest the tax money. Each step then unfolded the next step to him. In any challenging situation, *if you can see only the next step, that is all you need to see. Take that next step in faith, and it will lead you on.* In the process, remind yourself often, "FAITH MOVES ON SUBSTANCE TO PROSPER AND BLESS ME NOW."

HOW A DIVORCEE WENT THROUGH A STRINGENT FINANCIAL PERIOD, THEN REMARRIED WELL

A lovely lady in Southern California had endured a frustrating marriage with a very strange husband. His neurotic family had also joined him in making her life miserable. Finally he walked out and left her penniless. Although she received their house in the divorce settlement, it had not sold months later, and she was living from day to day financially. Although she had never worked, she finally secured a part-time job. But she was still living with only a small spasmodic cash flow while faced with numerous unpaid bills. Nevertheless, she tried to remain in an uplifted, prosperous state of mind: to see the good in the situation, to meet life one day at a time in the faith that the bitterness of the past could be forgotten, and that her life could still be transformed into one of happiness, abundance, and peace.

Six months after the divorce she wrote:

"Since having been divorced, I have resigned from two organizations in which I am no longer interested. I will concentrate on the one organization in which I am president. My daughter has invited me to spend a week with her. This is the first time in twelve years she has extended such an invitation.

"I contacted Social Security and they called back to say they would put through a request for my check (the one my former husband had tried to stop). I have just received checks from the work I did at several parties. I have been using the income that comes to me more wisely. I was invited out twice for dinner and once for lunch this week. It is wonderful to realize that I can still be prosperous and debt free; that I do not need to remain poor, stupid, or to handle money unwisely. *I am releasing all anxiety about the mistakes of the past. I have faith that God's good is coming to me now in wise and wonderful ways.*"

A year after the divorce she wrote:

"After my former husband left me without any funds, it was a test to my faith to keep believing that God's good could still come to me in wise and wonderful ways. But as I persisted in declaring those words daily, while meeting life the best I could one day at a time, it happened.

"Through mutual friends, I met a fine widower at a dinner party. He is cultured, refined, nice-looking, a kind man, and socially prominent. Now retired, he is comfortably fixed for life. Soon after we met, he asked me to marry him. After a short courtship, we had a lovely wedding in my home (which has now sold at a good price). We honeymooned in Mexico. Since our return I have enjoyed his beautiful home in a prestigious neighborhood, and we enjoy his boat on weekends. *It almost seems like magic, the secure life he has given me. Those words of faith worked.* God's good *has* come to me in wise and wonderful ways!"

This lady proved that it pays to take the next step in faith, in the knowledge that it will lead you on to something better. At a crucial time in her life, her words and acts of faith certainly moved on universal substance to prosper and bless her in countless ways, until her life had been transformed into the one of happiness, abundance and peace she dared to envision. And it all happened within the period of a year.

PART II: PROSPEROUS ACTIONS
FOR TAPPING UNRESTRICTED SUPPLY

THE SIXTH STEP IN THE "MONEY MIRACLE":
GO TO THE SEA OF RICH IDEAS

When the authorities inquired about the tax money, Jesus gave Peter specific instructions on how to meet this financial challenge. He told him to first "go to the sea." The "sea" symbolizes universal mind, that great realm of unexpressed ideas that contain all potentiality for good. The first thing you must have to meet any situation victoriously is *the right idea,* or the divine idea.

When confronted with a need, it is wise to ask specifically, "What is the divine idea that will meet this financial need?" or "What is the divine idea that will bring healing in this situation?" or "Let the divine idea *now* appear!" *Going to the sea of ideas is the way to begin successfully meeting every need in life.*

You can achieve whatever you want to achieve. You can be as successful as you want to be. *God will give you any good thing you desire, but in the form of an idea. There is nothing more tangible than an idea. If you take a divine idea that comes to you as the result of meditation, affirmation, inspirational study, or through association with other prosperous-minded people, and use it for all it is worth, there is no limit to the vast good you can derive from it!*

We all want to go to the sea of ideas, for that is where we find our unrestricted supply (as described earlier in Prosperity Steps 3, 4, and 5 of this chapter). The famous writer Napoleon Hill, who researched the secrets of five hundred of this country's most successful men finally surmised:[3]

---

3. Reprinted by permission of Hawthorne Books, Inc., New York, from *Think and Grow Rich,* by Napoleon Hill. Copyright 1967, 1966, 1960, 1937 by The Napoleon Hill Foundation. All rights reserved.

"If you are one of those people who believes that hard work and honesty alone will bring riches, perish the thought. It is not true! Riches, when they come in huge quantities, are never the result of hard work. . . *Ideas* are the beginning of all fortunes.''

THE SEVENTH STEP IN THE "MONEY MIRACLE": CAST A SPECIFIC HOOK

After going to the sea of ideas, Jesus told Peter to cast a hook. This is the only time in the New Testament when a hook was used in connection with fishing. To "cast a hook" meant that Peter, symbolizing faith, was to get definite about what he wanted. You, too, must get definite in your faith about what you want. To "cast a hook" is to get specific about what you want in your prayers, affirmations, meditations, list-making, visualization, and other prosperous-thinking techniques.Then get specific through your outer actions as well.

To "cast a hook" means to "cast a definite prayer or prosperity decree" into the sea of ideas. You cast your hook when you ask, "Father, what is the prosperous truth about this situation? What is the divine idea that will meet this financial need?" *You can always cast a hook in the sea of ideas, and bring forth the right results by asking Divine Intelligence to help you.*

In the booklet, *The Seven Main Aspects of God,* [4] Dr. Emmet Fox advised:

"When things in your life seem to be going wrong . . . when business or other conditions appear to

---

4. Published by DeVorss & Company, 1970 (pages 27–29). The booklet is taken from the book, *Alter Your Life* by Emmet Fox, published by Harper & Row, New York, 1950.

have reached a deadlock . . . when you seem to be up against a stone wall and apparently there is no way out, treat yourself for Intelligence. If you have to deal with someone who is seemingly very stupid or foolish, realize that Divine Intelligence works in him because he is a child of God. If you can get a sufficient realization, he will change for the better. It may sometimes happen, however, that *you* are the person who was at fault . . . and *you yourself will change.*

"If you are interested in a child at school . . . treat him several times a week for Intelligence. You will be surprised to find how his progress in his studies will increase. . . . If you are in business, treat yourself and your assistants for Intelligence several times a week. . . . The Intelligence aspect of God is very important in its relation to the health of the body. . . . *You should treat yourself for Intelligence at least two or three times a week by thinking about it, and claiming it for yourself. This practice will make every activity of your life more efficient.*"

FROM A SCREECHING HALT TO ABUNDANCE

A California housewife wrote:

"This is a learning period in my life concerning money. What an expanding process it has been! Every area of my life is growing better as my understanding of prosperous thinking widens to encompass more. *Every time I try to manipulate things and events, they tighten up and constrict. But when I turn a problem over to God, the perfect results are always revealed in glorious ways.*

"I am learning to trust more and have faith in Divine Intelligence to guide and direct my life in every area. Our prosperity had come to a screeching halt. As we called on Divine Intelligence to guide and direct us, here is what happened:

"*First*: After we had tried unsuccessfully to collect a check for $400 that had been owed us for more than a year, we received it within two days! *Second*: When my bank account statement arrived, I was overdrawn and couldn't cover it.

Then I found an error that easily covered it. *Third*: My husband received a call and got his first job in some time. *Fourth*: Our oldest daughter began college, and found a job that same day to supplement her income.

"We are realizing that we had given the outer appearances too much power by feeding them our full attention. Only by blessing them, then letting go, and calling on Divine Intelligence to do its perfect work, did things straighten out."

You can always cast a hook in the sea of ideas by declaring that Divine Intelligence is showing you the way. Then the *specific* laws of prosperity, which you should use, will be revealed to you. In some way your needs will be met.

IMPROVEMENT CAME ALONG ALL LINES WHEN SHE GOT DEFINITE

The main point about "casting a hook" is that it means *to get definite*. Many people go to the sea of ideas. They read and study along the lines of prosperous thinking. They may attend classes, seminars or lectures on the subject. They may even discuss at length the philosophy of prosperous thinking with other people. *But they never cast their hook in the sea of ideas.* They never get definite about the good they desire as a result of their prosperous thinking, so their good never gets definite about them.

An Arizona housewife wrote:

"Although I had been a student of prosperous thinking for five years, I had not gained either the understanding or the improved results in my life which I should have had. I discovered why: I had studied along *general* lines in the past. Since I have gotten *specific* this month and declared, 'I NOW OPEN MY MIND TO PROSPERITY,' here are some of the gratifying results that have occurred:

"A much-improved relationship has taken place in our family life. My husband had been under severe strain with a new job for over a year. His strain had affected everyone at home. We began studying *Open Your Mind to Prosperity* together this month, and using the specific methods described in it. We have become closer than ever before. My husband has relaxed and done many things needed around the house. There are freshly painted rooms and a new bedroom suite. Better still, *there is peace, harmony and contentment in our home atmosphere again.*"

WHEN A BANKRUPT CONTRACTOR CAST A HOOK, HE WAS PROSPERED

There once was a contractor who was having a hard time financially. He wasn't just broke; he was bankrupt. On the day when he was down to his last 45¢, he said to his wife, "We have just 45¢ left to our name. We both believe in God's bounty and we need to affirm His supply for us *now,* so let's make it systematic. Three times a day, let us sit down together and pray claiming His prosperity for us."

First they prayed, "Lord, we've done all we can see to do, and now it is up to You. *We will not push or pull in this situation. We will trust in Your supply.* THANK YOU FOR UNSEEN ABUNDANCE ON ITS WAY TO US NOW!"

The morning after they cast a hook in the sea of ideas by using this definite affirmation of abundance, the mail brought an insurance dividend check for $30. They gave thanks for it, and tithed from it. They blessed what was left and bought food with it. Then they continued to declare together at least three times a day: "THANK YOU GOD FOR UNSEEN ABUNDANCE ALREADY ON ITS WAY TO US NOW."

One evening the doorbell rang and a neighbor said, "Do you still have that power paint sprayer you talked about selling some time ago?"

They did.

"Do you still want to sell it?"

They did.

"How much?"

"$25."

"Sold!"

This man had considered trying to get a job outside his construction business. He applied for three different jobs, but nothing came through. As they kept affirming, "THANK YOU GOD FOR UNSEEN ABUNDANCE ALREADY ON ITS WAY TO US NOW," his previously bankrupt construction business became active again. Job after job began rolling in, so that he was soon busy and prosperous. But nothing good happened until this couple sat down together and regularly used prosperity affirmations.

A TWO-PART FORMULA FOR RESULTS

As I lecture on prosperity around the country, people often say to me, "I have an idea for prosperity, but I haven't done anything about it." A lady in Southern California talked about a wonderful mayonnaise dressing that she and her husband had developed while in the restaurant business. People all over that area loved her special homemade recipe, and wanted it for use in their own kitchens. But this lady had never done anything definite about it. She needed to go to the sea of ideas and cast a hook, asking Divine Intelligence to show her how to develop her special dressing for marketing on a wholesale basis.

A businesswoman in California wrote:

"Some people read all kinds of self-help books, but do not follow through and practice the simple techniques suggested.

They are the ones who say, 'It doesn't work.' They are wrong. *'It works, if you work it.*

"Perhaps the most important thing I have learned from my study of prosperous thinking is to practice these two disciplines daily: *First:* Speak prosperity decrees aloud each day. *Second:* Take time every day to go over my list of desires, and to meditate on the pictured desires that I have placed on my Wheel of Fortune. *Reading* comes first. Then *doing.* This assures results. I have had incredible prosperity come to me through use of this simple two-part success formula."

CAST SPECIFIC HOOKS TO PROSPER

"There is nothing so powerful as an idea whose time has come," is a well-known truth. Ideas are centers of consciousness. Hence a man's body, health, intelligence, financial affairs, and everything about him is derived from the ideas to which he gives his attention. *The idea is the most important factor in any act, and it must be given first place in your attention if you wish to bring about satisfying results of a permanent nature.* Ideas are truly the beginning of all fortunes, but you must follow through on the prosperous ideas that are revealed to you in order to reap results of abundance. The following people used specific methods—which anyone can use—for "casting a hook" in the sea of rich ideas.

THEY CAST A HOOK THROUGH LIST-MAKING

A BUSINESSMAN FROM TEXAS GOT A NEW HOME: "List-making is a mystical, yet scientific approach that works. The practice of writing down what we have wanted has brought results in many areas of our lives. The most recent result of our list-making is a beautiful new home.''

A BUSINESSWOMAN FROM ARIZONA GOT A JOB: ''I had made lists of the blessings I desired with good results in the past. Then I found myself in need of a job, so I made a new list for what I needed *right now*. On that list I wrote out the desire for a satisfying, well-paying job and the payment of some bills.

''While I was writing out my list of desires, the telephone rang, telling me I had been accepted for a job at the Medical Center, and that I was to begin work right away. This was a position I had applied for in the past. On that same day, I also received a second job offer. The following day I received an income tax refund check, which made it possible for me to pay the bills listed on my 'right now' list. *Within twenty-four hours of my list-making, the major items on my list had been fulfilled!*

A HOUSEWIFE FROM WISCONSIN WAS REUNITED WITH HER SON: *''It is true that if you write down your desires, something good will happen.* Three months ago I wrote out the desire to be reunited with my teenage son. The result? He is now living with my new husband and me. His father released him in a surprise action. My son is enjoying his new home, new family, and a happy new environment. I am a mother at peace.''

A DIVORCEE FROM MONTANA REMARRIED: ''After ten years as a divorcee, I married the most wonderful man, but not until I got definite. I typed on an index card specific ideas about the kind of man with whom I would like to share my life. Now when I study the power of prosperous thinking, my super new husband studies with me. What a thrill!''

THEY CAST A HOOK THROUGH AFFIRMATIONS

A BUSINESSMAN FROM OKLAHOMA WON $2,000: ''I had been using the statement, 'I AM BEAUTIFULLY

AND APPROPRIATELY SUPPLIED WITH THE RICH SUBSTANCE OF THE UNIVERSE NOW,' and I won a $2,000 prize! Since winning that amount, I have also won two very nice prizes in a national contest which required some effort to enter. I am also writing fiction again, and am back into sculpturing, so there's more prosperity and success to come.''

A LADY IN MASSACHUSETTS FINDS HER PLACE IN SOCIETY: ''At a time when I was getting settled into a new life and had been very lonely, I began to declare daily, 'DIVINE LOVE, EXPRESSING THROUGH ME, NOW DRAWS TO ME ALL THAT IS NEEDED TO MAKE ME HAPPY AND MY LIFE COMPLETE.'

''Two ladies, heading important social groups in this city, invited me to dine before two balls. They will provide me with suitable escorts. Three new friends have appeared who see me each week. They are opening new doors to me socially. The Center for International Visitors has arranged for me to take the Rector of Bangkok University for a delightful tour of the city. Two new jobs have been offered me. I may consider one of them in the fall. Best of all, I have been asked to act as Chairman of the Concert of the French National Orchestra's sole appearance here. All these results have come from the wonder-working power of words.''

SHE CAST A HOOK THROUGH PICTURING

A BUSINESSWOMAN IN COLORADO GOT THE APARTMENT SHE WANTED: ''I had just quit my job and moved back to my hometown, when I first read about the result-getting power that can be obtained through the act of deliberately picturing what you want: 'Picture a thing and bring it through, rather than trying to reason it through or force it through. You can hasten your good through picturing it.' This method was described as 'prayer in pictures.'

''The movers were due to arrive with my furniture in a few days, but the new apartment I had rented would not be ready for a couple of weeks. Since it was dark green with blue carpeting and not what I really wanted, I decided to picture what I truly desired.

"In meditation I pictured moving to an apartment in the same building with bright, cheery gold carpeting on the quiet side of the building with everything in it perfectly arranged. My landlady kept saying I would have to wait and take the apartment with the dark colors, but I kept calling every day to ask if I could move into my gold apartment yet. Finally she said she couldn't understand it, but there *had* been an apartment cancellation, and I could have a gold one that had just become vacant!

"That was just the beginning. *Since then I've had amazing results from my daily picturing, and I feel I am only beginning to change and improve my life. I could tell you story after story of how things have been eliminated, brought about, or transformed in every aspect of my life through picturing.*"

THE EIGHTH STEP IN THE "MONEY MIRACLE": HOW TO PROSPER FROM THE FIRST FISH

After going to the sea of ideas and casting a definite hook, Jesus told Peter to take up the first fish (idea) that came, and open its mouth. There he would find money with which to pay taxes.[5]

Fish symbolize ideas of increase. Often we take that first fish that comes up out of the sea of ideas, but we do not take the time to open its mouth and let it unfold its secrets to us. If Peter had taken the first fish that jumped out of the sea, and impetuously rushed off with it, the need would not have been met. He would never have gotten the desired coin.

---

5. This fish was later called "St. Peter's fish" because its male carried the eggs and the young in his mouth, just as the coin Peter found was carried in the mouth of such a fish.

If you have had a need, and an idea came to you that did not meet that need, it was probably because you rushed forth to use that idea before you had properly opened its mouth. You did not give that idea a chance to quietly unfold its secrets to you. An idea is like a child. It needs time to grow strong and then reveal its good to you.

An idea that comes to you, which you rush forth to use immediately, is like a child that is born prematurely and then dies. Your idea dies, too, if you do not give it time to grow and gain strength. You can open its mouth by pondering that idea, meditating upon it, and keeping quiet about it. *Privately keep mental company with your idea, and it will tell you its secrets.*

HE WAS TALKED OUT OF
BECOMING A MILLIONAIRE

When that first fish comes up out of the sea of ideas, keep quiet about it as you open its mouth. Do not let other people prematurely talk you out of your good. The rich substance of the universe exists in the realm of ideas. The ignorant open the *inner* valves of their minds and let ideas flow into an *outer* realm in which they have nothing in common.

Also, do not try to force the fish's mouth open, but allow it to gradually unfold its secrets to you. Only when its mouth is wide open, and it has fully shared its secrets, will you discover the coin within as the fulfillment of your need.

After inventing the telephone and placing his company on the stock market, Alexander Graham Bell realized that telephone stock was going to be a very good investment. So he went to the bank, drew out his life savings of $30,000 and started down to the stock market to invest in telephone stock. On the way he met a friend and made the mistake of sharing his idea with him. The friend only laughed at Mr. Bell, and then talked him into redepositing his $30,000 in the bank. Mr. Bell later mourned, "Thanks to my 'friend,' I just missed becoming a millionaire."

If, like Alexander Graham Bell, it seems that someone has talked you out of your good, or that you have lost your good through not keeping quiet about an idea, then your good can be divinely restored to you! Go back and use Jesus' famous prosperity formula all over again: (1) go to the sea of ideas; (2) cast a hook by getting definite; (3) take the first fish that comes up; (4) open its mouth gradually; (5) then keep quiet about the ideas you find there, as you begin to develop and use them.

HOW HE KEPT MENTAL COMPANY
WITH AN IDEA AND PROSPERED

A businessman in a mid-western city purchased a service station and opened a used car lot. He became a student of prosperous thinking, and took God as his Partner in this financial venture. For a time his business flourished. Then for no apparent reason, his business dwindled, and no matter how hard he tried, he met with failure.

Late one night after he had closed his station for the day, he sat at his desk going over the day's receipts, and again he prayed for guidance. The thought that came to him out of the sea of ideas was just one phrase, "time to grow."

He analyzed this idea of growth. The farmer plants the seed, but that seed has to have time to grow before there is a harvest. *Growth must come first.* He realized that since he had gone into business, he had been so busy in outer ways that he had not taken time to grow inwardly. He had not taken time to pray, meditate, study, or think along the lines of prosperous thinking. He realized *he must now grow if he was to outgrow his financial problems.* He also realized that the basic problem was *within him,* not within his business. So he began to trust God more; he stopped urging Him to greater speed. Instead of criticizing his financial affairs, he began to bless them: "I BLESS THE INCOME AND OUTGO OF ALL MONEY. I AM AT PEACE AS I TRUST IN GOD."

These inner actions led to a profitable harvest in his business. A prospect he had counted on, then lost, unexpectedly returned. This customer drew new business to this man's service station and used car lot.

Things are better for a period of seasoning. A period of growth gives substance to your life that cannot be crowded into the instant process. The season of harvest will come and in plenty of time. So regard the slow times in your life as periods of growth. You must never doubt that the harvest will come. but you should continue in your growth until the answer is revealed. This is how you can benefit from that "first fish," as did Peter and the disciples.

THE NINTH STEP IN THE "MONEY MIRACLE": WAYS TO OPEN THE FISH'S MOUTH

After Peter took the first fish that came up out of the sea of ideas, Jesus told him to open its mouth and there he would find the money with which to meet their needs. When that first fish (or prosperous idea) comes, you can slowly open its mouth and reap rich benefits in these simple ways:

First: If possible withdraw to some quiet place and dwell upon the idea that has been revealed to you. As you quietly think about it ask, "What is the Truth about this idea? Let the Truth about it be revealed to me now." Then quietly follow through on the guidance that comes as it is revealed to you.

Second: Get harmonious in your thinking. Dwell on peace, love and forgiveness. You cannot take new ideas into a mind that is cluttered with dissension, envy or jealousy. Clean out your thinking. Practice forgiveness and release of hurts of the past or present.

A businessman from Indiana wrote:

> *"Since I have taken up the daily practice of forgiveness and release, far-reaching changes for good have come into my life.* I have forgiven people for things done to me that I could never have forgiven a year ago. I have even been able to bless people who had done great harm to me in the past. I have now met new people, and have grown closer to old associations I had enjoyed over the years.
>
> *"Although I have been a church member for fifty years, the practice of forgiveness helped me to loosen up and begin to tithe for the first time.* As a result of forgiveness and tithing, I earned $36,000 between March 1st and December 1st, with $700 more to come before the end of the year. I now realize for the first time that God is not some far-off creature, but is close at hand to listen and guide me. Only since I took up the study of prosperous thinking have I realized that God is not only universal, but He is also *within* me. What a difference this has made. I shall continue to pray daily, 'CHRIST IN ME IS MY FORGIVING POWER. CHRIST IN ME IS MY PROSPERING POWER NOW.' "

Third: Stop envying the good of others and wondering where you have failed. Stop comparing your progress with that of other people. The progress of no two people is the same, even under identical conditions. If you expect to receive the prosperous ideas that will make possible a finer home for you, stop wondering why your neighbor's home may be nicer than yours. Stop thinking, "Why did he get

that promotion or raise in pay, when I received none?''
When you have attuned yourself to Divine Intelligence and
its realm of universal abundance, a rich and loving Father
will begin to pour into your own life an abundance of prosperous ideas that will lead to satisfying results which are just
right for you!

THE AUTHOR'S SINGLE PROSPEROUS SHEKEL

When Peter followed, in faith, the prosperity formula
given by Jesus, *only a single fish was caught. Yet what a fish it
was!* Never before or since in the history of mankind has a
single fish produced such far-reaching results. That fascinating fish's prosperity secrets have been closely studied
for twenty centuries.

After Peter opened the fish's mouth, he found a shekel
worth about seventy cents, took it, and paid the taxes. *This
first fish that came to Peter's hook contained the precise amount that
was needed.* The full shekel was just enough to meet the present necessity, no more, no less. You will probably find that
the rich idea that comes to meet your need will be just
enough, too, no more, no less. This is especially true when
you are first developing an *inner* consciousness of supply.
Later, as your prosperity consciousness expands, so do its
benefits expand in your life.

During the cold Recessional winter of 1958, the idea that
came to me out of the fish's mouth was to begin teaching
and writing about ''prosperity as man's spiritual heritage
from God.'' That prosperity idea was the only shekel I
found during that lean and challenging period. Like Peter, I
caught only a single fish. Yet what a fish it was! Over the
years that idea of prosperity has gradually opened its mouth
to me. Again and again, that single shekel has met my

needs, as well as the needs of countless others, while I have continued to work with and develop it, both from the lecture platform and in my writings. So often the shekel of prosperous thinking has provided me with the precise amount needed, no more, no less.

A much deeper understanding of the subject has evolved over the years as that fish has slowly opened its mouth, revealing more and more of the prosperous Truth to me. How grateful I am now that it did not open its mouth wide to me all at once. Had that happened, I would have doubtless missed much in the expansion of my understanding, and in the use of prosperous ideas. Had that divine idea opened wide its mouth to me all at once, how much I might have also missed that was needed to share with others. My prosperous shekel has become an evolving one which I trust shall continue to teach me its secrets for the rest of my life. That fish of abundance continues year by year to slowly open wider its mouth for me, and to share its countless secrets of abundance. Yes, I caught only a single prosperous fish in that severe economic Recession of 1958, yet what a fish it was!

THE TENTH AND LAST STEP IN THE "MONEY MIRACLE": USE WHAT COMES AS PROMISED

Jesus' last prosperity secret in this famous fish miracle was given in this instruction: Peter was to take the shekel he found in the fish's mouth and use it to meet their tax obligations.

When you pray to meet a need and the way opens for you to meet that need, be sure you take what comes and use it as you have promised to do—no matter how many other needs you have. *If you change your mind after your good comes, and you use that promised good in some other way, you will have to meet the challenge of that need again and again in various guises until you fulfill it.*

Also, if you have promised God certain things as He helps you, be sure to follow through on your promises, as your need is met.[6] *For instance, when one intends to make a gift of money in a certain amount and then mentally lessens it, or doesn't give it all, he is lessening his own receiving capacity.* So don't cheat yourself by trying to cheat on the situation. Play it straight and prosper.

HOW THEY STOPPED THEIR PROSPERITY

A BUSINESSMAN IN ILLINOIS LEARNED WHY THINGS GOT WORSE FOR HIM FINANCIALLY: "We were tithing faithfully and things were going well. But the first of this month, there were additional bills, and the money I had set aside for tithing was used to pay our car insurance. I now realize I should have mailed that tithe check immediately in the faith that God would provide for payment of the additional bills in His own wonderful way. I did not do this, and since I neglected to tithe, things have gotten worse financially. I realize now that we had better start tithing again, if we wish to be freed of financial problems and to prosper on a permanent basis. I have learned a valuable lesson from this experience: *When one lessens his giving, he automatically lessens his own capacity to receive, too.*"

A BUSINESSMAN IN NEW YORK OVERCAME FINANCIAL DESPAIR: "After learning about the prospering power of tithing, I progressed from greedy to modest to thankful. But then I got careless and stopped tithing. The first thing that happened was that I experienced a standstill in my job, and finally lost it. That was followed by weeks of

---

6. For this purpose you will enjoy making a Success Covenant. (See Chapter 6 in *The Millionaires of Genesis.*)

deep despair over money worries and near suicide. This brought me again to the Ponder prosperity books, especially *The Millionaires of Genesis, The Millionaire Moses,* and *The Millionaire Joshua.* I realized my mistake and have begun tithing again. Divine Order has replaced those depressed thoughts. A drinking problem has also cleared up since I have again begun to freely give a tenth to God. *It pays to honor our agreement with God if we wish to claim His blessings of abundance.*"

A BUSINESSMAN IN CALIFORNIA DISCOVERED WHY HIS GOOD HAD STALLED: *"When we were tithing on a regular basis, we always had whatever we needed when we needed it.* But three months ago, I decided to try a new method. I put aside my tithes in a special account, thinking I would pay them all at once at the end of each quarter. Now I realize my mistake in not tithing regularly as the income was received.

"We had applied for a loan that was needed to refinance our house. We needed the financing to pay off two second deeds of trust on the house totaling over $12,000. These must be paid before the end of the year. Yesterday a letter came that informed us our loan request had been disapproved. We decided that the first thing to do was to release the tithe money accumulated during the last three months, and trust God to prosper us and show us the way. Henceforth we will tithe regularly, not quarterly. *We have learned that to stall on God causes a stall in His good to us.*"

A REALTOR IN HAWAII MADE HER FIRST SALE IN FIVE MONTHS: "From August until the following May, I was without any income in my business. The tide turned in January after I entered into a Success Covenant with God. I first learned of the prospering power of Success Covenants when I read about them in *The Millionaires of Genesis.* I put my first sale in five months in escrow that same month, and closed the sale in May. *I will always tithe because of the way that first Success Covenant[7] came to my rescue and prospered me at such a crucial period in my life.*"

_____

7. A free Success Covenant is available upon request from the author.

IN CLOSING: THE RICH BENEFITS
TO BE FOUND IN THE FISH'S MOUTH

You can begin to experience the rich benefits to be found in the fish's mouth when you start thinking: "I AM ATTUNED TO THE INFINITE MIND OF GOD, AND I AM HEIR TO HIS UNIVERSAL ABUNDANCE." When you think in this way, you cannot fail. You can only go in one direction—forward. Your life will grow into one of ever-increasing abundance. You will exchange disharmony, worry, envy, fear and all the other troublesome, upsetting emotions for a life of perfect balance that is in Divine Order and perfect adjustment. All this you can achieve through the use of rich ideas found in the fish's mouth.

The basic prosperity teaching contained in the miracle of the tribute money is that you are to expect your good through all avenues of life. Not from one specified point, not from two or more, but from all points of the universe, your good is crowding upon you now in the sea of abundant ideas. Your good is as far reaching as the universe, and it can come to you in countless ways when you first look for it in the fish's rich mouth!

SUMMARY

The word "unrestricted" means "unlimited, not held down or confined." The prosperity law of unrestricted supply, which Jesus used to meet immediate financial needs was:

Part I: Prosperous *attitudes* for tapping unrestricted supply:

1. *The prospering power of nonresistance.* By being willing to pay temple dues for himself and his disciples, while passing through Capernaum, Jesus used nonresistance. He could have deferred payment until returning to his home town of Nazareth.

2. When a financial need arises, instead of grumbling or talking lack, *say "yes" to the need,* and the battle is half won! When asked, Peter quickly replied that Jesus paid taxes.

3. When faced with a financial challenge, make the effort to *get into an uplifted state of mind.*

4. Also, deliberately *get into a prosperous, Capernaum state of mind.*

5. *Use the prospering power of faith.* Peter, symbolizing faith, demonstrated the unrestricted supply. Since there is prospering power in faith, you should, like Peter, take one step in faith, and that will lead you on to unrestricted supply.

Part II: Prosperous *actions* for tapping unrestricted supply:

6. *Go to the sea of rich ideas* through: meditation, affirmation, inspirational study, or through association with prosperous-minded people.

7. *Cast a specific hook in the sea of rich ideas* by: asking divine intelligence to help you; through list-making, affirmations and picturing.

8. *Take the first fish (idea of increase) that comes up out of the sea of ideas, and keep mental company with it,* allowing it time to grow strong and reveal its secrets to you.

9. *Open its mouth gradually,* and keep quiet about the ideas you find there as you begin to slowly develop them.

10. *Use what comes as promised.* Otherwise you will have to meet that challenge again and again until you fulfill it. Peter carefully used the shekel to meet their tax obligation.

11. Only a single fish (idea of increase) was caught, yet it has produced a special fascination for, and a far-reaching effect upon, mankind for twenty centuries. Its prosperity secrets are still available to you!

THE PROSPERITY PARABLE OF RIGHT USE

FROM THE "RICHES-TO-RAGS-TO-RICHES" STORY

— Chapter 8 —

This seems to be the theme of the Bible's most famous prosperity parable:

> God is extravagant supply. He brings forth the best robe. He spreads the banquet table with good things on which we may feast. He overflows our cup. He opens the windows of heaven and pours out a blessing to those of us who are willing to receive it. *Why are you satisfied with such meager living when you may have so much?*

A parable is "an earthly story with a heavenly meaning," and Jesus often taught in parables. Furthermore, many of his parables were prosperity parables. Among his best known is the parable of the prodigal son. Although we have tended to regard this parable as a lesson in behavior and morals, it is also a riches-to-rags-to-riches story! The word

193

"prodigal" means "to waste." From this famous old parable, we learn how to stop wasting our substance in the far country of limited thinking. Among other things, we learn the prosperity law of right use.

One theologian has described the prodigal son parable as "the most divinely tender and most humanly touching story ever told." Charles Dickens described it as "the finest short story ever written." Along with its prosperity teaching, this parable also reflects the supreme expression of love, which is the heart of the gospel's good news. *This parable has probably touched the hearts of more wanderers in the "far country" than any other words ever written.* Indeed it *is* "an earthly story with a heavenly meaning" that belongs to all ages!

Regarding its prosperity teaching, Charles Fillmore has written:[1]

"WE CANNOT BE VERY HAPPY IF WE ARE POOR, AND NOBODY NEEDS TO BE POOR. *It is a sin to be poor.* You may ask whether Jesus cited any example of poverty's being a sin? Yes. You will find it in the story of the prodigal son. That parable is often used as a text to preach to moral sinners, but a close study of it shows that *Jesus was teaching the sin of lack and how to gain plenty.* . .

"The parable is a great lesson on prosperity, for it shows us that people who are dissipating their substance in sense ways are sinners and eventually fall into a consciousness of lack. It also proves that they may become lawful and prosperous again by returning to the Father Mind."

---

1. Charles Fillmore, *Prosperity,* (Unity Village, Mo.: Unity School of Christianity, 1936).

THE PROSPERITY PARABLE, PART ONE:
HOW TO GET OUT OF
THE FAR COUNTRY OF LIMITED THINKING

"A certain man had two sons; and the younger of them said to his father, 'Give me the portion of thy substance that falleth to me.' And he divided unto them his living.

"And now many days after, the younger son gathered all together and took his journey into a far country; and there he wasted his substance with riotous living. And when he had spent all, there arose a mighty famine in that land; and he began to be in want. And he went and joined himself to one of the citizens of the country; and he sent him into his fields to feed the swine. And he would fain have filled his belly with the husks that the swine did eat; and no man gave unto him.

"And when he came to himself he said, 'How many hired servants of my father's have bread enough and to spare, and I perish here with hunger.' I will arise and go to my father, and will say unto him, 'Father, I have sinned against heaven, and in thy sight; I am no more worthy to be called thy son; make me as one of the hired servants.' " (Luke 15:11-19)

The younger son was not a bad person when he left home. We can admire his ambition. He had initiative, daring and high resolve. *His intent was a healthy one, to win success and to become financially independent of his family.*

His great desire to prosper and succeed on his own is all the more understandable when you realize the customs of the East that prevailed in those times. The attention of the family usually centered around the firstborn son. To a great extent, the other children were disregarded. The best garments were made for the firstborn. A larger portion of food was given to him. The firstborn was empowered to act ir his father's absence: to buy and sell, to receive guests, to look after the servants and pay them, to hire and fire. He was even empowered to punish other members of the family.

In the face of these customs, it is easy to see why the younger son felt impelled to secure his property and leave home. This was often the only way a younger son could change his family's attitude toward him. So his intentions were good. Unfortunately, *he had not yet developed the understanding or maturity needed to succeed on his own. His zeal was not yet tempered with wisdom, and he had not yet learned the true Source of his supply.* (See chapter on Zeal in *The Healing Secrets of the Ages.*)

Most of us can identify at times with the ambitious young prodigal son off in the far country who wasted his substance in riotous living, because he did not yet understand the divine law of plenty.

People who waste their substance come to want in both physical and financial ways. Substance is very important to our world. The word "substance" was often used to describe one's wealth in Biblical times. The word "substance" means that which stands under all visible forms of supply. Substance as "the body of God" is the foundation of all true wealth. It is released through mind power.

THE MAGICAL POWERS OF DIVINE ORDER

There is a close relation between riotous living and want. The word "riotous" means "lacking in order," "lacking in peace." When you just rush into your day unprepared for it spiritually, mentally or emotionally—when you begin your day without first having a quiet time of prayer, meditation, affirmation, or study of some inspirational book or the

Bible—your day can become riotous, or lacking in order and peace.

You can, however, quickly learn how to handle periods of riotous living, which have seemed so lacking in order and peace. Things can straighten out and become orderly, when you begin to dwell upon "divine order."

DIVINE ORDER BROUGHT ABOUT REPAIRS THAT HAD BEEN DELAYED: A housewife wrote: "My house was such a mess. Something kept holding up the remodeling work that had been scheduled in our kitchen many weeks ago. After trying various other prayer methods without results, I began to affirm early one morning: 'DIVINE ORDER IS NOW ESTABLISHED AND MAINTAINED IN MY LIFE AND AFFAIRS.' The very next day the scheduled work was begun on the kitchen. It has now been finished and is beautiful, thanks to the power of 'divine order.'

HOW THE MAGIC POWERS OF THE UNIVERSE ARE RELEASED: A businesswoman wrote: "I was the daughter of a professional magician, but frankly never believed in magic. I have now discovered that *the universe is made up of a kind of magic.* In a sense we are all magicians who can release the magical powers of the universe in our behalves when we meditate often upon 'divine order,' and then get busy establishing it in our lives. I *now* believe in magic—the magical power of divine order."

THE SUCCESS POWER OF PEACE

Since the word "riotous" also means "lacking in peace," riotous living will hold no threat for you when you dwell upon thoughts of "peace."

A businesswoman from Mississippi wrote:

"Since I have practiced prosperous thinking in general, many of my prayers have been answered. I have recently received some lovely new furniture, over $700 from tax returns, and gifts of cash, clothes, and a car.

"I work for the police department; and *I am constantly decreeing 'peace and harmony' for my work. The results have been amazing:* the crime rate has fallen so low for our city that we have been unable to get government grants! The guys I work with are now complaining that our shift has become a dull and unexciting one. *This experience has proved to me how much power for good can be released when even one person declares 'peace and harmony.'* Imagine the good that could be accomplished worldwide today if people everywhere dared to do this."

NO ONE GAVE UNTO HIM

After the son wasted his substance in riotous living in that far country, there arose a mighty famine in that land. "No one gave unto him" and he quickly came into a state of lack. (Luke 15:16)

For a Jew, the feeding of the swine and the eating of their food was an experience in utter shame. It was the ultimate mark of degradation. Many of us have suffered at times from the misery of financial limitation. In our famine of loneliness and limitation, no one gave unto us; no one shared their abundance with us. It was a painful famine experience. Just as the marks of the far country probably remained with the prodigal son for the rest of his life, your own miserable famine periods may have been difficult ones to forgive and forget, once you overcame them.

Perhaps you've had painful periods in your life where no matter how hard you tried, your prayers seemed to go unanswered. You simply did not demonstrate the good you desired in life. If, at that point, you tried to force results on a human level, things just got more riotous and lacking in peace and order.

Like the prodigal son, you probably found that *the only solution was to release that which was unproductive and unrewarding.* Even though he was hungry and in rags, the prodigal son finally found the courage to say, "I will arise and go to my father." (Luke 15:18)

THE PROSPERING POWER OF RELEASE

You are in "the far country" when you are in circumstances that are lacking in harmony and peace (riotous), or when people, places, events or things in your world are no longer satisfactory, productive or rewarding. As in the case of the prodigal son, that is the time to release them; to arise in your thinking, and *make the effort to go forward* into a better way of life. However, *nothing happens until you first practice release of that which has been unproductive and unrewarding.*

RELEASE BROUGHT $2,500 TO A BUSINESSMAN IN NEW YORK: "Once when I was at the end of my rope financially, and felt that I could not go on, I just let go all my problems. When I stopped worrying about them, something wonderful happened: I won $2,500! That experience proved to me *the prospering power of letting go.*"

RELEASE BROUGHT THEIR OWN BUSINESS IN ARIZONA: "I am a registered nurse and my husband is a French chef who always wanted a restaurant of his own. I had resisted this because I loved my profession so dearly. *A wonderful change came in my thinking and in my life after I began to practice release of the situation, placing the matter in God's hands.*

"An opportunity arose for my husband to open a restaurant in a popular desert resort area of Arizona. The good Lord directed it all. The house we had owned in California sold in one day at the price we asked! We quickly moved to Arizona and everything was a miracle, with so many answers to prayer. Our restaurant has been a success from the start. This experience convinced me of the prospering power that lies in letting go.''

RELEASE BROUGHT HARMONY TO A WIDOW IN CALIFORNIA: ''I haven't called my son and his wife since she hung up the telephone on me. Instead, *I have practiced releasing, loosing, letting go, and letting God. I feel better than I have felt in years.* As I continue to practice loosing and letting go everything and everybody, some old friends have come back into my life and have told me how much they have missed me. I no longer beg for others' love like I used to do, and things are more harmonious and satisfying than ever in my life.''

Another way to practice release is by forming a vacuum and releasing those old (or new) items and possessions that no longer give satisfaction in one's life. Such release is magnetic and opens the way for new good to come to you.

RELEASE BROUGHT A POTENTIAL FORTUNE TO A HOUSEWIFE IN ILLINOIS: ''This morning I decided to practice release through forming a vacuum and cleaning up and cleaning out unneeded possessions to make way for new supply. After I had cleaned out one drawer in the bathroom, a telephone call came asking me to work several days. This will give me $90 I had not anticipated receiving. *At this rate, one drawer cleaned out and $90 returned, I must have a fortune in the rest of the house!*''

A HOUSEWIFE IN NEW MEXICO BROUGHT ABOUT FREEDOM FROM WORN-OUT POSSESSIONS: *''One of the most powerful success principles for experiencing happiness in the home and elsewhere is brought about through the practice of release.* For months I tried to get a second car in our family. Our old one spent more time in the repair shop than on the street. I also felt it a good idea to sell part of a certain investment on which we would not realize a good profit, so that we could pay cash for the new car. My husband wouldn't hear of it.

"Our old car kept going out. *It wanted to get away from us as much as I wanted to get rid of it!* After another large repair bill, it dawned on me that my husband was still emotionally attached to that old car. He had bought it in his home town, driven it across country, and enjoyed many adventures in it. I decided to speak these words of release: 'THIS CAR IS NOW RELEASED TO ITS DIVINE PLAN, AND WE ARE NOW RELEASED TO OUR DIVINE PLAN.'

"Within forty-eight hours my husband 'changed his mind.' We sold the investment at a profit, got an excellent trade-in for the old car, and purchased a new one that my husband can drive on his job as well as on camping trips. It will be a fine tax write-off, so that everyone is happy.

"I am continuing to speak words of release and I feel a vast inner freedom from old, unhappy memories. The practice of release is bringing peace and happiness into our lives. Regarding the tithe, I find the need to practice release there, too. It is not wise to keep God waiting on His tenth. He's one creditor we cannot afford to put off."

THE IMPORTANCE OF LITERALLY
GETTING BACK TO THE FATHER'S HOUSE

Getting back to the father's house can begin in a literal sense. When you search out other students of prosperous thinking and study with them, you have begun to get back to the Father's house, or into a consciousness of abundance and peace. When you attend classes, services, or lectures in the church of your choice that teaches prosperous thinking as a part of your spiritual heritage, you are getting back into the Father's house of abundance and peace. Perhaps this is why thousands of people who now attend churches that are allied with the International New Thought Movement[2]

---

2. For a list of such churches, write The International New Thought Alliance, 7314 E. Stetson Drive, Scottsdale, Arizona, 85251.

often report occurrences of vast good in their lives. The reports of miraculous happenings—such as mental and physical healings, increased prosperity, harmony, and spiritual illumination—are everyday occurrences in such churches.

A MINISTER REPORTS THAT A PROSPERITY CLASS IN TEXAS BROUGHT MIRACLES: "What a joy to report good news from the prosperity class held in our church based on *The Millionaires of Genesis*. After only three weeks of class study of that book, many wonderful reports have come in. Testimonies have been received of increased material wealth, increased pay, promotions, new job opportunities, the receipt of new furniture and cars. We have also received testimonies of some wonderful healings, which included physical healings, healings in relationships, and the establishment of peaceful, harmonious circumstances.

"Of our fifty-five enrolled students, we have three doctors, one engineer, three educators, many homemakers, and businessmen. Everyone is tuned in and turned on! Don't be surprised to hear of some 'new Texas millionaires'—thanks to *The Millionaires of Genesis*. They have had a dramatic effect upon our lives."

A BUSINESSMAN REPORTS ON A PROSPERITY CLASS IN ARKANSAS: "For over a year, I was privileged to moderate a group discussion class. We studied *The Dynamic Laws of Prosperity*, then *The Dynamic Laws of Healing*. After a short recess, we studied *Open Your Mind to Prosperity*.

"*In our pursuit of things spiritual, that year-long class study was one of the most gratifying experiences that my wife and I have ever had.* After the initial start, the class more or less ran itself. Not in any unruly way, but as if there were a Spiritual Power that took over. There was many a rich exchange of valuable ideas and experiences. It was not unlike an author that creates a character, and then loses control of his actions. Only in this case, it was all for the good. Our studies were so stimulating that my wife and I would take a day or so to "buzz down" after each session was over. The class discussion on tithing from *Open Your Mind to Prosperity* was one of the most thrilling, eye-opening and rousing that I can remember. It motivated most of the class members to begin tithing. Our studies together in that class have now passed, but a warm glow lingers on. The eternal truths we learned together there will benefit us for the rest of our lives.''

SHE WENT FROM ''RAGS TO RICHES'' BY GETTING BACK TO THE FATHER'S HOUSE

A retired businesswoman once told me a success story I have long remembered. This lady had become a student of prosperous thinking long before it was a popularly accepted philosophy. After she took up the study of prosperous thinking, she had literally gone from ''rags to riches.''

One reason she felt she went from ''rags to riches'' was because early in her study she made a rule, which was self-imposed. Her rule was that she would never allow people or conditions to keep her away from church services or weekly classes where the philosophy of prosperous thinking was being regularly taught and practiced. She felt that *the study of this priceless philosophy was the answer to every problem.* Instead of staying home with her problems when she felt low or discouraged, she knew *that* was the time she most needed to get to church. She realized that when she was confronted with problems. that was the very time when the study of Truth *must* come first in her life.

Her rule was such that even when she was tired, discouraged or not feeling well, she still made the effort to attend church anyway. There she found the uplifting and expanded spiritual consciousness needed, which made it possible for her to go forward and to overcome (or ''come up over'') all challenges.

Her rule also included people. She would not allow relatives or friends to keep her away from church on Sundays or from midweek lectures or classes. She would say to them, "You know I go to church every Sunday as well as to weekly classes. You know how much this means to me and you are always invited to attend with me, if you wish. But don't expect me to stay home and entertain you at that time. My study of the prosperous Truth must come first."

Once when a mistake had been made by the bookkeeper who worked in this woman's business, a great deal of money was involved. The bookkeeper finally gave up trying to find the accounting error. As the owner of the company, this lady had also searched the ledger all day trying to find the mistake, but to no avail.

That night was church night; there would be a class and midweek lecture. She kept thinking that she might have to break her rule for once and miss church. But as the time drew near, she felt impelled to go. As she relaxed in church for the first time that day, got quiet, peaceful, and into an uplifted state of mind—suddenly a ledger sheet flashed before her and she "saw" the bookkeeping mistake!

The word "religion" means "to bind man back to his source"—which is God the good. *When you put other things ahead of your religion—ahead of God and His goodness—you will have one problem after another. You will never find the solution until you are "bound back to your Source," or until you begin to put God first again in your life.*

As in the case of this businesswoman, any time your life seems lacking in order or peace, you are experiencing "riotous living." That is the time to get back to the Father's house in both *inner* and *outer* ways.

WHY A FAMINE OCCURS

Getting back to the Father's house not only symbolizes attaining an uplifted state of mind, it also symbolizes arriving at an awareness of God's abundant good for you. Sometimes we get away from the Father's house into that far country by putting people, conditions, or events in our life ahead of God and His goodness. When we are not putting God first in our allegiance, in our time, in our financial affairs, or in other phases of our lives, we often find ourselves off in a far country of lack and limitation.

Then some sort of famine occurs. It may be a famine of ill health, a financial famine, a famine in human relations conflicts, a famine of confusion, or a famine of loneliness. The word "famine" means "an acute and general lack of anything." In any event, the answer is to get back to the Father's house by beginning to put God first in your thoughts, time and money again. *One reason a person can experience a famine of lack is because he did not give what he should have given while he had his harvest.*

A businesswoman from Colorado wrote:

"I went through a period of resenting my tithes and doubting the good reasons behind tithing in general. *During this period, I seemed to be broke all the time, and a lot of unexpected bills arrived. Delays occurred suddenly in other areas of my life, too.* It feels good to 'feel good' about tithing again, and to be 'back in the Father's house,' where order and abundance prevail."

HOW TO OVERCOME FAMINE

Here is the way to overcome a famine: Begin each day with a quiet time of prayer, meditation and inspirational

study. This is a great way to get back to the Father's house
of unlimited abundance.

A businesswoman from Michigan wrote:

> *"I know my prosperity is permanent now as my inner work is con-*
> *stant.* God is filling my cup and it is overflowing in abun-
> dance of finances, employment and all good. I am so happy
> because this is a time of abundant energy and divine comple-
> tion for me."

Charles Fillmore has explained the "far country" and the
"Father's house" in these ways:

> "Our Father is always here and we are in a 'far country'
> only when we forget His presence. *He is constantly giving us*
> *just what we will acknowledge and accept under His law.* We can
> take our inheritance and divorce ourselves in consciousness
> from the Father, but we shall suffer the results, for then we
> shall not do things in divine wisdom and order, and there
> will be a 'famine,' or state of lack in our lives. Let us rather
> seek the divine wisdom to know how to handle our
> substance, and the law of prosperity will be revealed to us."[3]

As long as the son remained in the far country in a state of
riotous thinking and living, where there was no order or
peace, "No one gave unto him." (Luke 15:16) No one
helped him out. The privation he suffered seemed a cruel
experience. Yet that cruel privation served a divine purpose. Before anyone came to his aid, he was forced to make
the effort to return to the Father's house or achieve an
uplifted state of universal abundance.

A businesswoman started out making seven dollars a
week. Yet she later became the head of a 140-million-dollar-
a-year business. When asked the secret of her success, she

---

3. Fillmore, *Prosperity*, p. 63.

said, "God never made a nobody. God never made a failure. If you know you're special, created in the image of God, and that God has great plans for you, then you don't let someone else's opinion deflate you."

Here is the prosperity statement that can help you overcome any famine in your life: "I AM THE RICH CHILD OF A LOVING FATHER, SO I DO NOT DEPEND UPON PERSONS OR CONDITIONS FOR MY PROSPERITY. I LOOK TO GOD FOR GUIDANCE AND SUPPLY, AND I DARE TO PROSPER NOW!"

HOW $8,000 BECAME $25,000

I once lectured in a beautiful church that had been founded by a lovely minister. The church she served had just constructed an outstanding new building, but what was even more outstanding was the way it had been done. There had been no borrowing of money or selling of bonds. When sufficient money accumulated in the building fund, they had begun construction of the new edifice, which was located in a prominent area of the city.

Everyone was excited about the building program and contributed toward the new church. For a time everything went along fine. But—as often happens in a church building program—about halfway through the project, both the enthusiasm and the money ran out. When the bills started mounting, the board of trustees panicked. They reminded the minister that someone had given the church $8,000 in stocks as a tax write-off. They suggested that she sell the stocks for $8,000 and begin paying the bills. When the minister prayed about their suggestion, she did not feel led to follow through on it. She felt it would be far wiser to keep the $8,000 as a financial asset for the church rather than depleting it as their only cash reserve.

She reminded the trustees that the church had always paid its bills on time, and their creditors knew this. Their creditors also knew they were in a building program, and she felt they would cooperate. In faith, she assured the trustees that the bills would be paid, and the church would be finished if they did not panic.

At that point, the trustees were like the prodigal son off in the far country, as they dwelled upon the appearance of lack, and became riotous in their thinking. There was nothing unusual about their reaction. Until we have learned that there is a higher and better way to solve our problems, most of us have reacted similarly.

That minister refused to be pressured into sanctioning the sale of stocks. Instead, as her prayer ministry prayed with her daily affirming that God was the Source of their supply, substance began to flow again. The bills were paid. The fine new building was completed, and those stocks, formerly worth $8,000, soon rose in value to $25,000! That $8,000 became a $25,000 cash reserve. (On today's market, it would be worth much more.)

The human way is to force, rush, reason, judge by appearances, be afraid of them, be governed by them, and get into a state of riotous thinking where there is lack of order and peace. In this state of mind, things do not work out. "No one gives unto you." *But when you get back to the Father's house—into a state of peace and order—everything changes. Vast improvement often comes quickly.* It certainly did for the prodigal son.

THE PROSPERITY PARABLE, PART TWO: THE LAVISH ABUNDANCE THAT AWAITS YOU IN THE FATHER'S HOUSE

"And he arose and came to his father. But while he was yet afar off, his father saw him, and was moved with compassion and ran and fell on his neck, and kissed him. And the son said unto him, 'Father, I have sinned against heaven and in thy sight. I am no more worthy to be called thy son.'

"But the father said to his servants, 'Bring forth quickly the best robe, and put it on him, and put a ring on his finger and shoes on his feet. And bring the fatted calf and kill it and let us eat and make merry, for this my son was dead and is alive again. He was lost and is found,' and they began to make merry." (Luke 15:20-24)

Despite the rags, the father had recognized his son. While a person is yet a great way off in consciousness, a loving Father recognizes him as His own child. God's forgiveness is never mere pardon. It wipes out the sins (mistakes) of the past, and restores the soul, body and financial affairs of the one who is returning in consciousness to the Source of his supply. This segment of the parable points out that *God is a Father of love and forgiveness. No matter what we have thought, said, or done, the God of abundance still wishes to help and bless us.*

The Runner's Bible[4] explains:

"We can no more keep good from coming to us, if we are consciously at one with the Almighty, than we can hold back the tide with our hands."

In the gift of clothes and in the act of feasting, we see the restoration of dominion and prosperity. The prodigal son was no longer a poverty stricken slave in a far country. He was the son of a wealthy father again. The signet ring symbolized authority; the gift of this ring indicated that the son was still heir. The gift of shoes indicated that this son had been completely restored to favor in his father's house. In Biblical times, servants went barefooted, while their

---

4. Nora Holm, editor, *The Runner's Bible* (Boston, Mass.: Houghton Mifflin Company, 1913, 1943) p. 141.

master's children wore shoes as a token of their sonship. The best robe that was bestowed upon the returned son was usually reserved for only the most distinguished and honored guests. In preparation for some great occasion, the fatted calf had earlier been taken from its mother and specially fed. What a feast of thanksgiving it must have been! *Here is parabled the prosperity that ensues when man returns to the consciousness of God as his rich resource.*

In describing this segment of the prosperity parable of right use, Charles Fillmore has written:

"When he returned to his father's house he was not accused of moral shortcoming, as we should expect. Instead the father said, 'Bring forth quickly the best robe and put it on him.' That was a lesson in good apparel. *It is a sin to wear poor clothes.* This may seem to be a rather sordid way of looking at the teachings of Jesus, but we must be honest. We must interpret it as he gave it, not as we think it ought to be.

"The next act of the father was to put a gold ring on the prodigal's finger, another evidence of prosperity. *The Father's desire for us is unlimited good, not merely the means of a meager existence.* The ring symbolizes the unlimited: that to which there is no end. It also represents omnipresence and omnipotence in the manifest world. When the father gave that ring to the son, he gave him the key to all life activity. It was the symbol of his being a son and heir to all that the father had. 'All that is mine is thine.' The Father gives us all that He has and is, omnipotence, omniscience, all love, and all substance when we return to the consciousness of His house of plenty.

" 'Put . . . shoes on his feet,' was the father's next command to the servants. Feet represent that part of our understanding that comes into contact with earthly conditions. In the head or 'upper room' we have the understanding that contacts spiritual conditions, but when we read in Scripture anything about the feet, we may know that it refers to our understanding of things of the material world.

"The next thing the father did for his returned son was to proclaim a feast for him. That is not the way we treat moral sinners. We decree punishment for them; we send them to jail. But *the Father gives a feast to those who come to Him for supply.* He does not dole out only a necessary ration but serves the 'fatted calf,' universal substance and life in its fullness and richness.

"The parable is a great lesson on prosperity, for it shows us that people who are dissipating their substance in sense ways are sinners and eventually fall into a consciousness of lack. It also proves that they may become lawful and prosperous again by returning to the Father-Mind. When there are so many lessons in the Bible for moral delinquents, there is no need to twist the meaning of this parable to that purpose. It is so plainly a lesson on the cause of lack and want."[5]

CARRY YOURSELF AS ONE WHO
OWNS THE EARTH

A businesswoman from Oregon read these words, "Carry yourself as one who owns the earth, for you do!" Later she reported, "I am carrying myself as one who owns the earth, and to do this has worked for me. Today I am more prosperous than I have ever been before! I cannot find anything that I want removed from my life: no person or condition. I am very happy, prosperous, successful, and I am in perfect health. I am free in mind and spirit. *What a wonderful change from the past.*"

5. Fillmore, *Prosperity,* pp. 61, 62.

HOW A DIVORCEE AND HER CHILDREN
BUILT A SATISFYING NEW LIFE

A businesswoman from Idaho wrote:

"Last year I was living in a high crime area on the West Coast, unable to find work, and wanting a change. I began by changing my thinking after a friend gave me a copy of *The Dynamic Laws of Prosperity.* My sons and daughter wanted to live where they could hunt, fish, have animals—in a rural wooded area with mountains and snow. I wanted a teaching job in a safe atmosphere. We decided Idaho might be the state for us. I planned to leave in April to go there and take a temporary job while looking for something permanent. Then I got the inspiration to go earlier in January.

"With $400, our dog and cats, and everything we could pack into our station wagon, my children and I left for Idaho in January. We had no friends or relatives there, and went against the advice of everyone we knew. My mother got hysterical, and my ex-husband vowed he would send no child-support payments.

"Upon our arrival, we trusted God as the Source of our supply, and soon found a motel that accepted us with our animals. Next, we found a comfortable trailer to rent. Often on the day the rent was due, or just after we had eaten our last food, money would come in unexpectedly. I wrote to the Guardian Angel of my ex-husband, thanking him for providing for the children. A child-support check soon arrived!

"Within two weeks, I had a job, then a better one. But I was soon laid off. I decided this meant God had something better. So I praised Him for His Divine Plan for my life, and I thanked Him for divine guidance. I told Him we would continue to look to Him for guidance and supply. *As an act of faith, I then instructed the children to dress up in their best clothes so we could go out to dinner and celebrate the good that was on the way!*

"Within two days I found a teaching job to begin—not in September—but right then. We are now living in a wooded area even more beautiful than the one we had pictured, with each season more lovely than the last. As we have continued to look to God for guidance and supply, we have acquired eight acres of land and plan to build. This has turned out to be a fantastic year that my children and I shall always remember.''

SHE PROVED THAT YOU CAN HAVE EVERYTHING!

A businesswoman in California wrote:

"In 1967 I was alone, broke and suicidal. Five years earlier, I had had a serious automobile accident from which I still experienced a great deal of pain. There had followed such a series of tragedies within my immediate family that we were known as 'the crisis-a-week family.' Our friends even begged us to stay away from them because they couldn't take anymore of our troubles.

"Then a miracle happened. I got a job as a rehabilitation counselor with the State. One day, my supervisor, a warm-hearted person who was almost totally blind, said to me, *'Have you ever thought that you can have everything—everything you want in life?'* I said I supposed it was possible if a person were willing to pay the price. He replied, 'Then I want to lend you a book that will show you how to have everything you need and desire. Life's price is well within your ability to pay.'

"That book was *The Prosperity Secret of the Ages.* When I read it I thought, 'What have I got to lose? The rules are simple and not hard to follow.' *The most difficult thing was trying to decide what I really wanted out of life.* I was a forty-six year old widow with three grown sons who dreaded visiting me because of my constant complaining.

"I sat alone in my apartment and analyzed, out loud, just what I wanted to: (1) eliminate from my life, and (2) bring into it. I wanted the pain to diminish so I could regain my

verve for living. I wanted to remarry, but only to a definite
type of man with specific attributes. I wanted an attractive
home of my own. I wanted to be in an occupation in which I
could be of real service to others. I wanted to eliminate all indebtedness.

"It was a pretty large order. Yet *it has all come true, and
more!* The friends and family came back as I stopped whining
and complaining about my 'troubles.' Within six weeks of
my evening of self-analysis, I met the man to whom I have
been very happily married since 1968. I got a new job in a
new field, and was promoted from the entry level in 1969 to
the top position in the organization in 1973. I am out of
debt, and my health has vastly improved. My husband and I
have a lovely home, but are in the process of building a better one. My net worth has risen from zero in 1967 to well
over $100,000 today! I have given away more than one hun-
dred copies of that book to help others realize that they, too,
can have everything."

HOW HE BECAME A MULTIMILLIONAIRE
BY RETURNING TO THE FATHER'S HOUSE

In his book, *Wells of Abundance,*[6] E.V. Ingraham has written of the prodigal son's return:

"The Prodigal Son . . . said to his father, 'Give me that
portion of thy goods that falleth to me.' He understood that
certain things were naturally his. . . Up to this point, he was
entirely within his right. His mistake was in separating
himself and his inheritance from the father, spending it in
riotous living."

The author later explains that you must not sever your

6. E. V. Ingraham, *Wells of Abundance* (Marina del Rey, Calif.:
DeVorss & Co., 1938) pp. 48-49.

financial contact with your Source, God. Just as a farmer gives back to God at least one-tenth of his best seed to keep the soil enriched, so you should be giving back to God at least a tithe of your income to keep your own mind, body, affairs, and spiritual understanding enriched. Through your gifts, you also enrich the channel through which you receive spiritual help.

It is common knowledge that many of the most successful businessmen of the present day—great industrialists and captains of industry—attribute their success to having formed the habit of putting God first financially through consistent tithing. *Thousands of students of prosperous thinking have grown out of longstanding, and what looked like hopeless poverty, into security and comfort by the practice of tithing.* The reports I receive from people worldwide indicate that thousands more are doing so today!

The late R. G. LeTourneau called himself "the mechanic whom the Lord has blessed."[7] After early success and subsequent bankruptcy, he began to tithe and to prosper gradually on a secure basis. He later felt that the countless ideas which came for his inventions were a result of putting God first financially. He invented the famous earth-moving equipment that was used on the battlefields and in the jungles during World War II to clear the space for runways on which planes could land. He is probably best known for his vast achievements at Hoover Dam.

This businessman learned quite a lesson even after he had become successful through tithing. One year he had sold more machinery than in all his previous years in business combined.[8] It was projected that he would make at least $100,000 the next year—a lot of money in those days.

---

7. R. G. LeTourneau, *Mover of Men and Mountains* (Englewood Cliffs, N.J.: Prentice-Hall, Inc., 1960) p. 1.

8. Ibid., p. 173.

At this point he became over-confident. He decided to withhold the tithe because it looked like "too much" to give. His bargaining session with God went like this: "Instead of giving You Your share now, I'll put it all into expanding the business, and next year You will get a share to be proud of."[9]

What happened? Everything went wrong! There was unexpected bad weather, valuable employees got sick, and construction contracts fell through. He met delays, disappointments and failure at every turn. *Instead of making at least $100,000 that next year, he found himself exactly $100,000 in debt.* He learned an expensive lesson from this experience, but he learned it so well that he went on to become a multi-millionaire: He never again tried to cheat God out of His tenth. He gave it freely and on time, no matter what the amount. A foundation finally had to be formed just to handle the distribution of his vast tithes, which later ran into millions.[10]

In his book, *Mover of Men and Mountains,* R. G. LeTourneau wrote:

> "To what foolish lengths man will let his pride drive him. God does not do business that way. He keeps His promises. When you ask His help, He doesn't answer that He has a lot of pressing things to attend to, so come back next year. His time is *now.* In the early days, the true Christians gave God His share from the *first fruits* of their crops. They had faith. They didn't wait around to see if the later crops were to be destroyed by locusts or drought. *Let God's will be done and the rewards will be so great that there won't be room to store them.* But start to hedge, and wait to see how the whole crop turns out before giving God His share, and He knows you as a man of

9. Ibid., p. 173.
10. Ibid., p. 205.

little faith. . . *It's all right to give God credit, but He can use cash, too.* "[11]

The businessman proved that *when you violate the prosperity law of right use, you invite problems.* The solution is to get out of the far country of limited thought, and return to the Father's house of lavish abundance through both your *inner* and *outer* actions. It pays to put God first *financially* as well as to put Him first in other phases of your life.

THE PROSPERITY PARABLE, PART THREE: THE PROSPERING POWER OF JOY AND FORGIVENESS

"Now the elder son was in the field; and as he came and drew nigh to the house, he heard music and dancing. And he called to him one of the servants, and inquired what these things might be: 'Thy brother is come; and thy father hath killed the fatted calf, because he hath received him safe and sound.' But the elder son was angry, and would not go in; and his father came out, and entreated him. But he answered and said to his father, 'Lo, these many years do I serve thee, and I never transgressed a commandment of thine; and yet thou never gave me a kid, that I might make merry with my friends; but when this thy son came, who hath devoured thy living with harlots, thou killest for him the fatted calf.' And he said unto him, *'Son, thou art ever with me, and all that is mine is thine.* But it was meet to make merry and be glad: for this thy brother was dead, and is alive again; he was lost, and is found.' " (Luke 15:25-32)

We can regard the older son with sympathy. The calamity that befell him seemed worse than a famine. He had returned home tired from a hard day's work only to find the

---

11. Ibid., p. 173, 90.

house lit up, with welcome-home festivities going full blast for his wayward brother. He could not believe that a wastrel such as his "no-good" brother, was now being treated as an honored guest. He may have been harboring old resentments toward his brother that he himself did not understand. From a human standpoint, his resentment was understandable. The child who stays home is often taken for granted, or feels that he is. In the unredeemed part of his nature, perhaps the older son was jealous of the gaiety of his younger brother, and doubly jealous when this prodigal brother was welcomed with feasting.

Earlier, at the beginning of this story, the father may have been on the point of turning the management of the farm over to his two grown sons, along with its responsibilities and profits. When the younger son took his inheritance and left, the disappointed father had to go back to work. True, the prodigal's unruliness had brought grief to the father, bitterness to the brother, and had cast a shadow over the whole household. But from a financial standpoint, there was no need for the elder brother's distress. He was still entitled to two-thirds of the estate.

Perhaps by his rigid attitudes, the elder brother had helped unknowingly to drive the younger away in the first place. *Much that has passed for "religion" has been expressed in harsh, self-righteous, narrow attitudes.* The elder brother may have kept the letter of the law, while expressing none of its loving spirit. He had not been aware of his brother's suffering in a far country, nor had he shared in his father's grief. Although he was literally correct in all that he said about his wastrel brother, *that* was not the time to voice it to his jubilant father. The elder brother seemed merciless in his attitudes even though he was factually correct.

In some circles, the older brother appears as the type of villain who is unpopular in society because he still has many descendants among us, especially in some of our churches. The older brother had no patience with people who squandered time or money—especially money. He had a stringent "hard-work" consciousness.

When he upbraided his happy father, the reply had been a gentle one. The father had answered the elder son's harsh condemnation with generosity: "All that I have is thine." (Luke 15:31) A father with this attitude would hardly have overlooked the child at home, or have taken his loyalty and good works for granted.

THE DESTRUCTIVE POWER OF "INCURABLE CONDEMNATION"

Whether we like to admit it or not, most of us have been like that elder son at times. We have gotten critical, self-righteous, and unmerciful in our attitudes. *No one is less merciful than he who is unaware of any fault in himself.* Such attitudes can stop our own good. But something usually happens to bring our merciless attitudes to our attention.

When like the elder son, unmerciful experiences seem to come into your life, it is usually an indication that you have become unmerciful in your attitudes toward life in general, or toward specific people and situations. You may have become too rigid in what you expected of others. Or you may have become intolerant of them and unaware of their silent suffering, grief, or the desire to overcome their faults. If you have practiced such intolerance, this can draw intolerable experiences into your own life.

The damage that can be done to the body by "incurable criticism" is described in Chapter 4 of my book, *The Healing Secrets of the Ages.* It particularly affects the stomach, digestive and abdominal area. So-called "incurable" conditions are often the result of "incurable condemnation"—either that expressed by the sufferer, or from the chronic criticism of someone else directed toward him. The answer is to relax more, and judge or criticize others less. On one occasion, Jesus reminded his critics, "What is that to thee? Follow thou me." (John 21:21-23)

SHE WENT ON TO A WEALTHY LIFE STYLE
WHILE HER CRITICS REMAINED IN LACK

While a former husband did little to help, a courageous divorcee struggled to support herself and several small children. Behind her back, so-called "friends" kept criticizing her. They said, "What kind of a life can she ever have, as she struggles to raise all those children alone?" Almost as if looking forward to it, they would remark, "She'll never make it."

But this young woman learned about the power of prosperous thinking, and she began to practice it daily. Naturally. her life steadily improved. She soon took a job elsewhere and moved away. In her new surroundings she met and married a wealthy widower, who provided a good home for her children and helped her to raise them. While hers became a wealthy life style, her former "friends" continued to live in their self-induced prisons of doubt, criticism and financial limitation. Years later, when she was enjoying a life of abundance and happiness, her critics from the past continued to live lives of dismal lack. All the while they jealously lamented, "I don't understand how her 'luck' changed."

JOY PROSPERS AND LOVE ENVIETH NOT

Even though he lived in the midst of lavish abundance, one reason the elder son had not experienced greater good in his own life was because of his general attitude. He had served his father faithfully, but without joy. *If a joyous declaration has not been recurring throughout your life, then you, too, may have experienced a great deal of defeat, injustice, and unhappiness which you felt you were not entitled to. The joyous, happy state of mind is an attracting power for good. You can demonstrate through joy what you will never demonstrate through a strained, overserious, critical, judgmental, overworked state of mind.* The prodigal son certainly proved this while his elder brother experienced just the opposite result.

Yet our hearts go out to the elder son. Most of us have known what it was like to work hard, either physically or metaphysically, yet have seen someone else demonstrate good results when we did not. Perhaps that someone seemed to us to even be off in the "far country."

When it appears that others near you get the results you desire, it is an indication that your own good is on the way and getting very near. So there is never any need to envy anyone else their good. Just by relaxing and becoming more joyous, you open the way to receive your desires. "LOVE ENVIETH NOT. THE PROSPERING TRUTH HAS SET ME FREE TO PROSPER," is a powerful statement to use at such times.

You need not envy anyone else their good, since their good would not satisfy you anyway. Even if you momentarily demonstrated their good, it would be of no use to you. Instead, you would still have to demonstrate your own good according to your level of understanding and soul growth. As Dr. Emmet Fox has stressed, you can only demonstrate *on a permanent basis* that which is yours "by right of consciousness."[12]

A businesswoman from Washington wrote:

"A tragic, unhealthy love affair with a married man, plus

---

12. Emmett Fox, *The Ten Commandments* (New York, Harper & Row, 1953).

an abortion early this year, were the two worst exprience of my life. After the affair broke up, I began to turn to God again, and through my inspirational study, I was able to find the strength needed to go on.

"After my divorce three years ago, I managed to have affairs with the three loves of my teenage years. The *first* was a homosexual male, the *second* had been a drug addict, and the *third* was a man who had married someone else, instead of me, fifteen years ago.

"Through those illicit relationships, I learned these valuable lessons: (1) *You can't find your future in your past;* (2) *You can't find enduring satisfaction with a person who belongs to someone else.*

"Through my goofs, I also became aware of the incredible power of the mind. In the years of my own unhappy marriage, instead of using my mind power to try and solve or improve my unhappy relationship, I retreated into fantasies about all three of those former loves. And, lo and behold, my own marriage dissolved, and each old love again appeared in my life. I have now released all of the pain and heartaches I allowed myself to experience. I have released all three of those people to their own greater good elsewhere. Since doing this, I have literally become a 'new person.' For the first time, I have witnessed some profound happiness in my life, and some hope for the future."

RELEASE OF ENVY BROUGHT VAST IMPROVEMENT

A divorcee lamented what a bad life she had had, blaming it all on her former husband. Although she worked hard, she had an inadequate income, no social life, and a houseful of problem children. She lived a dismal existence.

Not only did she direct much condemnation toward her former husband, but also toward life in general. She seemed especially insensitive to the silent suffering and problems of others. In one instance she jealously said, "If only I had the good life that Professor Smith has. Along with a happy social life, he has a fine job and no family responsibilities. It must be wonderful."

A friend replied, "I am glad you think Professor Smith has no problems, and that his life is so carefree. But that is not the case. His parents died when he was young, and he raised six brothers and sisters alone. After he worked his way through college, he helped put each of his brothers and sisters through college. He still helps to support some members of his family. His life has hardly been a carefree one."

It was only after this self-centered woman began to stop envying the apparent blessings of others, and began to think more in terms of God's goodness in her own life, that things improved. Her daughters moved out and went to work. She developed a hobby into a thriving part-time business. She began to make new friends, and to expand her horizons in other ways. But *nothing happened as long as she sat in judgment on her own life, or silently envied the lives of those about her.*

IN CONCLUSION: THE PROSPERING, FREEING POWER OF FORGIVENESS

Just as the father had forgiven the prodigal son upon his return from the far country, so the eldest son needed to forgive both his father and younger brother. It was a big order because to all human appearances he had every right to forgive neither of them. However, it would be possible for him to practice forgiveness when he realized that *he was forgiving them for his own sake* far more than for their own.

Unforgiveness can rot your soul, destroy the cells of your

body, jam up your relationships, and stop the flow of prosperity in your financial affairs. *When you hold resentment toward another, you are bound to that person or condition by an emotional link that is stronger than steel. Forgiveness is the only way to dissolve that bondage and get free. You must forgive if you want to demonstrate over your difficulties and make any real progress in life.*

The word "forgive" simply means "to give up." Often the greatest way to forgive people is to give them up: first in your thinking, then from your life. *Setting others free means setting yourself free. The practice of forgiveness also sets free your good and brings it to you in countless ways.*

A businesswoman from Colorado wrote:

"Three years ago a friend gave me a copy of *The Dynamic Laws of Prosperity.* As I studied the chapter on forgiveness, miracles began to happen to me. I practiced forgiving my father. He quickly responded by giving me $300. Next, I released or 'gave up' my old clothes, and new ones quickly came. I released troublesome relationships, and got immediate deliverance from them. I clothed myself with the pure white Light of the Christ each morning before arising, and radiant health and new beauty enfolded me. *The practice of forgiveness and release has been the tool that unlocked many doors within my own consciousness as well as in the outer circumstances of my life.* Recently when my earthly father passed on, I inherited his thriving business. *How forgiveness has freed and prospered me!*"

Thus ends the most famous prosperity parable of all times. As you study this earthly story with a heavenly meaning, you will enjoy using "the dynamic laws of prosperity" it points out. That lady's last statement, "How forgiveness has freed and prospered me," might well be one of the basic success secrets we learn from the prodigal son's riches-to-rags-to-riches experience.

YOUR PERSONAL PROSPERITY PROMISE

I also invite you to meditate often upon that unlimited prosperity promise made to the older son by his father, "Son, thou art ever with me, and *all* that is mine is thine." As you claim this for your personal prosperity promise, declaring often: "ALL THAT IS THINE IS MINE," it can lead you into your own "rags-to-riches" experience!

SUMMARY

1. A "parable" is "an earthly story with a heavenly meaning," and the Prodigal Son parable is a riches-to-rags-to-riches story that teaches important prosperity principles.

2. The word "prodigal" means "to waste." This parable shows us how to stop wasting our substance through limited thinking, and how to return to the prosperity law of right use.

3. *The Prosperity Parable, Part One:* How to get out of the far country of limited thinking.

    a) When the younger son went off into the far country, his intention was a healthy one: to win success and to become financially independent of his family. But he had not yet developed the understanding to succeed on his own. He had not yet learned the true Source of his supply.

    b) The word "riotous" means "lacking in order and peace." No one gave to him in this state of mind, and he quickly came into a state of lack.

    c) There is a close relation between riotous living and want. Things can straighten out and become orderly when you dwell upon "divine order" and "peace," and establish them in your life.

d) When you are in the far country of lack, nothing works out until you first practice release of that which has become unproductive and unrewarding.

e) You can begin to again move toward God as the Source of your supply by getting into a consciousness of abundance and peace through: meditation, affirmation, inspirational study alone and with others; and by putting God first again financially. To do so can help you overcome any "famine" within or without.

4. *The Prosperity Parable, Part Two:* The lavish abundance that awaits you in the Father's house.

f) No matter what we have thought, said or done, the God of abundance and forgiveness still wishes to help and bless us.

g) The prodigal son proved that a rich, loving Father gives a feast to those who come to Him for guidance and supply.

h) You can return to the Father's house of lavish abundance through both your *inner* and *outer* actions. It pays to put God first *financially* as well as to put Him first in other phases of your life.

5. *The Prosperity Parable, Part Three:* The prospering power of joy and forgiveness.

i) Much that has passed for "religion" has been expressed in harsh, self-righteous, narrow attitudes, such as those displayed by the eldest son toward his prodigal brother.

j) If, like the elder son, you have become rigid, intolerant, or unaware of the suffering, grief and faults others are trying to overcome, your unmerciful attitudes can draw intolerable experiences to you again and again.

k) The solution is to relax more, and judge others less.

l) You can demonstrate through the prosperous attitudes of love and joy what you will never demonstrate through an overworked, critical state of mind.

m) When others near you get the results you desire, it is an indication that your own good is on the way.

n) To release envy and practice the prospering power of forgiveness can bring vast improvement quickly.

o) Dwelling often upon the Father's promise to the older son can lead you to your own "rags-to-riches" experience: "ALL THAT IS MINE IS THINE." You can personalize it by declaring, "ALL THAT IS THINE IS MINE."

THE PROSPEROUS MITE

ONE OF THE WORLD'S MIGHTIEST
FINANCIAL TRANSACTIONS!

— Chapter 9 —

In a book about the world's greatest millionaire, do you wonder why the author devotes an entire chapter to the subject of a "mite"? Because that is how it all begins: with the way one thinks about, handles, and uses prosperity in modest amounts. *The road to permanent, enduring riches begins with the mite.* It is like the manna in the wilderness that multiplied for the Hebrews when it was appreciated and used rightly on a daily basis. (See Chapter 4, "How to Gather Your Prosperous Manna," in my book, *The Millionaire Moses.*)

The story of the prosperous mite is described in only four short verses:

"And he sat down over against the treasury, and beheld how the multitude cast money into the treasury; and many that were rich cast in much.

"And there came a poor widow, and she cast in two mites, which make a farthing.

"And he called unto him his disciples, and said unto them. Verily I say unto you, this poor widow cast in more than all they that are casting into the treasury.

"For they all did cast in of their superfluity; but she of her want did cast in all that she had, even all her living." (Mark 12:41–44; also see Luke 21:1–4)

In the past, you may have disregarded the importance of this familiar old story. You may have felt it was tinged with poverty. Yet closer observation reveals that the fame of this incident spread far and wide over the centuries because *its message was not one of poverty, but one that is filled with prosperity—for you!* Yes, it has rightly been described as "one of the world's mightiest financial transactions!"

HOW SUPPLY CAN BE MADE TO INCREASE

It is significant that *just before Jesus' crucifixion—during Holy Week or Passion Week—he thought about prosperity and taught a simple, but powerful prosperity lesson.*

On his last visit to the Temple during Holy Week, Jesus sat among the alms boxes over against the treasury where he watched people make their contributions to the Temple. A "treasury" was a hall where voluntary offerings were received for the church. These offerings were placed in spout-shaped receptacles which had openings set in the outer wall of the sacred edifice at the visitors' entrance. Such offerings were purely voluntary, given over and above the required tithes. Like most voluntary offerings, they were not in large amounts.

And what a scene it was as Jesus observed a small woman in rags, with trembling hands, put two mites into one of the receptacles. That she made no effort to conceal the amount indicates that this widow was not ashamed of her small gift. As they were cast in, her two copper coins made a loud clanging of metal on metal. From a monetary standpoint, her two mites were almost worthless, because they were worth exactly two cents. Yet those two copper coins—the smallest in circulation—were actually big business. Jesus was so touched by this widow's brave offering that he called his disciples' attention to it. Out of all who contributed that day, only this one widow stirred and moved Jesus to exclamation.

As a rule, giving in Biblical times was done unobtrusively, not to be seen of men. However, *a person who is in a state of lack must go the second mile to get out of that state of lack. He must do more than the average person in order to prosper.* When she dramatically shared her two mites, this fearless widow was going all the way, that second mile, in an effort to activate her prosperity. She knew that *supply can be made to increase through sharing.*

When you pray to receive God's blessings, you must then be willing to share what He has already entrusted to you. By doing so, you show that you are capable of handling more, and you make yourself receptive to more of God's unlimited supply. However, if you do not share of what you already have, God will not do for you what you have been unwilling to do for Him, or for others.

THE WIDOW WITH THE
PROSPERITY CONSCIOUSNESS

Because she feels deprived of something, a "widow" symbolizes a belief in lack. She feels separated from her good. This was especially true in Jesus' time when a widow had no rights. She was denied the right to buy, sell, or own property. Should a husband die leaving no male heir, his property automatically went—not to his widow—but to his nearest male relative. In some instances, a widow was allowed to become the custodian of property on condition that a male guardian transact the business for her. In any event, many a widow got "ripped off" after her husband's death by those to whom she was forced to entrust her financial assets.

It is still true today that a "widow" is one who usually feels bereft of worldly protection and power. Having been widowed twice early in my life, I know some of the devastating feelings of lack and limitation one can experience under such circumstances, not only financially, but also emotionally.

This was no ordinary widow. It is true that she was in a state of lack and separated from her supply. But through her rather drastic act of giving away her last two mites, this dauntless woman was trying to overcome that belief in lack, and the poverty-stricken results that belief had caused in her life. Through this fearless act of giving, she was trying to develop a prosperity consciousness that would provide her with the divine protection and power she had previously lacked, so that she could rise out of limitation into abundance on all levels of life.

DO SOMETHING DRASTIC AND PROSPER

Most of us get into a "widow state of mind" at some point in our lives. Many of us are still trying to rise out of that belief in lack which the widow symbolized: (1) a feeling of being separated from our good, or (2) a feeling of being without worldly protection and power.

When you feel that you are in a state of lack and separated from your good, like this widow you need to do something drastic—first in your thinking, then in your actions—in order to rise out of that state of limitation.

This poor widow, who needed to buy bread, decided instead to put God first financially by giving away her last two cents to His work. What she gave left her in need of even the barest necessities of life. By all human calculations, the average person would have counted her conduct the height of folly, absurdity and extravagance. Yet Jesus considered hers not a foolish act, but quite the reverse. He called his disciples to him and said, "This poor widow cast in more than all they that are casting into the treasury. For they all did cast in of their superfluity; but she of her want did cast in all that she had, even all her living." (Mark 12:43-44)

We have often thought of a mite as a small amount worth practically nothing. Yet, in this instance, the mite was a very prosperous gift because it was her *all*. Why would she do such a drastic thing as to give away her last two cents? Because *she knew that giving expands us; that giving opens us up to receive more. Since she needed to expand her life in a big way she gave in a big way: all she had.*

The Persian philosopher, Kahlil Gibran, explained in his book, *The Prophet:*

> "There are those who give little of the much which they have. They give it for recognition and their hidden desire makes their gifts unwholesome. And there are those who have little and give it all. These are the believers in life and the bounty of life, and their coffer is never empty. . . *It is well to give when asked, but it is better to give unasked, through understanding. . . To withhold is to perish.* "[1]

---

1. Gibran, *The Prophet,* pp. 23, 24, 25.

THE MODERN WIDOW WHO DID
SOMETHING DRASTIC AND PROSPERED

On her way to lunch, Lucy, a modern-day widow, stepped into a church to pray. She was very unhappy and discouraged for she was working hard to pay off a debt of long standing, and it seemed as if she would never accomplish this. During her prayer time in church, she asked God to help her, and she soon felt a sense of peace and release from her worries. As she left the church, she felt guided to empty her purse into the "God box" she found there. A feeling of joy welled up within her as she declared, "I GIVE OF WHAT I HAVE LOVINGLY AND LAVISHLY."

Back on the street, Lucy realized that she had given away her last cent, and had no money left for lunch. At first she was concerned. Then she thought, "It won't hurt me to go without lunch today. I have been planning to diet and exercise for a long time, so this is my opportunity." Instead of sitting and eating all during the lunch hour, she walked, fasted, and quietly praised God for the opportunity. She soon realized she had never felt so happy and free.

When she returned to the office, her fellow workers commented on her uplifted, glowing appearance. She decided to make it a habit several days a week to give her lunch money to God's work and to fast. "GENEROUSLY I GIVE, AND RICHLY I RECEIVE," was her daily affirmation. In a short time she looked better as she lost weight and her health improved. Her mind became clearer, her work more efficient, and her attitude changed so much that she soon became the most popular girl in the firm.

As a result of these events, she was promoted several times within the next year. Her debts were all paid and she even had money in the bank toward a long-dreamed-of vacation trip. The vast improvement in her life had begun with that first act of giving her "mite." Not only was she rewarded with material blessings, but her acts of giving made her happier within herself. This modern-day widow proved that *the act of giving was a freeing act to the mind. Her generosity also led to growth and expansion on all levels of her life.*[2]

WHY THE WIDOW WAS ONE OF THE
GREAT PERSONAGES OF HER TIME

It is significant that the widow at the Temple was considered one of the greatest personages to be found in both of the Gospels according to Mark and Luke; and that Jesus made such a fuss over her actions. The word "poor" comes from a Greek root that suggests "one who has to labor hard for a living." Even in her poverty, this widow gave everything she had. Hers was a gift of adventurous faith for she gave "out of a deficit"—not from a surplus. *The gift that counts is the gift which costs!*

Many rich persons may have cast much into the receptacles at the Temple that day, and Jesus found no fault with their giving. However, they cast in of their abundance. What they gave they could easily spare, feeling no financial inconvenience. What you have left *after* you cast into God's treasury denotes the importance of your gift—whether you give out of your faith, or out of an abundance you would never miss.

In this instance, the rich were merely drawing on what remained to them as a surplus—the "over and above"—after

---

2. This experience first appeared, entitled "The Magic of Giving," in the July 8, 1965 issue of *Weekly Unity*. It was written by my good friend, Countess Viola Lukawiecki, and is used here by permission of the author, and Unity School of Christianity.

all their own needs, and probably most of their desires, had been met. Theirs was ''conscience money'' or giving ''what was expected.'' Giving of such a surplus is not missed. Casting it into the treasury costs nothing. The rich are often inclined to give to God's work only *after* all of their obligations have been met, rather than putting Him first financially *before* everything else, whereas, the widow gave *first* of all she had to God's work. She gave everything she could lay her hands on.

People have sometimes been ''turned off'' by this famous old story, because they thought Jesus expected them to give away everything they had to their church, thereby hoping to be prospered in return. But this is not what Jesus meant to imply. Instead, he was trying to emphasize the importance of giving initially out of your sense of need rather than from a sense of abundance, because it is that which is given in faith that prospers you. Your act of faith moves on the rich substance of the universe, causing it to fill your life to overflowing with its abundant blessings.

When you put God first—and not last—financially, your consciousness expands and becomes a magnet for attracting additional bounty. Yes, *the gift that counts is the gift which costs*—especially in your initial acts of spiritual giving, when you are just beginning to recognize God as the Source of your supply. *As you continue in the practice of consistent sharing, you will grow out of giving from a sense of need, and you will give from a consciousness of grateful abundance.* Such is the expanding power of the prosperity law of giving.

HOW TO OBTAIN SPECIAL BLESSINGS

The word ''tithe'' means ''tenth,'' and the ancients felt that ''ten'' was the magic number of increase.'' They freely gave the tenth in happy expectation of lavish increase. *The age-old practice of sharing ten percent of* all *one receives with God's work and workers still has an unprecedented prospering power— unequalled by any other method!*

"Giving" was a household word in Biblical times. The four Gospels are filled with Jesus' promises on the subject. His most famous prosperity promise was very definite:

> "Give and it shall be given unto you: good measure, pressed down, shaken together, and running over, shall they give into your bosom. For with what measure ye mete it shall be measured to you again." (Luke 6:38)

In Jesus' time, just as in the Old Testament era, a faithful Jew continued to give three tithes (the Levites' tithe, the festival tithe, and the charity tithe) plus many other offerings, all of which added up to between one-third and one-fourth of his income. (See Chapters 3 and 6 in *The Millionaires of Genesis* and Chapter 7 in *The Millionaire Moses*.) *None appeared before God empty-handed.*

During the New Testament era, the worldwide practice was still prevalent from Old Testament times, of paying vows or "faith offerings" *before* meeting any severe challenge. Also, "thank offerings" were given *after* victorious results had been obtained. (See Chapter 8 in *The Millionaire Moses*.) There was also the practice of paying tithes and offerings in the face of disease, in the belief that giving had healing power, and could even save one from death. Over and over, it had proved to be so. (See Chapter 13 in *The Dynamic Laws of Healing*.) In Old Testament times, the spoils of war had also been considered holy unto Jehovah —the same as a tithe offering. To have withheld such a tithe for one's personal use would have been punishable by death. (See Chapter 6 in *The Millionaire Joshua*.) Instead, they were ceremoniously presented to the priests. This form of giving also carried over into the New Testament as was later evidenced by the early Christians. (Acts 5:1-11)

When the widow dramatically gave her last two mites, she shared the popular Biblical belief that *the giving of tithes and offerings to God's work and workers was a means of obtaining special blessings.*

A person is usually in financial straits when he begins to tithe. Like the widow, by all human standards he cannot afford to share. His tithe of ten percent of his income to God's work is an act of faith, given out of his need and not out of any sense of abundance. Yet this method of systematic sharing ten percent of *all* one receives with God's work—beginning when one is in financial straits—has a mighty prospering power! Yes, *tithing is an act of faith that helps one to grow out of longtime financial limitation into a happy, prosperous way of life.*

A lady in England wrote:

"I have a ninety-four year old mother for whom I must care, so I cannot do a lot of work to earn a living. In spite of this, *I find I am given all I need as I give to God.* And I never miss my gifts to Him."

A MODERN BUSINESSMAN'S
PROSPERITY SECRET

A successful California businessman wrote:

"Enclosed is my biggest tithe check to date. This tithe is from the sale of some property. I bought a dilapidated house two years ago for $18,000, worked hard to make it a dream house, and just sold it for $40,000! I netted a profit of $22,765.29 on it. What a joy it is to give thanks to God through sharing the tenth from this magnificent increase.

"Also noteworthy is the fact that I put this property on the market with only one realtor, permitting no multiple listings, or 'for sale' signs out front. The realtor sold the house to a lovely couple on his first showing—*for cash!*

"When I first started studying and applying prosperous thinking almost twenty years ago, I never dreamed I would someday be able to joyously and freely tithe on a profit of more than $22,000 in one transaction alone. As I recall, my first tithe check was for only $10, and the giving of that amount was a big step for me to take in consciousness. I have shared consistently of my tithes since that time, and they have increased mightily over the years. *It is amazing to observe the inner and outer growth that has taken place in my life since I began a program of consistent sharing.*"

HOW JESUS TRIED TO PROSPER THE POOR

People sometimes say, "I do not tithe because I am 'a new Testament Christian' and neither Jesus or Paul emphasized tithing." The reason they did not stress tithing was because it has been a required Temple practice since ancient times. Jesus and Paul were both tithers. When Christianity appeared in Palestine, tithe-paying was inseparably intertwined with almost every important act in the daily life of a religious Jew.

Jesus was born at a time, in a country, and into a devout Jewish family where the law of tithing was strictly observed. Jesus' enemies, who monitored his behavior in an effort to find fault, never accused him of not paying tithes or other ecclesiastical dues. Yes, both Jesus and Paul grew up as tithe-payers.

Jesus proclaimed at the outset of his ministry that he came not to destroy the law, but to fulfill it. Although Jesus seemed to criticize the Pharisees for many things, he was actually criticizing them in matters of conduct rather than in principle. The Pharisee said, "I give tithes of all that I get." (Luke 18:12) Jesus said, "Woe unto you scribes and Pharisees, hypocrites! For ye pay tithes of mint, anise, and cummin, and have left undone the weightier matters of law, justice, mercy and faith." (Matthew 23:23) Yet Jesus did not disapprove of their tithing. Far from it, he expressed approval, "These ought ye to have done." (Matthew 23:23) He not only expressed approval of the payment of tithes and offerings, which amounted to between one-third and one-fourth of a Pharisee's income, but he told his own disciples that their righteousness ought to exceed that of the Pharisees.

In modern times, there may have been some confusion about the tithing practices of Jesus' time because of the political situation of that era. Whereas the Jews of the Old Testament had been ruled by Jewish monarchs and so were required to pay tithes—in New Testament times, the political situation was different: The Jews were then under Roman rule. Although tithe-paying was a well-known practice to the Roman government, they did not require the Jews to tithe. Because of this, many of the less-than-devout Jews had become lax in their observance of tithe-paying and other religious duties.

However, according to Jewish law, and from a religious standpoint, a devout Jew in Jesus' time was still required to tithe three-tenths as in the time of Moses; as well as to share many other offerings—giving between one-fourth and one-third of his total income to God's work and workers. Thus, tithe-paying was still a general practice among the mass of devout Jews.

In Jerusalem the Hebrews tithed to the Temple. But in Galilee, where a number of Jesus' followers were far away from the influence of Temple practice, many had stopped the practice of tithing, or of systematic religious giving. This is why so many of Jesus' parables, sayings and teachings, delivered in Galilee, emphasized the importance of giving. *He was trying to lead the poor of his time back to the prospering power of systematic religious giving.* Jesus knew that *throughout Hebrew history, when they had given not the last and the least, but the first and the best to God's work, their giving had made them rich!* This is why he made so many promises concerning the importance of giving throughout the four Gospels.

THE EARLY CHRISTIANS' SECRET FOR THEIR VAST SUCCESS

Later, the early Christians certainly did not stint in their giving. Tithing was practiced in full force by tens of thousands of Christ's early followers, and the practice continued for many years.

Soon after Jesus' resurrection, on the day of Pentecost, the early Christians were so excited about their new religion that they gave not merely one- or more-tenths of their income and property, but during that exciting period, each one gave *all* he had. (Acts 2:44,45) Because of the wholesale giving of the early Christians, officers had to be appointed to handle the vast gifts received by the early church.

Just as with the Hebrews of the Old Testament, so with the early Christians: *They knew that tithing was the best investment they could ever make because tithing put them in touch with the ceaseless flow of universal supply. Every phase of their lives reflected the wealth that tithing—and their other acts of generous giving—could bring. Just as in Old Testament times, the early Christians never complained about their giving. They never said it was a burdensome or oppressive practice to give so much. Throughout the Acts of the*

Apostles, as well as in the four Gospels, no request was ever made to lessen or to repeal the practice of tithe-giving. The practice of giving vast amounts of one's income was never rescinded.

Instead, when giving was at its height among the early Christians throughout Palestine (which included Judea, Galilee, and Samaria), their payment of tithes and offerings brought peace and plenty over and over. The act of tithing was believed to be so powerful that it could purge one of sin, sickness and even deliver from death, whereas to withhold tithes was counted as robbery (the same as in Old Testament times). Giving was considered to be a method for getting one's prayers answered. The early Christians looked upon right giving as an important part of right living, and the more closely the tithing law was kept, the more prosperous they became!

Tithing and systematic giving have been considered a *required* part of spiritual worship since ancient times. Even primitive man practiced it. *The reason that tithing and systematic giving has always been a first requirement for spiritual growth is because the act of systematically putting God first financially opens you up to grow, expand and to receive spiritually.*

The fantastic success power that tithing can bring into one's life is shown in the history of the early Christians. *The fast rise of the early Christian church can be traced to the abundant tithes and offerings of the faithful that made it possible to spread the Gospel so quickly throughout the ancient world!* Thus, systematic giving and tithing played an important role—not only in Jesus' time, but the practice contributed greatly to the vast success of the early Christian church throughout the ancient world. *The act of putting God first financially through tithing still plays an important part in the success of those who practice it to this day; and of churches which still teach this proven ancient practice.* In this realization lies one of the most powerful prosperity teachings of Jesus, as handed down to him from the high-powered spiritual leaders of the Old Testament!

HOW OTHERS HAVE PROSPERED THROUGH
USING THIS ANCIENT SUCCESS PRINCIPLE

A BUSINESSWOMAN IN ILLINOIS RETIRED AT 55: *"I began the practice of regular tithing many years ago, and I have not had an empty wallet since!* My savings have increased, and I have even been able to retire at the age of 55—by choice—and not by necessity."

WHY A TEXAS BUSINESSWOMAN'S SUPPLY WAS CUT OFF: "I decided to experiment with tithing to see if it really works. After having tithed for a long time, my experiment was to stop tithing in order to compare the results. As soon as I stopped tithing, we had one misfortune after another: I lost my job, my daughter was in a car accident, our main water line broke, and our hot water heater went out. The list of problems was endless.

"As soon as I decided I had 'had enough,' and began to put God first financially again, good things started to happen. Almost before I could get that first tithe check in the mail, I was reinstated to my former job with an increased salary! My daughter also found a good job. Many other happy things have occurred. Prosperity is on its way to our house again. This experiment proved to me that *when you delay your giving, you delay your receiving, because the return waits upon you.* Tithing really works when applied with love."

HOW A BLESSED PENNY
MULTIPLIED TO BECOME MILLIONS

Many theologians have emphasized the fact that the widow in the Temple gave all she had to the church, period. Although her motive for giving was important, it is also important to note the *attitude* in which she gave her last two cents.

From a human standpoint, this widow might have reasoned, "What difference can my two cents make? So small a gift will count for nothing. Let those give far more who can afford it. I haven't a penny to spare."

Instead, we have every right to believe that this widow first blessed her last two cents as she fearlessly gave them away. The act of blessing was practiced in Biblical times, and the word "bless" means "to make happy and prosperous." (See Chapter 2 in my book, *The Prosperity Secrets of the Ages*) Whereas what you curse or condemn dissipates, your blessed money can multiply because, as the ancients knew, what you bless increases.

It seems amazing now that the building program of the nondenominational Unity movement was started with only a blessed penny. The people who gave that single penny to Charles Fillmore in 1902 considered their insignificant gift to be a joke. But Mr. Fillmore took their one-cent gift seriously as he graciously blessed it. He knew that a mere penny had multiplying power when it was blessed. By the end of 1903, that blessed penny had grown to only twenty-five cents in the building fund. Yet by 1905, it had multiplied to $601. In 1906, the building program of Unity Society was launched with that humble amount applied toward the purchase of buildings located on Tracey Avenue in Kansas City, Missouri, which housed both Unity School and Unity Temple. The Unity headquarters remained at that location, grew and prospered until Unity School was finally moved to a thirteen-hundred acre tract known today as Unity Village. That incorporated village is now worth so many millions of dollars that appraisers have been unable to estimate its true value. The prestigious Unity Temple is now located on beautiful Country Club Plaza in Kansas City. Yet both of these impressive organizations began originally with a single penny that was blessed in 1902!

What is equally as interesting is that over the years the nondenominational Unity work has been sustained and prospered, not so much by large gifts, as by the humble offerings of the blessed pennies, dollars, five, ten, twenty, fifty, and hundred dollar offerings that have been gratefully shared by those people who have been helped by Unity's positive thinking outlook on life. When a rumor circulated in 1926 that Unity School had been given three million dollars, Charles Fillmore explained (in the Unity publications) that it was not so. He said the most Unity School had been given up to that time in a lump sum was $1,500. So the prosperous mite, in the form of blessed tithes and the offerings of ordinary people, have carried the nondenominational work of Unity forward over the years.

Not only is this true of Unity School, but it is true of most churches and religious organizations. One churchman said, "How great and many have been the gifts which have come out of poverty. The support of the church throughout the world has come far more from the two coppers of the poor and working class than from the relatively few large gifts given only spasmodically by the rich."

From almost twenty-five years' experience as a minister who has founded three churches from "financial scratch," without financial underwriting from *any* organization, I can add an emphatic "Amen" to that churchman's comments. (The establishment of new Unity churches is not financially underwritten by the Unity movement. Each church is considered a separate entity and must make its own way financially.) *Often churchmen have been dazzled by the one-time or spasmodic gifts of the rich. Yet many a poor widow, obliged to work long and hard for a mere pittance, has given far more—and far more consistently in proportion!*

HOW YOUR MONEY CAN DO FAR MORE
FOR YOU THAN YOU THOUGHT POSSIBLE

The prosperity law is that *it is better to give small gifts consistently than to wait hoping to be able to give large gifts spasmodically. You can estimate what you would give when you have much by what you give when you have little.* So never underestimate the true value of a gift you personally consider to be small, especially if you bless it.

The simple act of blessing your money stamps it with increased value on all levels of life. A dollar which has been blessed is capable of bringing you (and the recipient of it) much greater good than the dollar which has not been blessed.

As you bless the money that you give away, you will discover that *the money that comes to you in return will do many things for you which you would not have dreamed it could.* When the word of blessing is placed upon tangible objects, those objects are then surrounded with the quickening power of divine substance, causing that substance to work its multiplying power for good through every phase of your life.

I suspect this is what that humble, but illumined, widow may have said: "A SIMPLE WORD OF BLESSING POURED OUT UPON WHAT I HAVE, OR UPON WHAT I CAN CONCEIVE OF AS POSSIBLE FOR ME AS A CHILD OF GOD, NOW RELEASES THE SUPERABUNDANT SUBSTANCE OF THE UNIVERSE TO ME, AND THROUGH ME, IN STREAMS OF PLENTY."

Your money will do far more for you than you thought possible when you: (1) bless the good you have; (2) bless the good you want or expect to have. (See Chapter 8 in *The Millionaires of Genesis.*) *When you think of something you need, bless that need. Your act of blessing will open the way for that need to be met.*

HOW A YOUNG GIRL FOUND
WORK AND PROSPERED MIGHTILY

There once was a young girl who was without employment, funds, or a home. She had looked for work for many days to no avail. Finally, in desperation, she prayed one night asking God to forgive her of past mistakes by giving her a chance. She asked Him to lead her to the right job, and to please do it soon. That very evening a neighbor told her about another neighbor who was looking for a secretary. That same night she visited the second neighbor, and was hired on the spot!

Her new boss was a student of prosperous thinking who told her that health and prosperity were her divine right. She decided to brighten up her office, and to make it look more prosperous. She reasoned that a more cheerful office would not only make her feel happier, but it would attract more business to her employer. This, in turn, could mean more income to the business, and a larger salary for her.

Her boss knew the power of blessing what he had and of blessing what he wanted to have. He brought some plants into the office one day and informed his secretary that if she would make a practice of regularly blessing those plants, they would soon produce an abundance of beautiful blossoms.

As predicted, they soon produced such colorful flowers that she called them her "prosperity blossoms." People even came in off the street to inquire about where they could buy such plants. The secretary began to bless God as the Source of her abundant prosperity. She blessed the increased abundance she felt should be hers. She reasoned that since universal abundance was omnipresent, she did not have to limit her financial income to her pay envelope.

She began to also bless everything and everybody that passed through her life.

The blessing method increased her good in several ways:(1) She gained in health until she looked like a different girl from the one that was originally hired; (2) A new sense of happiness and well-being welled up from deep within her consciousness; (3) A prominent merchant contacted her employer with the request that she be allowed to keep his books. This meant two pay envelopes instead of one! (4) In response to the many requests for her beautiful plants, she also started a little florist business on a part-time basis, and her abundance increased mightily. She soon had more work than she could handle, so she had to hire an assistant!

But *all this abundance came only after she had blessed what was on hand, and had given thanks for the increased supply she had desired, even before it appeared.* She learned to bless and give thanks for every penny, dime, and dollar that passed through her hands. As she continued to use the power of blessing in every phase of her life, this previously shy young girl, who had been without a job, funds or home, grew into an unusually successful businesswoman. She now has such an abundance of funds that she has become independently wealthy. She and her husband own one of the finest estate-homes in their city! She has also taught all of her employees, including her staff of household servants, how they can prosper themselves and others through the act of blessing.

THE PROSPERING POWER OF EXPECTATION

The widow with the prosperous mite doubtless knew about the prospering power of expectation, too. *When you give out, be sure that you expect increased supply to return to you—not increased lack—since what you expect comes back.*

There once was a farmer who for years thought the world was not giving him a square deal. He expected hard times, disappointment, and failure. He anticipated that unpleasant things would happen to him, and happen they did! He said his livestock would never do well, so a horse met with an accident, and a fine colt died. Another horse, which he had planned to exhibit at the county fair, broke its hip. *He went through life experiencing one disappointment after another, because he expected it.*

But this man had a neighbor who felt he would succeed in a perfectly natural way. The result was that the neighbor was blessed with a fine family and many true friends. His crops prospered, his cattle thrived, everything came his way. He expected all these blessings, and they appeared in his life over and over.

The widow of old seemed to know about the prospering power of expectation as she gave away her last two cents. She gave fearlessly and freely, expecting increased supply, because she knew that giving is the first step in receiving.

DO NOT HURRY PAST YOUR SUPPLY

We cannot expect in just a few minutes of occasional reading, or by attendance at an occasional prosperity lecture, to develop a full consciousness of supply. Instead we need to remind ourselves daily of the great prosperity laws of life, because repetition is the mother of wisdom.

A builder does not erect a beautiful building without first providing cross-braces to hold each wall. Stone by stone each wall is then built slowly. We build a prosperity consciousness the same way: by working with the prosperity law daily, proving it step by step. *People are often in too big a hurry. They are not willing to do the simple, ordinary things that must be done to develop an understanding of supply.*

Where the act of giving is concerned, many people are like the little boy in Sunday School. When the offering plate was passed, this youngster did not put his money in the plate. Realizing the omission, his Sunday School teacher said, "Son, the money that goes into this plate is an offering to God."

"In that case, I'll give it to Him myself," the boy quickly replied.

We might regard him as a "Sunday School dropout." Well, there are a lot of "prosperity dropouts," too, who are not willing to do the simple, ordinary things that must be done in faith on a day-to-day basis in order to develop an enduring consciousness of supply.

Not so with the widow. She gave freely and boldly because she knew that by giving in a certain attitude of mind, those two cents would come back to her greatly increased. There is a saying, "Poor men have poor ways." This widow was trying to overcome those poor ways that had separated her from her good. She had learned that giving boldly, fearlessly, and freely would help her to overcome such poor ways. As she gave her two mites, her prayer might have been, "ALL THE WEALTH THAT THE UNIVERSE HAS FOR ME NOW COMES TO ME SPEEDILY, RICHLY, FREELY."

Many people feel that they can bypass the law of giving and receiving. In the process, what they bypass is their good. A mother heard her baby crying. Rather crossly, she said to the nursemaid, "Haven't I told you to let my baby have what he wants?"

"Yes, ma'am," replied the nursemaid. "I followed your instructions. There was a wasp in the window. The baby wanted it, and I gave it to him. That's why he's crying."

If you are not willing to discipline your thoughts, feelings and actions to follow the prosperity law, you, too, may get stung—by the wasp of lack.

THE INVALUABLE PROSPERITY
LESSON HE LEARNED EARLY

The widow had learned that *you must share your supply if you wish to insure continuation of your supply.* A successful businesswoman said, "I have developed a marvelous prosperity formula. When anything negative happens to me, I know I have not been giving enough, so I ask myself, 'What can I give?' and I give it. I have found that I always have something to give. This prosperity practice has made me financially independent." You, too, must share your supply if you wish continuation of your supply, and *you always have something to give!*

Dr. Ernest Wilson once described an invaluable prosperity lesson he learned early in his career. He bought a fine new car. An expensive wire wheel and tire were soon stolen from it, and he could not understand why. Then a second spare wheel and tire were stolen. He first wondered if he should have insured the car. He next wondered if he should have had stronger locks placed on it. He finally sought the advice of a wise friend who said, "If some good is taken forcibly out of your life, that indicates that you are receiving faster than you are giving. The channel has gotten clogged somewhere. What have you withheld that you should have given?"

Dr. Wilson concluded, "That experience helped to awaken in me a new consciousness of giving. I have made sure that I have given generously ever since, and nothing else has ever been forcibly taken from me."

If some unpleasant experience comes into your life, ask yourself what you have been withholding that you should have given. Then get busy sharing it. Yes, *not your possessions, but your attitude toward your possessions and the way you use them, makes you rich or poor.* In the process, your attitude attracts either enriching or depleting experiences to you.

WHEN THEY USED WHAT THEY
ALREADY HAD, THEY BECAME MILLIONAIRES

The widow knew that *when you share what you already have, your prosperity begins.* In most of the prosperity stories in the Bible, the user started with what he had. As he shared his good, it multiplied. As stated in Chapter 6, Jesus started with only five loaves and two fishes. Yet when he blessed and shared them, they multiplied to feed a multitude with an abundance left over. As the widow in Elisha's time started pouring forth the oil from her pot, it multiplied, paid all her debts, and provided her with an income for life. What an annuity that pot of oil proved to be for her—but only *after* she began to share it! (II Kings 4:1-7) Elijah was fed at Zarephath in a similar way. (I Kings 17:8-16) Yes, when you share what you already have, your prosperity begins.

A lady in financial difficulties developed her talent for making jam. From this talent she built up a thriving business. A firm recently paid her a vast sum of money for her jam recipes, as well as for her professional name and reputation. After she used and shared that simple jam recipe, it brought her millions.

When you pray for supply, God usually asks, "What talent, idea or tangible thing do you have that you can share with others? Share it and your prosperity will begin."

A great showman decided to make a fresh start after he had lost everything. He wanted to take over a business, but lacked the money with which to purchase it. The owner of the business asked the showman if he had any collateral, such as real estate. He suddenly remembered that he *did* own what he considered to be an insignificant strip of swampy land in Florida, which had been his since boyhood. He was able to use that strip of swampland as financial collateral. So he bought the desired business, and built up what became known as "the greatest show on earth." What he had considered worthless swampland on the rich Florida coast is today worth millions! This man's popular business is worth many millions more. *When, in faith, you use what you already have, your good multiplies.*

HOW A GOLD NUGGET MANIFESTED

The widow knew that *no place is barren of supply; that right where you are, you can be prospered.* A man bought an old carpenter's tool chest. It had four feet with knobs, one at each corner of the chest. After the man had owned the chest for some time, he decided to move it. In the process, one of the knobbed feet was knocked off and he noticed that this knobbed foot was hollow. When he inspected the other three knobs, he discovered that each one was hollow, too. In one of those hollow knobs he found a nugget of gold and sold it for hundreds of dollars!

There is no numbering of the avenues through which supply can come to you. No place is barren of good, and your resource is as far-reaching as the universe.

HOW A $100 GIFT BROUGHT
A $1,000 RETURN

Stop trying to figure out or reason through how increased good can come to you. Your supply is omnipresent. It is everywhere. Declare often: "MY SUPPLY COMES FROM THE INFINITE."

The widow knew that the way to overcome the belief in lack was to keep her supply in circulation by sending out. Ask yourself often, "How can I get my supply into circulation? What do I have that I can send out?" You must do something in faith to move the rich substance of the universe into activity. As you fearlessly send out, you can then expect replenishment.

A lady recently said, "I thought if I studied and learned more about prosperous thinking, and then earned more, *later* I could give. But the moment I reversed this process and began to give first of what I already had, the way to all of life's blessings opened to me. My mistake had been to think I had to receive *before* I could give."

The prosperity law of sharing *first* works to prosper organizations as well as individuals. A minister related how his church had been having financial difficulties, so he convinced the trustees that the church should tithe to its spiritual headquarters, giving a "tithe of the tithe" (known in Old Testament times as a "heave offering") to the mother church with which it was affiliated. Soon after his church had mailed out their first tithe check of $100, a lady walked in and gave that same church a check for $1,000. But nothing happened until that organization had given *first*!

TO OVERCOME THE CONSCIOUSNESS OF LACK:
SEND OUT IN FAITH, THEN EXPECT REPLENISHMENT

The widow knew that the way to overcome lack was to keep supply in circulation by sending out or giving *first*. When you put God first financially, that opens the way for Him to put you and your business affairs first financially.

You can estimate what you would do with much by what you do with little. If you feel you cannot share, you are poor in mind and you will remain poor financially. Furthermore, if you say you are too poor to share now, you will find other reasons for not sharing if and when your supply ever becomes greater (which is doubtful). A famous churchman recently said, "The person who goes through life doing nothing for others is doomed."

A couple had a bank account they had always called "the Lord's account." It contained several hundred dollars, and they realized they must get that supply into circulation. They did so by sharing it with the church of their choice where they had learned this prosperity principle. Soon afterwards, more than that amount came back to them in the form of a much larger income tax refund check than they had expected to receive. *The way to overcome lack is to keep supply in circulation. Send out in faith. Then expect replenishment, and it will come.*

GIVING THANKS IN ADVANCE
DRAWS HAPPY RESULTS TO YOU

One last way to overcome the consciousness of lack is that when you give in an *outer* way, then also give thanks in an *inner* way that you have already received, that you have your increased good *now*. *This mental agreement that it is already yours is the power back of all results.* The giving-thanks-in-advance attitude draws your good to you.

HOW A BUSINESSMAN IN MISSOURI SHARED IN AN INHERITANCE: "This is a happy letter. A few weeks ago, I sent an 'advance offering' in anticipation of increased prosperity. Sure enough, something beautiful happened. I was called long distance by a dear friend who needed my help with a tragic event in her life. I talked with her twice within a few days, and wrote her a letter.

"In due time she called to tell me she had received an inheritance and was sending me a portion of it—simply because I had helped her in a spiritual way through a very trying time! I am overwhelmed. She studies the Ponder books diligently and knows we must give to keep the channels to our good open and flowing. Of course, I plan to tithe from her prosperous gift in appreciation. But I have learned from this experience that there is prospering power in giving *first* in faith and thanksgiving."

When the enlightened widow of old gave her last two mites, she doubtless gave them in joy, thanking God that she had already received additional blessings; that she had her increased good *now*!

HOW A MUSIC TEACHER IN CALIFORNIA EXPERIENCED HER MOST ENJOYABLE VACATION: "The day we left on our vacation, I sent a small 'faith offering.' I know that's why we had the most enjoyable vacation my husband and I have ever experienced! I am still on Cloud Nine. I could enumerate a dozen things that took place which were unexpected and most enjoyable. I am now sending another 'faith offering' in appreciation not only for all the good that has come to us recently, but also in expectation of the new blessings that are on the way."

JESUS' LAST PROSPERITY LESSON
AT THE END OF HIS EARTH LIFE

This simple and beautiful "prosperous mite" incident, which occurred just prior to his crucifixion, sums up Jesus' prosperity philosophy at the end of his earth life. Again he was emphasizing: put God first financially. Do not depend upon persons, conditions or possessions for your good. This incident is a beautiful example of the spirit of the gospel message of "good news," and of Jesus' intention to form a generous spirit in his followers, one of large and noble generosity.

Of course, the "widow's mite" symbolizes more than a contribution of money. It includes the giving of our all: love, obedience to spiritual law, service to God, and to others in His name. In return, a rich and loving Father shares unstintedly with us on all levels of life.

As Jesus and his disciples left the Temple, they turned and gazed once more at all of its splendor. It was a magnificent structure, rebuilt by Herod, that radiated a lavish prosperity consciousness. The Temple had a number of beautiful gates: One was of solid brass; others were overlaid with gold and silver. The building had graceful, towering arches, blocks of marble, cloisters, and stately pillars. It occupied 35 acres, was one of the wonders of the ancient world, and an appropriate setting for Jesus' last prosperity parable at the end of his spectacular *earth* life.

Note: Dr. Wilson's experience given on page 250 was first related in an article entitled "How Much Shall I Give?" in Unity magazine, July, 1931.

A SPECIAL NOTE FROM THE AUTHOR

Through the generous outpouring of their tithes over the years, the readers of my books have helped me to financially establish three new churches—the most recent being a global ministry, the nondenominational *Unity Church Worldwide,* with headquarters in Palm Desert, California. Many thanks for your help in the past, and for all that you continue to share.

You are also invited to share your tithes with the churches of your choice—especially those which teach the truths stressed in this book. Such churches would include the metaphysical churches of Unity, Religious Science, Divine Science, Science of Mind, and other related churches, many of which are members of The International New Thought Movement. (For a list of such churches write The International New Thought Alliance, 7314 Stetson Drive, Scottsdale, Arizona, 85251.) Your support of such churches can help spread the prosperous Truth that mankind is now seeking in this New Age of metaphysical enlightenment.

SUMMARY

1. It is significant that just before Jesus' crucifixion, he thought about and taught a simple but powerful prosperity lesson.

2. The message of the widow's mite is not one of poverty, but one that is filled with prosperity—for you! One's success begins with the way one thinks about, handles

and uses prosperity in modest amounts. The road to permanent, enduring riches begins with the mite.

3. Most of us find ourselves in a "widow state of mind" at times, feeling separated from our good, bereft of worldly protection and power. Like the widow, we, too, must do something drastic, first in our thinking, then in our actions, in order to rise out of that limitation.

4. Through the drastic act of giving away her last two cents, this dauntless widow was attempting to overcome the belief in lack, and its results in her life. Through her fearless act of giving, she was trying to develop a prosperity consciousness that would provide her the protection and power she had previously lacked; a consciousness that would help her rise out of limitation into abundance.

5. The widow was considered one of the greatest personages of her time because she gave out of her need—not out of a sense of abundance, as did the wealthy. She knew it is that which is given in faith that prospers us.

6. She also knew that giving expands us; that giving opens us up to receive more. She needed to expand her life in a big way, so she gave in a big way *all* she had.

7. Giving was a household word in Biblical times. The word "tithe" meant "tenth," and the ancients felt that "ten was the magic number of increase." In Jesus' time, as in the Old Testament era, none appeared before God empty-handed, and a faithful Jew tithed.

8. Jesus was trying to lead the poor of his time back to the prospering power to be found in systematic religious giving. When you, too, practice consistent sharing, you grow out of giving from a sense of need into giving from a consciousness of grateful abundance.

9. Later, the fast rise of the early Christian church could be traced to the abundant tithes and offerings of the faithful, which made it possible to spread the Gospel quickly throughout the ancient world.

10. Often churchmen have been dazzled by the one-time or spasmodic gifts of the rich. Yet many a poor widow, obliged to work long and hard for a mere pittance, has given far more—and far more consistently—in proportion.

11. Of course, the "widow's mite" includes more than a contribution of money. It includes the giving of our love of Truth, obedience to spiritual law, service to God and man in His name.

12. It was appropriate that Jesus' last prosperity parable at the end of his *earth* life was given in the magnificent Temple, which radiated a consciousness of lavish abundance.

THE PROSPERITY LAW OF
THE RIGHT SIDE

FROM THE HUNGRY FISHERMEN
AND THE PROSPEROUS CHRIST

— Chapter 10 —

What you need to realize above all else is that a rich and loving Father has provided for the most minute needs of your *daily life.* If you lack anything, it is because you have not used your mind to make right contact with the realm of universal abundance, both within and all around you. Jesus' bountiful breakfast feast, which took place after his resurrection, shows you how to do this.

Yes, Jesus was so interested in prospering his followers that he even appeared to his disciples *after* his resurrection, and showed them how to turn their failure into success. *Thus Jesus both began and then ended his ministry with "fish miracles" of abundance.* (Luke 5:1-11; John 21:1-14)

As mentioned in Chapter One, Jesus' first *private* prosperity miracle occurred after Peter, James and John had fished all night without results. Jesus then manifested fish for them in such abundance that they had to ask fishermen in a second boat to help bring in the catch. Still their boats almost sank with the abundance! As a result of this *first* fish miracle, Peter, James and John were so impressed with Jesus' ability to demonstrate prosperity that they unhesitatingly left their boats—bulging with an abundance of fish— and became Jesus' first disciples. (Luke 5:1-11)

From the standpoint of practical mysticism, I find it intriguing that one of the *last* things the resurrected Jesus did before making his ascension into the universal ethers was to perform a final prosperity miracle. *Through these two fish miracles, performed at the beginning and end of his ministry, Jesus "sealed" his great contribution to mankind with abundance.*

Although John was considered the most spiritual of all the disciples, he was the only one to close his gospel with an account of Jesus' *last* fish miracle. John was a practical mystic who wished, in closing, to emphasize the prospering power that lies in the Name and Presence of Jesus Christ. A "mystic" is one who has a metaphysical thirst for Truth, and learns how to live from the inside out through the action of the mind. You, too, can become a "practical mystic" as you avail yourself of the prospering power to be found in the Name and Presence of Jesus Christ. The success formula related in this chapter shows you how.

As mentioned earlier, *Jesus did not despise either money or business, and he did not hesitate to use his deeper senses to promote earthly prosperity. He knew that no greater work could be done for the kingdom of heaven than to show people how to gain success in the business world through the use of spiritual methods.*

THE PROSPERITY MIRACLE
OF THE SECOND DRAUGHT

Jesus' *last* prosperity miracle is a dramatic story vividly told as it relates to the night's failure, the word from Jesus to lower the nets on the right side, and the astonishing haul.

Seven of the disciples had gathered at the Sea of Tiberias. Peter said to them, "I go a fishing." The other six disciples replied, "We will come with thee." (John 21:3) They entered a boat, went forth, fished all night, but caught nothing. When day was breaking, Jesus asked from the shore, "Have you anything to eat?" When they answered, "No," he instructed them, "Cast the net on the right side of the boat, and ye shall find some." (John 21:5-6)

When the hungry fishermen again cast their nets as instructed, they were not immediately able to draw in the multitude of fish! Later Jesus said, "Bring of the fish ye have now taken." (John 21:10) The net which they drew to land was now full of fish, one hundred and fifty-three in all. Jesus, whom they now recognized as the risen Christ, had already made a fire on the beach and had placed fish on the coals. He shared bread and the fish with them after their arrival.

STEPS THAT CAN LEAD
YOU TO THE RIGHT SIDE OF LIFE

STEP ONE: ASK THE HELP OF THE
PROSPEROUS CHRIST

HOW TO TAP A SUCCESS POWER FOR
OVERCOMING LIFE'S HARD EXPERIENCES

The first thing we learn from this *final* prosperity miracle of Jesus is that *there is prospering power in the Name and Presence of Jesus Christ.* Jesus Christ is still your helper, if you will but look to him for help. Whoever you are, wherever you are, Jesus Christ in his spiritual consciousness is waiting for your mental recognition. *Whatever your object, he will show you how to attain it if you ask his help.*

When his Presence is recognized and used, the success power of Jesus Christ can still produce outstanding results today. Remember that the name "Jesus Christ" also symbolizes the divinity in you that is never poor. The former Kansas City realtor, Charles Fillmore, was once asked how he had been able to gradually demonstrate such abundant prosperity for the nondenominational Unity School of Christianity, which had started financially with nothing. He replied, "I have found that asking in the Name of Jesus Christ immensely strengthens my consciousness of substance, which is so necessary for demonstration."

If life has seemed hard for you so that you are uncertain what you should do next, begin by declaring: "I ASK THAT THE SUCCESS POWER OF JESUS CHRIST NOW GO BEFORE ME, GUIDING AND UPHOLDING ME, AND MAKING ALL THINGS RIGHT."

If you have a health problem that you have tried to overcome to no avail, pause for a moment in your efforts, lift your thoughts to a higher level, and boldly declare: "I ASK TO BE STRENGTHENED, RESTORED, AND MADE WHOLE IN THE NAME OF JESUS CHRIST." Your prayer can be answered as you follow the guidance that comes.

Or if you have been struggling against lack, limitation, or seeming failure, take your courage in your hands and say in faith: "I ASK TO BE INSPIRED, PROSPERED, AND BLESSED WITH ABUNDANCE IN ALL MY WAYS, IN THE NAME OF JESUS CHRIST."

THE SUCCESS POWER THAT WAS POURED
OUT UPON A BUSINESSMAN'S LIFE

A businessman was very discouraged. He had once had a chronic drinking problem which he had been able to curb, but now the strong desire to drink had returned. He had other health problems, and trouble was brewing in his marriage. Since his sales were down, he also had financial difficulties.

He finally sought the advice of a friend, who listened while he poured out a long list of woes. Then the friend quietly began to talk about the success power to be found in the name and presence of Jesus Christ.

The troubled businessman exclaimed, "*That* is the answer! For many years I meditated nightly on the name and presence of Jesus Christ. I sent him before me into my business day and I did well. My marriage was peaceful, and I had no health problems. *It was when I stopped doing this that all these problems appeared.*"

Together they quietly meditated and declared that this man, his wife, and his business were all surrounded by the pure white light of the Christ into which nothing negative could penetrate, and out of which only good would come. They invited the success power of Jesus Christ to take control of his health, his marriage, his sales, and to guide him every step of the way. Then they spoke words for the perfect outworking of the prosperous Christ in his life. With a sense of peace he had not known for months, this businessman went on his way. As he meditated nightly on these ideas, improvement came in all areas of his life. Peace was established in his marriage. The desire to drink faded away and his health improved. He again became successful in his sales work.

STEP TWO: GO TO GALILEE WITH HIGH VISION AND ORDERLY THOUGHTS, WORDS, AND ACTIONS

Jesus' last prosperity miracle took place in a prosperous setting: at the Sea of Tiberias, commonly called "the Sea of

Galilee." *Jesus' ministry had begun in thriving Galilee, and it was fitting that the Sea of Galilee, in which fish were found in abundance, should also be the setting for his final prosperity miracle.*

The Sea of Tiberias symbolizes high vision and its orderly expression through your prosperous thoughts and words. Galilee symbolizes constructive action. *It is in an uplifted state of mind that you begin to experience prosperity when you express your high vision in prosperous thoughts and words (Tiberias). But do not expect permanent results unless you follow through on those prosperous thoughts and words with orderly action (Galilee).*

Many people get the high vision of prosperity, but nothing happens because: (1) they talk their good away by speaking negatively of themselves or others, or (2) they talk idly about their vision of prosperity, so that they dissipate it. They should have kept quiet, and taken action.

You can get the high vision of prosperity and express it through verbally declaring these orderly thoughts and words: "I SET THE PROSPERING POWER OF JESUS CHRIST BEFORE ME TO GUIDE, GOVERN, PROTECT AND PROSPER ME. MY WORDS ARE CHARGED WITH PROSPERING POWER." Then follow through, as you are guided, with constructive action.

A businessman from California wrote:

"I needed to use these two disciplines stressed in your books: (1) To take time every day to go over my prosperity decrees, my list of needs, and to meditate on the pictured desires on my Wheel of Fortune. (2) I also needed to *speak aloud* the prosperity decrees—not just read them, or meditate silently on them.

"In my previous study of prosperous thinking, I had not received results because I had not done these things. The statement 'Some people read all kinds of self-help books, but do not follow through on the prosperity techniques suggested,' surely applied to me. *I have seen vast improvement in my life since I have been practicing constructive thought and action.*"

STEP THREE: INSTEAD OF TRYING HARD
FROM A HUMAN STANDPOINT, LOOK UP FROM
YOUR TASKS, AND REAFFIRM YOUR FAITH

WHY THEY DID NOT IMMEDIATELY PROSPER

Earlier Jesus had made startling promises to his disciples:
"He that believeth on me, the works that I do shall he do
also; and greater works than these shall he do; because I go
unto the Father." (John 14:12) Yet after his crucifixion,
days crept by and nothing happened. The uncertainty about
their future, and the strain of delay was trying for them.
Finally, while watching other fishing boats sail out on the
Sea of Galilee, Peter said, "I will go fishing, too," and the
other disciples decided to accompany him. Peter knew that
*while you are waiting to be prospered, it is wise to do something in
faith.* He also knew that all true work is sacred. It is not only
through prayer and literal spiritual activities that we glorify
God's goodness in our lives, but also through the sanctity of
ordinary work.

So they left the shore, hoisted the sails, and had the feel of
the ropes in their hands again. They were happy to be back
at the familiar, long-deserted task of fishing. After witness-
ing apparent defeat through seeing the crucifixion of their
beloved leader, to get back to work as fishermen was a wise
and therapeutic move. Symbolically they were fishing for
prosperity, abundance, and success.

To human appearances, everything was in their favor:
the night was a most favorable time to fish; they knew the
lake well; and they were experienced fishermen. Yet when
they did their best from a human standpoint and fished all
night, they caught nothing.

Why?

Peter, who symbolizes faith, had said, "I go a fishing" The other disciples had replied, "*We* will go, too." These two simple statements explain why they may have toiled all night without success. How often have you rushed forth into some task and confidently said, "*I* will do this," rather than asking for divine guidance and help in the matter.

You can try so hard from a human standpoint that you become hypnotized by it when you seem to fail. Then you see nothing else. If so, like Peter, you may feel in your human faith that you toiled long and hard without results. It is only after the disciples heard the voice of the resurrected Christ calling to them from the shore, then looked up from their task, and followed his instructions to cast their net on the right side, that they met with success.

It is necessary, at times, to look up from your tasks and reaffirm your faith. Looking up in this sense does not mean a mere physical looking up with the eyes. It denotes a turning away from the appearance of lack, and lifting up your thoughts to higher levels of universal abundance; therein dwells the prosperous Christ consciousness which will help you as you become attuned inwardly to its guidance.

HOW TO MAKE YOUR CATCH
OF UNLIMITED ABUNDANCE

Like Peter, *while you are waiting to prosper, it is wise to do something in faith.* These are the things you can do in faith: (1) Turn away from the appearance of lack; (2) Lift your thoughts to higher levels by dwelling upon the prospering power in the name "Jesus Christ." One of the seemingly audacious promises that Jesus had earlier made to his disciples was, "If ye shall ask anything in my name, that will I do." (John 14:14); (3) Declare that Jesus Christ is with you showing you the way.

Charles Fillmore has promised:

> "The mightiest vibration is set up by *speaking* the name 'Jesus Christ.' This name holds all power in heaven and earth. This name has power to mold universal substance. When *spoken,* this name brings results."[1]

In all kinds of situations on all levels of living, you will find yourself getting on the right side of life if you begin to recognize that the prosperous Christ is right there with you to help you. Just as he appeared to those discouraged fishermen when needed. Jesus Christ still lives in the spiritual ethers of this universe, and is in constant contact with those who prayerfully raise their thoughts to him and ask his help.

Once, after a strenuous period of work, I was suffering from near physical and mental exhaustion. While vacationing, I kept trying to unwind mentally and to relax physically, but had been unable to let go.

One afternoon I was visiting with an old friend, who had just come through some trying experiences. When I asked her secret for having met such vicious circumstances victoriously, she replied, "I couldn't have done it had I not prayed daily that Jesus Christ was with me, and that he was meeting those experiences for me and through me."

When I confided to her my pent-up mental and physical state, she prayed with me, declaring that Jesus Christ was in our midst relaxing, renewing and healing me. After our quiet prayer time, I felt in need of an afternoon nap. This was a luxury in which I had seldom indulged.

Later that afternoon, as I was coming out of a deep sleep, I glimpsed the filmy form of Jesus Christ at my bedside bending over me. By the time I was fully awake, he was no longer visible. But the healing work had been done. My

---

1. Fillmore, *Prosperity,* p. 36.

mind cleared and my body relaxed. That experience convinced me that the living presence of Jesus Christ is still in our midst; and that when we recognize his presence, and call on him for help, he is then freed to meet our needs, no matter what they may be—just as he met the needs of the multitudes twenty centuries ago.

So don't be like the well-meaning but over-zealous Peter who said, "I go a fishing." Instead, *ask the presence and power of the prosperous Christ to help you. To do so can guide you to the right side of life where you will make your catch of unlimited abundance!*

STEP FOUR: CAST YOUR MIND IN A SEA OF RICH IDEAS BY GETTING DEFINITE

THE PROSPERING POWER OF RIGHT ATTITUDES

In the grey light of dawn, a voice from the beach called to Peter and the other disciples: "Have you anything to eat?" When they replied, "No," Jesus' prosperity message to them was, "Cast the net on the right side of the boat, and *ye shall find.*" (John 21:6) When the disciples followed his instructions, they were not able to pull up the net because of the multitude of fish it contained! (John 21:6)

The right side has always been regarded as the side of good luck. It is the side on which man realizes that *inexhaustible resources are always present, and can be manifested as visible results by those who put their faith into action. Those who patiently and persistently seek supply through spiritual methods will ultimately succeed. The peace, health and plenty of true prosperity will follow!*

Most of us know people who appear to abide on this favored side of life. Everything works out well for them.

They enjoy splendid health, their relationships are harmonious, and the good things in life come their way. No matter what happens, such fortunate people always seem to be blessed.

Just as there was a right side to that boat, so there is also a right side of life for you, too. *Your attitudes of mind actually cause the good things of life to either gravitate to you, or to move away from you.* You may be much nearer to your good than you think! Yet in spite of your efforts, that desired good may not have materialized. If not, you can still step over to the right side of life by cultivating prosperous attitudes of mind. As you do so, the good you seek will come streaming into your life. *Success in life depends not so much on external things, persons, or conditions, as it does on right attitudes. This was Jesus' last success message to the world, and what a powerful message it was!*

SHE WENT FROM A RENTED HOUSE TO HER OWN ELEGANT HOME

What is the basic success attitude that can help you cross over to the right side of life? It can be found in the prosperity formula that I discovered when I taught my first prosperity class during the severe recession of 1958:

"Turn the great energy of your thinking upon *ideas of plenty,* and you will have plenty—regardless of what people about you are doing or saying."

In my books, *The Dynamic Laws of Prosperity, Open Your Mind to Prosperity,* and *The Millionaires of Genesis,* I have recounted some of the immediate, as well as long range, results that came to those who used this success formula; thereby *casting their minds into a sea of rich ideas and pulling in abundant results.*

The word "cast" means "to put in motion." Casting a net into the sea of ideas on the right side means to put in motion definite prosperous ideas and techniques. When this is done, you are then able to make contact with a multitude of fish, or prosperous ideas, that will produce bountiful results for you.

A California housewife wrote:

"When working in cosmetic sales about two years ago, I was encouraged by my beautiful sales director to read the book, *Open Your Mind to Prosperity*. That book showed me how to turn the great energy of my thinking upon ideas of plenty, and put in motion specific prosperity methods such as forming a vacuum, practicing forgiveness, list-making, picturing, using prosperity decrees, and tithing.

"That was the beginning of an exciting new life for me. *On pure faith, I applied the principles as set forth, and results were inevitable.* Within a few months my business prospered. I, too, became a sales director, and soon met my husband-to-be. Although I had previously lived on meager means in a small rented house, we now have a beautiful home in the exclusive Bel Air section of Beverly Hills. Johnny Carson, the Gabors, and many famous show business personalities have estates nearby.

"Since I no longer have to work, I now devote most of my time to my first love, the spiritual path. I spend my time helping others learn how to apply the power of prosperous thinking to their own lives. What a joy!"

STEP FIVE: MAKE THE EFFORT TO MOVE TOWARD YOUR GOALS IN FAITH

WHY PETER HAD TO MAKE THE FIRST MOVE TOWARD RESULTS

Fish dealers usually waited on the shore to greet the fishermen upon their return from the night's toil, and to buy

their fish. So Peter and the others did not immediately recognize Jesus in the misty dawn. When the disciples exclaimed, ''It is the Lord,'' Peter, in his excitement, hastily
donned his outer garments and flung himself into the sea on
the landward side where he was clear of the net. He swam,
splashed and waded to the shore. The other disciples followed in the boat, dragging their net with its great haul of
fish behind them.

*If you want to obtain successful results in your life, like Peter you
must have the courage to do something in faith first. You must make
the effort to swim, splash, wade, or move toward the good you desire.
Only then will you be able to pull in a net full of abundance out of the
bountiful sea of ideas.*

SHE MOVED FORWARD INTO
SUCCESS ONE DAY AT A TIME

*One of the ways you can move forward in faith is to begin asking
that the prospering power of Jesus Christ guide you, help you and
show you the way to succeed one day at a time.*

There once was a young businesswoman named
Charlotte, who felt she had every strike against her. She had
had a hard life filled with unhappiness. Everything seemed
wrong. There had been no money for an education so she
worked as a clerk in a store, but she resented her mundane
job. She was unattractive, colorless, unsure of herself, and
she had an unhappy home life with her family.

One day when the problems of life seemed too much for
her, she went to see a lovely friend who was gifted, popular,
successful, and who seemed to live on the right side of life.
To this friend she poured out her story of poverty, ugliness,
and disappointment.

The friend calmly replied, *''You can change all that if you
really want to.''*

"How?" the young girl eagerly asked.

"It is not hard, but it will take time. *You must sow the seed for another kind of life, and wait with patience for it to grow.* The secret is to live twenty-four hours at a time as if the prosperous Christ were right beside you, seeing everything you do, and showing you the way. Try it, and come back in twenty-four hours to tell me what happened."

Charlotte was surprised that her lovely friend spoke of Christ as if He were a neighbor one might speak with and visit. When she arrived home in the late afternoon, she noticed that the tablecloth was soiled. "If Christ were going to eat with us tonight, we would not use soiled linen," she thought. On a fresh table cloth, she arranged a small vase of flowers from the yard. She set the table with care, and even put the butter on a fresh plate. Instead of serving the potatoes boiled, she mashed them until they were fluffy. Then she carefully made gravy that was smooth and rich. "If I had known Christ would be here tonight, I would have managed to make a nice dessert," she mused.

When her father arrived home from work he asked, "Company tonight?"

"No, just you, Daddy," Charlotte replied as she thought, "If Christ were here, I would smile at my family and display my best manners."

Her tired mother came to the table in her work dress and said skeptically, "I don't know what's gotten into Charlotte to fix up so just for us. I suppose she's expecting someone to drop in before we finish."

Charlotte bit back a hasty reply and smilingly said, "I don't know of anyone I would rather fix things up for than my own folks."

The family stared at her in disbelief until her father finally said, "That's right, daughter. It's too bad we don't think of that more often." But her little brother only snickered. Again, her anger almost flared. Just in time she said to herself, "Christ is here." The family was soon talking quietly together.

Later her sister said, "It's your turn to wash the dishes." That remark usually brought a sharp reply. but this time Charlotte nonresistantly got busy with the dishes, and her sister quickly confessed, "It was really my turn, so I will do the dishes tomorrow night and the next."

Later in the evening Charlotte began to read a trashy magazine. Then she thought, "I wouldn't be reading this if Christ were here with me looking over my shoulder." As she put the magazine in the wastebasket, voices were heard at the door.

"Come on, Charlotte. We're having an impromptu party," they called.

Should she go? Yes! Christ went to parties and he helped other people have a good time. All through that festive evening she kept thinking, "Christ is beside me."

Charlotte disliked her job very much. If only there had been money in the family for an education, she would have gone to college to become an interior decorator. Instead, she worked in what she regarded as an unimportant job in a commonplace store.

The next morning things seemed different as she said, "Christ is beside me." When she entered the store, she smiled at all her fellow employees, who only looked at her in disbelief. Then she noticed that one employee, whose mother had been sick, was crying.

"How is your mother?" Charlotte asked.

"She's bad today and I need to be at home."

"Don't cry," replied Charlotte. "I'll ask the boss if I can do your work along with mine."

In a few minutes it had been arranged. As the relieved employee left for home, Charlotte said to her, "Let us both pray for your mother today. Christ is right at hand, and he wants her to be well because he cares about suffering people."

"Yes, I'll pray with you all day," came the glad reply.

Charlotte usually had little patience with fussy, rude customers. But when the first one of the day appeared, she said to herself, "Christ is beside me. He would be kind even to people like that," and she smiled at the customer. After she had met this demanding customer's unpleasant request, the troublesome woman asked, "Why don't they have more clerks like you?"

When Charlotte realized that the head of the department had been watching her, she commented to her superior, "You get along better with the rude ones if you're pleasant to them. There's nothing that wears one out like fighting your job."

The rest of the day went smoothly and that evening she reported the first twenty-four hours' progress to her lovely friend: "I have tried your success formula. It made everything different, but I still have problems."

Her friend replied, "When you first plant seed, the garden doesn't look different right then. But it's on the way to becoming different. Instead of the dull, brown earth which you first saw, within three months that same garden will be bright with bloom. *As you change inwardly, the outer problems in your life will start to change. As you persist in daily living as if Christ were with you, you will cease to be poor and without opportunity. Friends will be drawn to you. Doors will open before you. Your surroundings will blossom with beauty. You have the magic words, 'Christ is here.' Fretting inwardly or even making extreme outer effort doesn't change things very much, but Christ does.*"

STEP SIX: TO MAKE THE EFFORT TO SHARE WHAT YOU ALREADY HAVE, DEVELOPS YOUR PROSPERITY CONSCIOUSNESS, STRENGTHENS YOUR CHARACTER, AND OPENS THE WAY TO SUPERABUNDANCE

THE SECRET OF THE BOUNTIFUL BREAKFAST FEAST

On land the hungry disciples were greeted by the resurrected Jesus who had prepared a breakfast feast for them with his own hands. Knowing they would be cold, wet, and famished, he had laid fish on a fire of coals. He also had bread. But Jesus did not immediately offer them the bread and fish to eat. Instead, he extended to them a prosperity invitation, "Bring of the fish which ye have now taken." (John 21:10)

In faith, Peter then went into action and made the effort to draw the net full of fishes to land. And what a catch it was: one hundred and fifty-three fish in all. In such a catch there was an abundance and to spare. Many of the early church fathers had mystical interpretations for those one hundred and fifty-three fish, but basically they symbolized *abundant prosperity in large, definite numbers.* Even though there were so many fish, the net did not break (as it had done in the first "fish miracle" in Luke 5). This time, none of their abundance was wasted or lost, probably because they had now gained an inner hold on substance through an evolving process.

When Jesus invited them to make their own contribution to the feast, it was for the purpose of developing their prosperity consciousness and strength of character. They needed to make the effort to first share of the abundance they had received. When they willingly did so, the prosperous Christ then added his abundance to theirs, and a superabundance resulted. Thus, the wonder of this scene is not the net full of fish which Peter pulled in, or even the fire of coals with Christ's fish already upon it, but Jesus' prosperous invitation, "Bring of the fish which ye have now taken." (John 21:10)

You must share what you already have before the superabundance being offered you by the prosperous Christ can truly be yours. This is why many people do not prosper as they should after they take up the study of prosperous thinking. They try to get without giving. They reach out for the fish on Christ's coals without first sharing from their own nets of abundance. *Sharing is always the beginning of permanent financial increase. Without consistently sharing first of the prosperity you have already caught, there can be no enduring financial increase.*

HOW SHE FINALLY GOT A JOB

A businesswoman from Missouri wrote:

"I have a job, and I must tell you exactly what brought it to me. I recently relocated here in the faith that I could build a new life. I had applied for several local jobs. Although everyone was extremely pleasant and encouraging, nothing had come through.

"This morning I sat down, and in faith, I made a new Success Covenant (which I had learned about from *The Millionaires of Genesis*). I wrote out my desire to find a job and get free from debt. I then wrote out my promise to return to God a tenth of everything I received from any or all channels of supply. Next, I wrote out a tithe check for ten percent of what was left in my out-of-state checking account.

"As I finished writing that tithe check, the telephone rang. It was the head of public relations at one of the firms where I had applied for work. He asked me to come in for an interview this very afternoon. I tucked my tithe check in an envelope, and mailed it on my way. My interviewer was very kind, but said he wanted to 'sleep on it.' However, late that afternoon he called and said, 'Can you start tomorrow morning? You're hired. Welcome aboard!' *Of all the jobs I had applied for, this was by far the best one. Yet nothing had happened until I first shared of what I had on hand. What a comfort to know that the prosperity law is inexorable, and always works when we work it.*"

WHAT JESUS' LAST MYSTIC
PROSPERITY FORMULA CAN DO FOR YOU

Even though Jesus had prepared fish and bread, and shared them at other times (Luke 24:30–35; Mark 6:41; 8;6), his last act of abundantly sharing bread and fish with his disciples had prosperous significance. Indeed, *it is of special importance that Jesus' last earthly act, before making his ascension, was to offer the formula for enduring prosperity not only to his disciples, but to all mankind.* Because that prosperity formula was clothed in mystic symbology, relatively few people have recognized the prospering power it contained.

I have been working with Jesus' mystic formula for prosperity for more than twenty years. It consists of appropriation of the bread (rich universal substance), and appropriation of the fish (prosperous ideas), offered by Jesus to the disciples at the last bountiful breakfast feast. It is a soul-satisfying process to develop your prosperity consciousness through: (1) dwelling upon divine substance (bread) as the foundation of your supply, and then (2) using prosperous ideas (fish) to activate that rich substance and increase your supply.

Once a person learns this inner, mystical method of prospering, no lesser means seems satisfying or lasting. To practice using this mystical method for abundance takes away all fear of lack, inflation, recession, or other economic inconsistencies that may seem to be affected by changing national politics or unstable world conditions.

The inner, mystical method of prosperity, which Jesus emphasized at the close of his earthly ministry, does not always produce quick results because it works deep in consciousness to supply and provide. Yet through use of this method, one's needs are always met as the needs arise on a day-to-day basis. And the financial results are far more lasting than the usual "get-rich-quick" methods used by those in human consciousness. The soul satisfaction that accompanies the use of Jesus' mystical prosperity methods gives a sense of inner security and satisfaction that nothing else can.

When long-time friends recently visited me in the Palm Springs area where I now live, they commented, "What a thrill it is to see your life today, Catherine, compared to what it was when we first met you twenty years ago. What's an even greater thrill is to know that your busy work schedule combined with a *Social Register* life style in this beautiful desert resort is the result of your use of the *inner* methods of prosperity—not the usual blood-sweat-and-tears methods used by those who are still functioning from a material consciousness of supply."

It has been amusing to realize that the *inner* mystical methods of prosperity can generate an aura of abundance that sometimes causes those about us to think we are far more prosperous than we may literally be. Perhaps the reason this is true is because when you work from this *inner* level, you do not fear lack or feel bound to limitation. So you are inclined to be more generous in your giving, and to feel freer in receiving the bountiful blessings of life. The result is that those who are still in a material, human consciousness of supply may literally have far more, yet enjoy what they have far less. By comparison, those who are working with mystical prosperity methods may actually have far less in a literal sense, yet they dare to enjoy what they have to the fullest. So to all appearances, they are far more prosperous than their literally rich brethren!

STEP SEVEN: DIVINE SUBSTANCE (BREAD) THE FOUNDATION OF ALL WEALTH, IS A RICH GIFT THAT CAN BRING A FEAST OF ABUNDANCE

THE PROSPERING POWER OF THE MYSTICAL BREAD MADE ONE FAMILY RICH

The *bread* that Jesus shared in that bountiful breakfast feast symbolized *divine substance,* or the body of God, which is the foundation of all wealth. You can appropriate divine substance and reap its rich results through recognizing it as the foundation of your wealth, and calling on it to prosper you.

At the turn of the century, there was a businessman who learned that substance was the basis of all wealth. He became so fascinated with this mystical success method that he began to declare daily: "DIVINE SUBSTANCE CANNOT BE WITHHELD FROM ME. DIVINE SUBSTANCE CANNOT BE TAKEN FROM ME. DIVINE SUBSTANCE IS THE ONE AND ONLY REALITY IN MY FINANCIAL AFFAIRS NOW. DIVINE SUBSTANCE IS MANIFESTING THE WEALTH OF THE UNIVERSE FOR ME IN RICH, APPROPRIATE FORM HERE AND NOW. I AM SUSTAINED AND PROSPERED BY THE INFINITE RICHES OF DIVINE SUBSTANCE."

The result was that he prospered when business associates all about him did not. People who came into his store to shop were surprised when he did not give them a "hard sell." Fellow merchants were even more surprised when this man's business prospered through good times and bad, until he finally was able to open several more thriving stores around the city.

When a friend asked how this man prospered—in spite of his apparently casual approach to business—he replied:

"I know the secret of the ages: that 'divine substance' is the foundation of all wealth. So I do not depend upon customers, economic conditions, or any outer situation for my supply. Instead, I think prosperity, and I daily call on 'divine substance' to prosper me. This method has freed me from all the usual concerns about business."

Later, this man's daughter also learned that same secret: that divine substance is the foundation of all wealth, and she meditated upon it daily. When she inherited her father's thriving business, it continued to prosper under her leadership until she became a very rich woman. When friends would ask the secret of her success, she always replied, "From my father I learned about the prospering power of substance."[2]

STEP EIGHT: IDEAS OF INCREASE (FISH) ARE A RICH GIFT THAT CAN BRING A FEAST OF ABUNDANCE

WHAT A PROFESSOR LEARNED FROM THE PROSPERING POWER OF THE MYSTICAL FISH

The *fish* that Jesus shared in that bountiful breakfast symbolize *ideas of increase* which can also be activated through prosperous thinking, and more specifically through the use of prosperity decrees.

---

2. See Chapter One of *The Millionaires of Genesis* for a full explanation of substance, and how to activate it as wealth in one's affairs.

Can prosperity decrees actually produce visible, tangible results of prosperity? Yes! In fact, *the results that come through the use of prosperity decrees can be far more satisfying than those results that come through the usual human methods of blood, sweat and tears.*

A college professor was asked to visit leading universities in a dozen cities throughout America in order to study their architecture. He was to report his findings to the officials of the university for which he worked, since they were planning new buildings on campus. Because this professor was a student of prosperous thinking, he decided that in each city which he visited on university business, he would also visit the local New Thought church.

He was very excited when he returned home from his trip. After reporting the technical findings of the trip to his university superiors, he reported these metaphysical findings to a friend: The most outstanding university he had visited was one of the best known in America. It was located in one of this country's major cities. The architecture of this prominent university was considered so outstanding that millions of dollars had been spent to erect its new buildings. Yet he found these ''architectural wonders'' cold and impersonal. The beautifully landscaped grounds surrounding the area were littered with trash left there by students. The behavior and attitude of many of the students on campus also disappointed him and left much to be desired. Their general untidiness and lack of respect for others was displayed in numerous ways. This professor of architecture left that famed multimillion dollar university feeling sad and frustrated that, in an over-all way, it did not live up to its great name and vast potential.

In that same city was located what had been reported to be one of the most outstanding New Thought churches in America. He hesitated to visit it since he did not wish to be bitterly disappointed twice in the same city. Yet what a contrast in consciousness he felt when he walked into that church for a mid-week service. Hundreds of people had crowded in and were singing, meditating upon, and affirming prosperous words of Truth.

The visible, tangible results of prosperous thinking, and the use of prosperity decrees, were obvious. Although there had been no dramatic fund-raising drives nor millions of dollars spent in its buildings, this bright, beautiful church radiated an aura of abundance, happiness and peace he had not previously found. Those in attendance joyously shared with each other the results they were obtaining through their study of prosperous thinking. That church, its architecture, and its people were a revelation to this previously despondent professor.

After that mid-week church service, he boarded his homeward bound flight with a song in his heart and a conviction that "the prosperous Truth works" to provide for and bless those who use it. On that flight he reflected that whereas millions of dollars had been spent to raise up the first set of buildings he had viewed in that city, millions of prayers, prosperous thoughts, and prosperity decrees had been used to raise up the second set of buildings he had seen. Thanks to the power of prosperous thoughts and words, the second set of buildings, radiating light and enlightenment, had cost much less. Yet they were a far greater architectural feat. (This thriving ministry has since added other beautiful buildings to its complex, through the use of these same *inner* methods of prosperity.)

Thus we see the prospering power of the mystical fish that was offered by Jesus to his followers at that *last* feast of abundance, as it works in modern times to move through thoughts and words of prosperous increase to produce satisfying, visible results of abundance.

STEP NINE: THE PROSPERING POWER OF RELEASE

JESUS' LAST PROSPERITY MESSAGE

The first and last "fish miracles" of Jesus ended by bearing the same message: We should hang onto or clutch nothing to us in the way of possessions. *There is prospering power in release.*

Whereas, the first fish miracle concluded, "They left *all* and followed him," (Luke 5:11), the last fish miracle ended with Jesus' question to Peter, "Loveth thou me more than these?" (John 21:15), meaning "Loveth thou me more than these boats, nets and fish?" They did and to prove it, they left their old jobs forever.

It is significant that at the close of this last "fish miracle," the disciples again released the abundance gathered, along with their boats and nets, never to return to them. Instead, they went forth to become fishers of men, as they spread the gospel of the prosperous Truth throughout the ancient world. In the process, they were well sustained by the tithes and offerings of those whom they served.

In the development of your prosperity consciousness, you, too, may seem to go through cycles of growth and-development, which you eventually outgrow. You may develop a prosperity consciousness and enjoy its visible results. Then you may feel guided to leave it all to begin a whole new cycle of development, perhaps even starting all over again from a financial standpoint. At such times you may carry with you very little except what you learned in a previous cycle. Yet such knowledge is an invaluable asset as it helps to successfully launch you in a new cycle.

HOW THE PROSPERING POWER OF
RELEASE WORKED FOR THE AUTHOR

I recall working literally around the clock for almost a decade in the business world. Yet when I had reached the top in that job and was just beginning to enjoy some of its rewards, I felt guided to give a two-weeks notice, leave it all behind me, and begin again from financial scratch as a minister-in-training. This meant living in one room and gaining experience in every phase of church work: from helping with the cleaning to serving as secretary to a minister; doing on-the-job teaching and counseling, while at the same time completing my ministerial training through correspondence courses and attendance in ministerial school. It was a demanding, challenging period, to say the least.

After becoming an ordained minister, I was asked to take a troubled church and restore it in both inner and outer ways. Several years later, when that assignment had been accomplished, and I was just beginning to feel financially secure in that job, I released it in order to found a new church elsewhere from financial scratch. This project took almost ten years. When I felt that mission was accomplished, and both that ministry and I were beginning to be prospered for the first time, again I felt guided to release it in order to found a second new church. My loyal board of trustees strongly objected to my leaving: "Why would you leave us just when everything is beginning to thrive and prosper, and there are no problems? You have been with us for almost ten years, through a very challenging period, and you are loved and appreciated here. Why can't you be satisfied to remain on indefinitely, and let someone else pioneer that new church?" For a variety of reasons, there was no one else to pioneer that new church, and I felt irresistibly called to the task.

Within a few years, when I had founded the second new church, again I felt that the time had come to move on to found still a third new ministry in another part of the country. At this point it was a bigger decision to make than ever before because for the first time, I had a home and some possessions, plus more family ties than previously. Nevertheless, after praying about it, my family and I did a lot of releasing and made the long-distance move in faith. We have never regretted it.

Each time I have left old nets filled with abundance in order to move on to new fields of service, the challenges involved have caused me to grow deeper in my understanding of prosperity. As I have moved on, it has been a test to develop my prosperity understanding anew at deeper levels of consciousness, through meeting the *inner* and *outer* demands that the new experiences presented. Yet my experience seems not to be an unusual one for those who are prospering along *inner* lines. We learn to hang onto or clutch nothing. There is prospering power in release. To practice it, under divine guidance, not only brings greater freedom and expansion, but a deep sense of inner security which no lesser experience can provide. It is soul-satisfying to prove God as the Source of one's supply at deeper and deeper levels of consciousness.

THE LAST STEP: AFTER RELEASE, COMES
NEW SUCCESS AND SATISFYING ABUNDANCE

THEIR SUCCESS STORY WAS JUST
BEGINNING, AND SO IS YOURS!

Had the disciples been humanly successful on that last fishing expedition, it might have been difficult for them to renounce their former craft forever. Their lack of success by their own human efforts in their last fishing venture made them more willing to give up their prior trade and proceed with the work of the prosperous Christ. When they had followed Jesus' instructions and cast their net on the right side, great material abundance was theirs. It seems ironic that they were then freed by that *outer* success to leave their fishing boats and nets forever.

Yet their success story was not ending; it was only just beginning. This previously nondescript handful of ordinary men were among those who became the illumined apostles of the early Christian era—one of the most exciting periods in all of church history. They were destined to perform the colossal task of spreading the gospel of the prosperous Truth to the entire ancient world.

In later centuries, when the gospel of the prosperous Truth seemed to have been lost from the attention of the masses, it continued to be taught in secret to only a privileged few. But in this present age of metaphysical enlightenment, the world is again ready to hear and learn the inner message of the prosperous Truth as given through Jesus' life and teachings. Thus, Jesus ended his ministry as he had begun it: at the Sea of Galilee with fish and fishermen—both of which are eternal symbols of true prosperity and abundance.

I trust that something of the prosperous truths shared with you in this book have begun to open your mind to the unlimited abundance that can be yours as you, too, avail yourself of the *inner* prosperity methods that Jesus taught and demonstrated. *May his formulas for experiencing universal prosperity fill your consciousness "to the brim" with the peace, power and plenty of true abundance! Thus, also leading you to the right side of life.*

SUMMARY

1. Jesus was so interested in prospering his followers that he even appeared *after* his resurrection, and showed them how to turn failure into success.

2. Through the two "fish miracles," performed at the beginning and end of his ministry, Jesus "sealed" his great contribution to mankind with abundance.

3. Jesus knew that no greater work could be done for the kingdom of heaven than to show people how to gain success in the business world through the use of spiritual methods.

4. Prosperous steps that can lead you to the right side of life:

   a) Ask the help of the prosperous Christ, because there is success power in his Name and Presence.

   b) Jesus' ministry began and ended in prosperous Galilee. You, too, can go to prosperous Galilee through your high vision, followed with orderly thoughts, words and actions.

   c) When Peter and the disciples tried all night from a human standpoint to catch fish, nothing happened. It was only after they heard Christ call to them from the shore, then looked up and followed his instructions that they met with success. Instead of trying hard from a human standpoint, look up from your tasks, and reaffirm your faith. Then you will hear the inward guidance of the prosperous Christ leading you to success.

   d) Jesus promised if they would cast their net "on the right side" that they would get results. You, too, can cast your net (mind) in a sea of rich ideas through the use of right attitudes. That success in life depends on right attitudes was Jesus' last basic success message to the world.

e) When Peter (symbolizing faith) recognized the prosperous Christ, he made the effort to get to shore. The other disciples followed, dragging a great number of fish behind them. When you make the effort to move forward in faith toward your goals, your desired abundance also appears, often in great numbers.

f) Even though Jesus had prepared a breakfast feast for the wet, hungry disciples, he invited them to share first of the large number of fish they had caught. There was a reason for this: To make the effort to share what you already have develops your prosperity consciousness, strengthens your character, and opens the way for your own superabundance to manifest, too.

g) The *bread* that Jesus then shared in that bountiful breakfast feast symbolized *divine substance,* which is the foundation of all wealth. When you call on divine substance to prosper you, it is a rich gift that can bring a feast of abundance to you.

h) The *fish* that Jesus shared in that bountiful breakfast feast symbolized *ideas of increase.* When they are activated through prosperous thinking and the use of prosperity decrees, they are also a rich gift that can bring a feast of abundance to you.

i) The first and last "fish miracles" of Jesus ended with the same message: we should hang onto or clutch nothing to us. There is prospering power in release, which can lead to new cycles of expanded growth and abundance.

j) The disciples' lack of success by their own human efforts in their last fishing venture, made them more willing to release their prior trade and proceed with the work of the prosperous Christ, in which they became far more successful than ever before. After our release of former ways of living, which we have outgrown, comes new success and satisfying abundance. It is thus that we are led to "the right side" of life.

IN CONCLUSION . . . .

When I finally got busy writing this book—after thinking about and preparing to do so over a twenty-year period—I had a surprise. When I wrote about money appearing in the fish's mouth, and the loaves and fishes increasing to feed a multitude—that very thing began to happen in this manuscript, as the prospering power of the Christ consciousness quietly went to work.

The more I tried to "cram" the prosperity secrets of Jesus into these pages, the more prosperity secrets appeared and multiplied. I began to realize that the four Gospels were so filled with prosperous truths that there would be no way to get more than some of the major ones described in this *first* book on the subject. I now suspect that what started out to become one book on "The Millionaire from Nazareth" may later become a series.

In any event, the theme of this book might be taken from that saying quoted earlier: "Give a man a fish and you feed him for a day. Teach him *how* to fish and you feed him for a lifetime."

I bless you as you now get busy using some of the ideas of increase (fish) described herein, thereby opening the way to reap a lifetime of soul-satisfying results in your mind, body and financial affairs! As you begin using these ideas of increase in *"Nazareth"*—or through your daily, commonplace experiences—may your life also be "crammed" to the hilt with abundance! May your good just multiply and multiply. You can commence confidently with Jesus' promise ringing in your ear:

"He that believeth on me, the works that I do shall he do also; and *greater works than these shall he do.*" (John 14:12)